KW-481-257

W.I.T.

2 4 FEB 1999

LIBRARY

CONTENTS

30.88

Connect Your LAN to the Internet

Cost-Effective Access for Small Businesses and Other Organizations

Thomas W. Madron

WILEY COMPUTER PUBLISHING

John Wiley & Sons, Inc.

New York • Chichester • Brisbane • Toronto • Singapore

W.I.T.

3 9003 00096279 4

Publisher: Katherine Schowalter
Editor: Phil Sutherland
Managing Editor: Angela Murphy
Text Design & Composition: Benchmark Productions, Inc.

Designations used by companies to distinguish their products are often claimed as trademarks. In all instances where John Wiley & Sons, Inc. is aware of a claim, the product names appear in initial capital or all capital letters. Readers, however, should contact the appropriate companies for more complete information regarding trademarks and registration.

This text is printed on acid-free paper.

Copyright © 1996 by John Wiley & Sons, Inc.
All rights reserved. Published simultaneously in Canada.

This publication is designed to provide accurate and authoritative information in regard to the subject matter covered. It is sold with the understanding that the publisher is not engaged in rendering legal, accounting, or other professional service. If legal advice or other expert assistance is required, the services of a competent professional person should be sought.

Reproduction or translation of any part of this work beyond that permitted by section 107 or 108 of the 1976 United States Copyright Act without the permission of the copyright owner is unlawful. Requests for permission or further information should be addressed to the Permissions Department, John Wiley & Sons, Inc.

Library of Congress Cataloging-in-Publication Data:
Madron, Thomas William
    Connect your LAN to the Internet : cost-effective access for small businesses and other organizations / Thomas Wm. Madron.
        p.   cm.
    Includes index.
    ISBN 0-471-14054-6 (pbk. : alk. paper)
    1. Internet (Computer network)   2. Local area networks (Computer networks)--Management.   I. Title.
    TK5105.875.I57M34 1996
    004.6'7--dc20   95-50056

Printed in the United States of America

10 9 8 7 6 5 4 3 2 1

PREFACE

A preface is always difficult to write. It is difficult because it can be the most important single document in a book. On the other hand, any writer has a suspicion that prefaces are not read with any care. In this case **it will be of benefit to you to read this preface.**

This book explains (or attempts to explain) the strategies and techniques for connecting your local area network (LAN) to the Internet. As I explain elsewhere, such a connection becomes desirable when your company or organization grows (or has grown) to more than about ten people who use the Internet regularly. For smaller organizations, although the solution is elegant, it is probably less expensive to simply get several individual accounts with an Internet Service Provider (ISP). Assuming that you meet this criterion, or that for some other reason you determine you want to connect your LAN to the Internet, then you can find out how to do it here.

Chapters 1–3 cover some important, but more general, networking concepts. Chapter 2, in particular, discusses the role and importance of *routers* in this process. The issue of routers and routing is recurrent throughout the book. In Chapter 3 we take a look at hardware and software requirements that will allow you to manage the task. The second part of the book, Chapters 4–7, focus on several specific ways to handle the task of connecting your LAN to the Internet. The one primary omission is that I have not discussed a Novell NetWare solution. This was omitted because first, there are already good guides in your bookstore that can assist you; and second, because most NetWare LANs exist in large organizations which are outside the specific scope of this book. Chapter 8 deals with the software you will need on each workstation in order to complete your setup.

In order for any solution to work, you must have acquired some IP addresses. These are usually (today) obtained from your ISP. If you have a permanent connection through the use of a leased line to your ISP, then properly assigned IP addresses are mandatory. Your ISP should also be able to obtain a domain name for you, as well. These issues are more extensively discussed in subsequent chapters. When you have SLIP or PPP connections, as is common among smaller organizations, then a company-specific domain name is desirable, although a permanent IP address may be optional. The reason I even mention these issues in this Preface is to emphasize the importance of understanding your options.

Much of the discussion in subsequent chapters is based on the premise that you will have a properly registered domain name and several permanently assigned IP addresses. Even with a dial-access connection, having permanent addresses simplifies configuration and routing. These accoutrements come with a price, however. There is usually a surcharge for permanently assigned (static) IP addresses (as compared with dynamically assigned addresses). Furthermore, not all ISPs offer static IP addresses for dial access so you may have to shop around more extensively for an ISP. Even with dial access service you can perform most Internet functions when you have static IP addresses. If you elect not to have static IP addresses, there are some Internet services that you will not be able to offer to users of your LAN, but the price is lower.

When you use a service with dynamically assigned IP addresses you must still assign IP addresses to each of your LAN workstations for them to have access. And you *do not* dream up these addresses. The Internet Assigned Number Authority (IANA) has reserved three blocks of IP addresses for use with private (i.e., not connected to the Internet) networks:

10.0.0.0	-	10.255.255.255
172.16.0.0	-	172.31.255.255
192.168.0.0	-	192.168.255.255

The first is a single class A network number, the second is a set of 16 contiguous class B network numbers, and the third is a set of 255 continuous class C network numbers. These classes are explained in some detail later. You will need all or part of a single block of class C addresses (256 addresses with 254 usable for individual devices).

When you elect to have a dynamically allocated IP address assigned when you phone your ISP, you will have to configure your LAN as if it were an *unconnected* IP network. *Never* will you be able to broadcast your workstation addresses to the Internet. There are, however, techniques available by which you can isolate your internal LAN IP addresses from the Internet, yet still allow those workstations to do useful work on the Internet including electronic mail and other forms of access. The downside of this approach is that certain services *will not* work. The services that will usually work are TELNET (terminal emulation) and http (World Wide Web access). FTP *may* work if a workstation can force the server into "PASV" mode. If these restrictions are acceptable, then you can use almost any ISP that offers a SLIP or PPP service and still connect your LAN to the Internet. There are ways, for example, to configure both Linux-based and Windows NT Server-based routers to handle these conditions. It may be possible to configure some of the stand-alone dial-access routers in this manner, as well.

In any event, as you read this book, regardless of any IP addresses I may use for purposes of illustration, please keep the foregoing comments in mind.

During the writing of this book I have consulted many sources, most of which have found their way into end notes for each chapter. For further information, consult those end notes. I have tried to test out the procedures in each chapter. Do not depend on slavishly following examples given, however, for published examples rarely work completely in other contexts. Some *experimentation* is typically required in order to get some of these techniques working properly. If you are an experienced network person, then the suggestions offered in this chapter may give you some ideas about how to configure a particular Internet connection. If you are a novice at networking, then, by all means, plan to read other books and articles on networking as well as this book.

I do wish to thank those who have reviewed this book as well as my wife Beverly, who put up with me as I was doing the writing. Any errors of judgment or fact are, of course, my own responsibility. Good luck on your quest to connect your LAN to the Internet.

1

WHAT, WHEN, WHERE, AND WHY?

As a reader of this book you have probably already reached the conclusion that your company or organization needs access to the Internet. For that reason I will not spend much time providing yet another rationale for Internet access. Suffice it to say that access to the Internet will improve the ability of your organization to communicate with those people with whom you need communication. In order for you to connect your local area network (LAN) to the Internet, however, it will be necessary to learn some common network terminology. It is not possible today to do networking at this level without an understanding of some of its technicalities. Learning what you need to know is not terribly difficult but it is necessary. At the outset we should note the difference between an internet and the Internet.

The term *internet* is a shorthand form of *internetwork*, a network with two or more (sub)networks connected by an internal or external router. We will have more to say about routers later. The Internet (and some enthusiasts pronounce it so that we will all know it is capitalized) is the series of interconnected networks that includes local area, regional, and national backbone networks. Networks within the Internet use the same telecommunications protocol (TCP/IP) and provide electronic mail, remote login, and file transfer services. The Internet is the largest internet in the world. It has a three-level hierarchy composed of backbone networks (e.g., NSFNET, MIL-NET), midlevel networks, and stub networks. The Internet is a multiprotocol internet. The Internet grew out of the Advanced Research Projects Agency Network (ARPANET) of the U.S. Department of Defense. It served as the basis for early networking research as well as a central backbone during the development of the Internet. Today the Internet consists of many public and private networks in many different nations around the world.

Getting Started

Before you can get very far with connecting your LAN to the Internet, you will need to communicate with a variety of people and they almost universally prefer that communication to take place by electronic mail (email). Consequently, the first thing you should do is get an email address (CompuServe, America Online, or a personal subscription with one of the many public Internet providers). Many service providers today sell internet services designed to handle anything from individuals to multinational corporations.

The Varieties of Access

The second thing that you should do is decide what your intended use of the Internet will be because that will determine the kind and quality of access you will procure. It will also determine how much you will pay for that access. The following are some possible options (see Figure 1.1):

- Option A: Send and receive email only, or
- Option A: Provide your employees or members the resources to surf the Internet for information important for your business, plus email, but do not allow external access to your LAN.
- Option B: Provide your customers or other people external to your location an information resource regarding your activities, but allow no one in your organization to use other Internet resources, plus (perhaps) email.

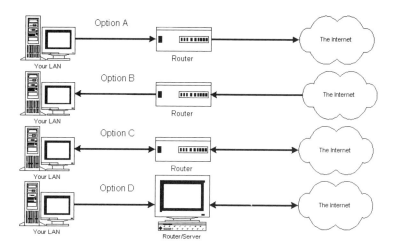

▬▬▬▬ **Figure 1.1** Varieties of LAN access to the Internet.

- Option C: Provide both your employees and your customers complete access to Internet resources both internal and external to your LAN.

- Option D: Provide your employees surfing capabilities, provide your customers access to your information, but do not allow customers or others access to your LAN. This option requires a somewhat more elaborate configuration of the router than do the previous options and that router may need to be a computer running a more powerful operating system, such as Unix.

There are other options as well, a few of which will be discussed in the context of security issues.

The choices outlined above should be a *business* decision. Based on the costs of potential use and how you want to use the Internet, what is the most cost-effective way to connect your organization? The break-even point between multiple individual subscriptions to an Internet provider and some sort of a LAN connection, at 1995–96 prices, is probably about nine active Internet users. Part of that business decision also revolves around what you want to do with an Internet connection.

Deciding What You Want

Before you do *anything* you must decide on what kind of access to the Internet you want or need. If you want *only* electronic mail (email), then there are three basic approaches that can be used, although not all Internet providers sell all three of these services: 1. Unix-to-Unix CoPy (UUCP)[1]; 2. POP3 mail access; 3. full mail transfer through a LAN linked via a router to a provider. If, in addition to email, you want to use other Internet services, such as FTP, TELNET, SMTP, and World Wide Web (WWW) access, then only a LAN linked to a provider through a router is an acceptable alternative. This book is based on the assumption that you wish to have relatively full access to the Internet, thus requiring a router. All of this jargon will be explained in due course, so forge on. There are techniques for using UUCP and POP3 mail access for transferring mail to multiple LAN users, but email is then the *primary* Internet service you can use. For use on a LAN both would require some sort of email server that may involve costs equivalent to more extensive Internet access.

Individual Dial Access

The cost of an individual Internet subscription is a combination of the monthly cost of the service and the telephone toll charges incurred to use the service. Although cut-rate services are now being advertised, across the United States the average monthly cost for an individual subscription to access the Internet is probably about $30. This figure may be larger if your provider charges by the hour and/or if you have to pay for telephone toll charges to use the service. If you can keep the costs down to about $30 per month, however, nine users will cost you $270 per month.

On-Demand Dialup

Once you jump up to ten users ($300 per month), you should be able to connect your LAN to an Internet provider for around $285 per month fixed fee for on-demand dialup service (unlimited use), plus whatever telephone toll charges you may incur. Some providers will include 800 access in that fixed fee; some will not. Some may provide access through public switched networks and others will not.

A further fee you might decide is worthwhile is rental of some disk space at your Internet provider for the purpose of maintaining a World Wide Web (WWW) home page (more of this later). Five megabytes or so typically rents for about $30 per month. This is a fee you might wish to accept regardless of whether you have individual accounts or have your LAN connected, since a Web page could become an important marketing tool.

We assume that as a reader of this book you have already decided to move to a form of access that allows you to connect a proposed or existing LAN to the

Internet. Regardless of whether you use an occasional dialup link or a permanent connection, the logic of what you will be doing is illustrated in Figure 1.2. The key to success is the box marked "Router." In order for you to communicate from your location with some other location, a *route* must be established. A route is an ordered sequence of nodes and links that represent a path from an origin node (location) to a destination node (location) traversed by the traffic exchanged between them. The device that we use to accomplish this task is called a *router*. A router is a software and hardware connection between two or more networks, usually of similar design, that permits traffic to be routed from one network to another on the basis of the intended destinations of that traffic. Another way of thinking about a router is to imagine it as any machine responsible for making decisions about which of several paths network traffic will follow. In the Internet, every IP gateway is a router because it uses IP destination addresses to choose routes. The terms *gateway* and *IP addresses* will be clarified below. The bottom line is that in order for you to connect your LAN to the Internet, you will need a router.

There are devices that we will discuss that are dedicated routers, built only for that purpose. Such devices are connected to your LAN on one side and to the telephone

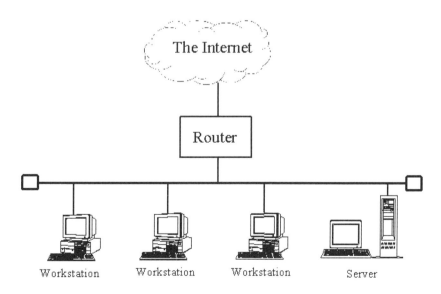

■■■■■ **Figure 1.2** A LAN linked to the Internet.

line on the other. It is also possible to configure some computer systems as routers if those computers are running under an appropriate operating system such as Unix, Windows/NT, or even MS-DOS. In each of these cases the correct routing software is necessary, of course. If you have a Novell NetWare network, you may be able to use your file server as the router, again with the appropriate software. Regardless of what you end up using for a router, routing is accomplished when there is the assignment of the path by which a message will reach its destination. A significant proportion of this book will deal with how to set up routers, their costs, and related issues.

When dial access is used to connect to the Internet there is always a question of the speed at which data can travel from one place to another. Speed is measured in bits-per-second (bps), kilobits-per-second (kbps), and megabits-per-second (mbps). A *kilobit* is 1,024 bits, while a *megabit* is 1,048,576 bits (1,024 × 1,024 bits). To give you some idea of what this means, one alphabetic character, such as the letter *A*, is defined as 7 *bits*. A *byte* contains one character (7 bits) plus a parity (error-checking) bit for a total of 8 bits. When you use a standard asynchronous modem to connect to some service, each byte is preceded by and succeeded by a *stop bit*. Stop bits represent transmission overhead since for every character transmitted a total of 10 bits are transmitted. High-speed, permanently linked modems usually operate in a synchronous communications mode and do not have the stop bits. Dialup options now widely available include standard asynchronous services and Integrated Services Digital Network (ISDN) services. ISDN is a high-speed alternative that requires special telephone lines and still may not be available everywhere. For the most part, the discussions in this book will center on standard asynchronous communications, although you should be aware that in virtually all cases ISDN may be a higher-speed alternative.

Continuous Access

Of course, if your organization is large, then an economy of scale may enter in. If you have 200 active Internet users at $30 per month, the yearly cost would be about $72,000. It is possible to obtain a yearly service for about $9,500 plus a leased high-speed telephone line (about $3,500 per year for short lines to the nearest node running at 56 kbps) for a total of about $13,000 per year for unlimited use. It does not take a rocket scientist to figure out that a yearly bill of $13,000 is preferable to $72,000. In this case you could maintain Web pages on your own in-house computer. This book, however, is geared toward smaller companies and organizations. The typical speeds for leased lines are 56 kbps and 1.44 mbps (T1 service). Although leased-line service costs more, and larger organizations will almost always opt for such service, if a small company or other group has very high use, then even they may find leased lines are more cost-effective than dial access. The break point, depending on actual local costs, is between about 8 and 12 hours per day of continuous connection.

Understanding TCP/IP

Among the things with which you need a nodding acquaintance are *networking standards*. The Internet was founded upon, and continues to use, the Transmission Control Protocol and the Internet Protocol, usually referred to as TCP/IP. The definition of TCP/IP and other things related to the Internet are contained in documents called *request for comment* (RFC). To the extent that the various RFCs define the way in which the Internet will work (the *protocols* of the Internet), and to the extent that those RFCs are widely accepted, TCP/IP and its multitude of related procedures constitute a standard. Although it is somewhat of a misnomer, we will refer to this set of networking-related protocols as TCP/IP. The problem with this is that no officially recognized national or international standards organization has ever adopted TCP/IP as a standard.

When it comes to an official set of standards we must look at the Open System Interconnection (OSI) model and the set of standards that have been derived from it. The objectives of OSI and TCP/IP are similar: to provide open systems architectures that large numbers of manufacturers can use as the basis for their own products. The resulting products should, as a result, be able to communicate with one another. Technically, the Internet is protocol independent, yet today it is predominantly oriented toward TCP/IP. Much of European networking is, however, moving toward networks based on the OSI model, and in the United States it is clear that a similar transition is at work. The U.S. Department of Defense, the originator of TCP/IP, has announced its intention to move to OSI-based networking in the not-too-distant future.

The consequence of all this is that manuals for Internet-oriented networking products usually contain a mishmash of references to both OSI and TCP/IP procedures
and protocols. If you currently have a LAN in your office, you probably already
use a fragment of an OSI standard network. If you have a token ring or Ethernet
(more properly, an 802.5 or an 802.3) network, you probably have a somewhat
proprietary network operating system (NOS) built on top of the 802.3 (Ethernet) or
802.5 (Token Ring) standards. Today an 802.3 LAN is probably the most common
base for a TCP/IP network even though TCP/IP is not part of the OSI model.
Before presenting a brief discussion of TCP/IP, therefore, we will take a look at the
OSI model because it can aid your understanding of TCP/IP and because it is
becoming increasingly important.

Networks in the Context of the OSI/ISO Model

To understand some of the issues involved in network planning and to lend credi-
bility to the project itself, it is useful to take a quick look at some of the relevant
standards available. There are several standards organizations in North America
and Europe that seek to rationalize electronic systems. Among those organizations
are the International Organization for Standardization (ISO) and the Institute of
Electrical and Electronics Engineers (IEEE). Standards of any kind for networks are
of recent origin, a situation that has led to an almost chaotic array of network
products.

In 1977 the ISO chartered a committee to study the compatibility of network
equipment, a development that eventually led to the publication of the Open
System Interconnection Reference Model (OSI). In this context, *open system* refers
to a network model open to equipment from competing manufacturers. As Frank
Derfler and William Stallings have noted, the OSI "reference model is useful for
anyone involved in purchasing or managing a local network because it provides a
theoretical framework . . ." by which networking problems and opportunities may
be understood.[2] The OSI model divides networking issues into functions or layers.
These layers are depicted in Table 1.1.

▮▮▮▮▮ **Table 1.1** OSI Model

Layer	Function
Layer 7 Application	End-user and end-application functions, such as file transfer (FTAM), virtual terminal service (VTP), and electronic mail (X.400)
Layer 6 Presentation	Data station for use by Layer 7, such as protocol conversion, data unpacking, encryption, and expansion of graphics commands.
Layer 5 Session	Provides for the establishing of a session connection between two presentation entities, to support orderly data exchange.
Layer 4 Transport	Transparent transfer of data between session entities, relieving the session layer of concerns for data reliability and integrity.
Layer 3 Network	Contributes the means to establish, maintain, and terminate network connections among open systems, particularly routing functions across multiple networks.
Layer 2 Data Link	Defines the access strategy for sharing the physical medium, including data link and media access issues.
Layer I Physical	Definition of the electrical and mechanical characteristics of the network.

▮▮▮▮

Overview of OSI

The reference model was devised to allow "standardized procedures to be defined enabling the interconnection and subsequent effective exchange of information between users."[3] "Users," in this sense, means systems consisting of one or more computers, associated software, peripherals, terminals, human operators, physical processes, information transfer mechanisms, and related elements. These elements together must be capable of "performing information processing and/or information transfer."[4] The importance of the reference model is that it will permit various networks of the same or different types to easily communicate with one another as if they constituted a single network.

At the outset it is important to keep in mind that conformance with the reference model does not imply any particular implementation or technology. It does not, in other words, specify a medium (such as fiber optic, twisted pair, or coaxial cable) or a specific set of recommendations, such as the IEEE 802.3, 802.4, or 802.5 networks in the United States. The reference model is designed to support standardized information exchange procedures, but provides neither details nor definitions or interconnection protocols.[5] The model, therefore, is a frame of reference for open systems with implementation details being left to other standards. Because the model is a frame of reference, it provides the framework for the definition of services and protocols that fit within the boundaries established.

Open Systems Interconnection Environment

It is important to understand that OSI is concerned with the exchange of information among open systems—not with the internal functioning of each individual real open system. A real system is, therefore, a set of "one or more computers, associated software, peripherals, terminals, human operators, physical processes, information transfer means . . . that forms an autonomous whole capable of performing information processing and/or information transfer."[6] Within an open system an application process performs the information processing for a particular application.

Aspects of systems not related to interconnection are outside the scope of OSI. This still leaves broad scope for OSI, for it is concerned not only with the transfer of information among systems but also with their ability to work together to achieve a common or distributed task. This is implied by the expression "systems interconnection." The fundamental objective of OSI is to define a set of *recommendations* to enable open systems to cooperate. Cooperation involves a broad range of activities:

1. Interprocess communication—the exchange of information and the synchronization of activity among OSI application processes

2. Concern with all aspects of the creation and maintenance of data descriptions and data transformations for reformatting data exchanged among open systems

3. Concern with storage media and file and database systems for managing and providing access to data stored on the media

4. Process and resource management by which OSI application processes are declared, initiated, and controlled, and the means by which they acquire OSI resources

5. Integrity and security of data during the operation of open systems

6. Program support for comprehensive access to the programs executed by OSI application processes

Because some of these activities may imply exchange of information among the interconnected open systems, they may be of concern to OSI.

Concepts of a Layered Architecture

In a layered architecture each open system is viewed as logically composed of an ordered set of subsystems.[7] The seven subsystem layers of OSI have been depicted in Figure 1.3. Subsystems that are adjacent to one another in the vertical hierarchy communicate through their common boundary.

A layer may have sublayers. Sublayers are small substructures that extend the layering technique to cover other dimensions of OSI. A sublayer, therefore, is a grouping of functions in a layer that may be bypassed, although the bypassing of *all* the sublayers of a layer is not allowed. A sublayer uses the entities and connections of its layer. The IEEE 802 standards, for example, deal primarily with the data link layer, and that is divided into the Logical Link Control (LLC) and Media Access Control (MAC).

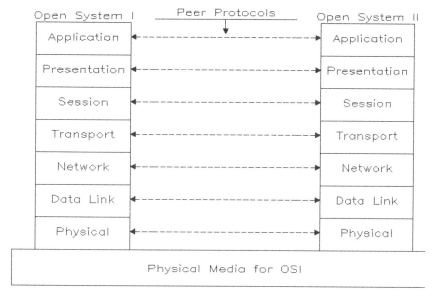

████████ **Figure 1.3** Seven-layer reference model and peer protocols.

It is important to understand that an open system can be OSI compatible without providing the initial source or final destination of data. In other words, an open system need not contain the higher layers of the architecture. The IEEE 802 standards, for example, apply only to the lowest two layers, data link and physical. This is often the source of significant confusion because when we talk of 802.3 (commonly called Ethernet) or 802.5 (token ring) the discussion sometimes proceeds to commentaries on TCP/IP or XNS or some other protocol. TCP/IP and XNS exist at layers beyond the physical and data link (although TCP/IP and XNS are not OSI standard protocols). Peer entities communicate through peer protocols at the appropriate layer of the OSI architecture (Figure 1.3).

Not all open systems provide the initial source or final destination of data. The physical media for OSI may not link all open systems directly. Some open systems, therefore, may act only as relay open systems, passing data to other open systems. A related concept is *routing*. A routing function within the *n*th-layer enables communication to be relayed by a chain of entities. Neither lower nor upper layers know that a communication is being routed by an intermediate entity. An entity participating in a routing function may have a routing table. The functions and protocols that support the forwarding of data are provided in the lower layers: physical, data link, and network. This forwarding function is illustrated in Figure 1.4.

There are a number of layered data communications architectures around but, other than OSI, they are often proprietary and were not originally designed to promote the interoperability of networks. The three best known examples are TCP/IP, IBM's SNA, and DEC's DNA. DNA, like SNA, was originally proprietary, but in recent years it was completely reworked in order to be OSI compliant. It is possible, therefore, to formulate alternative layering strategies. In the construction of the OSI model, however, some general principles were developed to guide the process.

The Seven Layers of OSI

The OSI seven-layer model has evolved. It might be useful to review Table 1.1. Layers 1 through 6, together with the physical media for OSI, provide a step-by-step enhancement of communication services. In the OSI model layer 1 is the hardware base for the network but does not include the physical communication media. Layers 2 through 7 are implemented in software. Table 1.2 is a list of

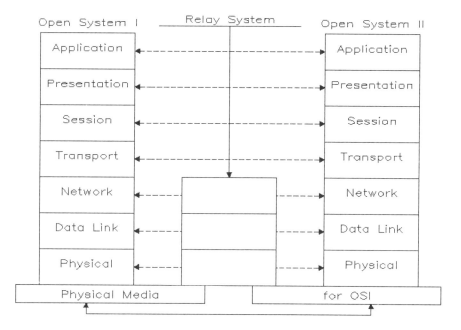

Open System I   Relay System   Open System II

Application	Application
Presentation	Presentation
Session	Session
Transport	Transport
Network	Network
Data Link	Data Link
Physical	Physical

Physical Media   for OSI

▬▬▬ **Figure 1.4** Communication involving relay open systems.

some of the protocol standards (either already adopted or in the process of development) by layer. This table is presented only for illustrative purposes. The adoption of protocol standards is ultimately what makes competitive products possible.

Throughout the discussions of standards in this book two concepts recur and need to be defined here: *connectionless* and *connection-oriented* services. These are also sometimes referred to as *datagram* and *virtual circuit* services, respectively. Generally, a datagram may be defined as a finite-length packet with sufficient information to be independently routed from source to destination without reliance on previous transmissions. Datagram transmission typically does not involve end-to-end session establishment and may or may not entail delivery confirmation acknowledgment. A connection-oriented service establishes a virtual connection that gives the appearance to the user of an actual end-to-end circuit. Datagrams are sometimes called *packets*.

■■■■■■■ **Table 1.2** OSI Intra-Layer Standards

Layer	Standard Name	Number
Application	Office Document Architecture (ODA)	ISO 8613
	File Transfer, Access, & Management (FTAM)	ISO 8571
	Virtual Terminal	ISO 9040
	Network Management	ISO 9595/96
	Manufacturing Message Specification	ISO 9506
	Distributed Transaction Process	ISO 10026
	Document Filing and Retrieval	SC 18N 1264/5
	Remote Database Access Protocol	ISO 9576
	Job Transfer and Manipulation	ISO 8832/33
	Document Transfer, Access, & Manipulation Prot.	CCITT T.431/433
	The Directory	CITT X.500, ISO 9594
	Message Handling Service	CCITT x.400, ISO 10020/21
	Common Service Elements:	
	Association Control Service Elements (ACSE)	ISO 8649/50
	Reliable Transfer Service Elements (RTSE)	ISO 9066
	Remote Operations Service Elements (ROSE)	ISO 9072
Presentation	Connection-oriented Presentation Protocol	ISO 8823
	Connectionless Protocol	ISO 9576
Session	Connection-oriented Session Protocol	ISO 8237
	Connectionless Protocol	ISO 9548
Transport	Connection-oriented Transport Protocol	ISO 8073
	Connectionless Protocol	ISO 8602
Network	Connectionless Protocol	ISO 8473
	X.25 Packet Switching Protocol	ISO 8208
	End System to Intermediate System Exchange Prot.	ISO 9542
	Use of ISDN in OSI and OSI in ISDN	ISO 9574
Data Link	Logical Link Control	IEEE 802.2, ISO 8802/2
	Media Access Control:	
	CSMA/CD	IEEE 802.3, ISO 8802/3
	Token Bus	IEEE 802.4, ISO 8802/4
	Token Ring	IEEE 802.5, ISO 8802/5
	Fiber Distributed Data Interface	ISO 9314

■■■■■■■■ **Table 1.2** Continued

Layer	Standard Name	Number
Physical	CSMA/CD	IEEE 802.3, ISO 8802/3
	Token Bus	IEEE 802.4, ISO 8802/4
	Token Ring	IEEE 802.5, ISO 8802/5
	Fiber Distributed Data Interface	ISO 9314
	Slotted Ring	ISO 8802/7
OSI Model Related	Application Layer Structure	ISO 9545
	Procedures for OSI Registration Authorities	ISO 9834
	Security Architecture	ISO 7498-2
	Naming and Addressing	ISO 7493-3
	Management Framework	ISO 7493-4

Note: While many of these standards are completed, some may still be under development. Enhancements and additional standards are being reviewed constantly, however, so this list must be regarded as incomplete, while others were intentionally omitted.

■■■■■■■■

The virtual connection contrasts with a physical circuit in that it is a dynamically variable connection where sequential user data packets may be routed differently during the course of a virtual connection. A connectionless service does not set up a virtual or logical connection between hosts and does not guarantee that all data units will be delivered or that they will be delivered in the proper order. The advantages of connectionless service are flexibility, robustness, and connectionless application support. Connectionless applications are those that require routing services but do not require connection-oriented services.

A datagram service, such as that provided by the Internet Protocol (IP), is a connectionless service. Likewise, in the context of OSI, some protocols provide connection-oriented services while others provide connectionless services. Moreover, both these services can exist at several levels. The ISO 8473 standard, for example, is a connectionless protocol for the network layer and functions similarly to IP, while ISO 8073 is a connection-oriented protocol at the transport layer. The IEEE Std 802.2 (ISO 8802/2) Logical Link Control standard can be implemented as either a connectionless or connection- oriented service in the data link layer.

Typically, if a network is configured to handle connection-oriented services at, say, the transport layer, the protocols at the network and data link layers would likely be implemented as connectionless services.

At least in the United States a significant literature is developing concerning the relationship between TCP/IP and OSI. The reason for this is that a great deal of internetworking in the United States is currently being accomplished through the use of TCP/IP. The DOD, along with the U.S. Government in general, has committed itself to moving from TCP/IP to OSI. That movement will likely continue well into the twenty-first century, but it requires that the relationship of TCP/IP to OSI be well understood. Some parallel comment on OSI and TCP/IP standards is necessary because plans are already in place in the United States to migrate from TCP/IP to OSI. This planning includes both the Department of Defense and the National Science Federation. It is important, therefore, to understand where parallel protocols fit and how we get from one standard to the other.

Compared with TCP and IP, OSI standards provide equivalent or superior functionality. X.400, the international message transfer standard, provides significantly greater capability than the Simple Mail Transfer Protocol (SMTP), which is a part of the TCP/IP protocol stack, for example. A standard since 1984, X.400 is gaining significantly in vendor support. The international standards corresponding to TCP/IP's File Transfer Protocol (FTP) and virtual terminal services (TELNET) are FTAM and VTP, respectively. These were not yet widely available at this writing, but will provide much greater capability when implemented. The National Research Council (NRC, U.S.) has detailed many of the reasons for migration from TCP/IP to OSI.[8] With respect to the U.S. Department of Defense the NRC study produced three findings:[9]

1. DOD objectives can be met by international standards.
2. TCP and OSI transport are functionally equivalent.
3. There are significant benefits for DOD in using standard commercial products.

In the long run the cost of OSI products should be lower than corresponding TCP/IP products. There are, however, some functional benefits in addition to lower cost:

1. The variety of commercial products integrated with OSI-related standards will continue to grow and expand.

2. OSI counterparts to FTP, SMTP, and TELNET do not suffer from the same limitations.

3. OSI-related standards extend far beyond the DOD standards in areas such as document architecture, network management, and transaction processing.

During the period of transition it will be necessary for many TCP/IP networks to operate in parallel with OSI networks, using application layer gateways that map between TCP/IP and OSI applications. As networking becomes more global and as TCP/IP runs out of addresses, OSI will become the dominant internetworking standard.

Layer Functions

Each layer in the OSI reference model defines a layer or level of function. Compatibility of equipment can be defined within a layer, or lower-level implementations can be hidden to achieve compatibility at some higher level. The dual purposes of the model are to ensure information flow among systems and at the same time permit variation in basic communications technology. Moreover, in any given organization, it might be possible to have one network take care of the lower levels and another network the higher levels, using gateways among the networks.

In the ISO model, layer 1 is the hardware base for the network. Layers 2 through 7 are implemented in software. The application layer (layer 7) provides services for network users. The responsibility for the initiation and reliability of data transfers takes place in layer 7. General network access, flow control, and error recovery are, in part, a function of this layer. Tasks are performed at the level of layer 7 and all lower levels are designed to support the applications. Electronic message systems, terminal emulation capabilities, and file transfer programs are illustrative of the software operating at layer 7.

Translation of information for use by layer 7 is accomplished in the presentation layer (layer 6). Such services as protocol conversion, data unpacking, translation, encryption, character set changes or conversions, and the expansion of graphics commands take place in layer 6.

Of particular importance to local area networks is layer 5 (the session level). Recall that one major reason for implementing a LAN is connectivity—the ability for any two (or more) devices to connect with one another. When a link is made between two devices, a session is established. In a somewhat more technical sense, the session layer provides for the establishment and termination of streams of data from two or more LAN connections or nodes. When a network maps network addresses on specific connections, a level 5 function is taking place.

The purpose of the transport layer (layer 4) is to provide an additional lower-level of connection than the session layer. Within the transport layer issues dealing with a fundamental level of reliability in data transfer are confronted. These issues include flow control, error handling, and problems involved with the transmission and reception of packets. We will return to a more detailed discussion of packets in a later chapter so suffice it to say that a packet is composed of user-originated data plus information the network needs to transport user data from one network node to another.

In many local area networks a functional layer 3 (network layer) is not needed. Networks that require routing mechanisms among nodes require layer 3. LANs, however, in some implementations, have data broadcast to every node and a particular connection collects those packets properly addressed to it. Baseband LANs, such as Ethernet, typically broadcast on only a single channel and require no routing. Broadband systems, however, are often designed with frequency agility (the ability to use more than one channel) and therefore require some bridging mechanism—that mechanism requires some routing technique.[10] When LANs are connected via gateways to one another, however, a functional layer 3 is required.

The data link layer (layer 2) defines the access strategy for sharing the physical medium (the cable of whatever variety). We will discuss such access strategies at greater length later in this chapter but common LAN techniques include Carrier Sense Multiple Access/Collision Detection (CSMA/CD) and token passing schemes. Techniques for network-specific information in data packets, such as a node address, are functions of layer 2.

Layer 1 is the physical layer—the layer that defines the electrical and mechanical characteristics of the network. Modulation techniques, frequencies at which the network operates, and the voltages employed are all characteristic of layer 1. Because all networks must implement layers 1 and 2 they have received the most attention from network vendors. If the attention paid to these layers results in compatible components, then we will know whether the concept of standards has been useful.

Standards are often less a technical accomplishment than they are the illustration of some vendor's ability to lobby a standard to success.

The development and implementation of OSI standards promises to make new and expanding networks easier and less expensive in multivendor environments. With increasing frequency, OSI is the model being followed by manufacturers and by requirements of governments and user organizations worldwide. In the United States, OSI standards have been incorporated into the National Bureau of Standards (NBS) Federal Information Processing Standards. OSI is a key factor in the development of the Manufacturing Automation Protocol (MAP), developed by General Motors. And the U.S. Department of Defense has reviewed OSI protocols for suitability for its requirements, although it supports its own Transmission Control Protocol (TCP). Other standards, such as those of the IEEE, are integrated into the OSI scheme.[11]

LANs and the Internet: TCP/IP

Both TCP/IP and OSI are, of course, layered protocol stacks. The TCP/IP protocol set consists of four layers that might be labeled *physical*, *routing*, *service*, and *application*.[12] OSI is structured around the seven-layer OSI reference model. The physical layer is not actually specified by TCP/IP. The user is free to use any physical transmission including wide-, metropolitan-, and local-area-based networks. The most common networking systems at this writing were X.25 and IEEE 802.3 (Ethernet), both of which are explicit parts of the OSI framework. Remember in the discussions of the IEEE 802.x networks the 802 specifications dealt only with the OSI physical and data link layers, with the logical link control (LLC) sublayer providing a standardized access to the network layer. It is at the rough equivalent of the OSI network layer that TCP/IP begins.

The TCP/IP Internet Protocol (IP) is more or less equivalent to the network layer of the OSI model, while TCP corresponds to at least the transport layer and in some ways to the transport (4) through the presentation (6) layers. The comparable international protocols are the "Connectionless-Mode Network Service" (OSI 8473) for the network layer and the "Connection-Oriented Transport Protocol Specification" (OSI 8073) for the transport layer. The other TCP/IP-related protocols are related to the application layer and include the File Transfer Protocol (FTP), the Simple Mail Transfer Protocol (SMTP), and the Terminal Emulation protocols (TELNET). Approximately equivalent international standards include File Transfer, Access and Management (FTAM, OSI DIS 8571), the Message Handling System (X.400), and the Virtual Terminal Protocol (VTP, OSI DIS 9041). In general the OSI protocols are richer than those of TCP/IP. Moreover, related international protocols exist in the layers between transport and application that support a wide variety of services.

The Relationship between TCP/IP and OSI

Before going into discussion of the relationship between OSI and TCP/IP we should clarify the use of the abbreviation OSI. OSI is sometimes used to refer to the Open Systems Interconnection Reference Model, described earlier in this chapter. It is also used to designate a more detailed set of protocols to be used as guidelines for configuring a real OSI network. It is in the latter sense that we will use it in this section. When we use OSI to mean the reference model it will be modified appropriately. In Table 1.3 I have attempted to display the relationship among the layers of TCP/IP, the OSI reference model, and the actual component standards for guiding the development of real systems.[13]

On the right side of Table 1.3 is displayed the seven-layer names of the OSI model. Also given are ISO standard names or numbers of some of the standards for each layer. It may be helpful to look back at Table 1.2 for a more comprehensive listing of OSI standards. On the left side of Table 1.3 are some layer names for the four levels of TCP/IP and in the boxes the names of the TCP/IP components at those levels. The TCP/IP protocol stack has been equated to the appropriate layers of the OSI model, but bear in mind that it is easier to draw such figures than to actually make such components equivalent. In general, the OSI standards are much richer both in number and in functionality than the TCP/IP standards. One of the challenges for users of TCP/IP networks over the next few years will be the need to migrate to OSI standards.

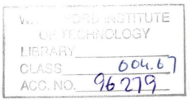

W. ...ORD INSTITUTE
OF TECHNOLOGY
LIBRARY
CLASS _____ 004.67
ACC. NO. _____ 96279

Table 1.3 TCP/IP-OSI Architectures

TCP/IP Layers	TCP/IP Applications	OSI Applications	OSI Layers
Application	telnet, FTP, smtp	VTP, FTAM, X.400	Application
Service	TCP	ISO 8823	Presentation
		ISO 8327	Session
		ISO 8073	Transport
Routing	IP	ISO 8473	Network
Physical	Note 1	LLC/MAC	Data Link
		Note 2	Physical

X.400	= Message handling service
ISO 8823	= Connection-oriented presentation protocol
ISO 8327	= Connection-oriented session protocol
ISO 8073	= Connection-oriented transport protocol
ISO 8473	= Connectionless protocol
LLC	= Logical Link Control
MAC	= Media Access Control

1. TCP/IP does not specify any physical layer, although the data link and physical layers standards are most frequently IEEE 802.3 (Ethernet) and X.25 and these are used only to deliver TCP/IP packets to IP for routing purposes.

2. The Physical Layer in OSI parlance includes various modem standards, IEEE 802.x LANs, and the 8802/7 slotted ring standard.

Migration from TCP/IP to OSI

The purpose of both TCP/IP and OSI is to provide a set of communications protocols that are manufacturer independent. The motive of the U.S. Department of Defense when it started developing TCP/IP in the late seventies was to broaden the base of hardware and software from which they had to choose for purposes of competitive bidding, rather than be stuck with a proprietary networking system such as IBM's SNA. With the development of international standards, however, it has become clear that over the decade of the 1990s far greater numbers of manufacturers will support international standards than TCP/IP as the major approach internetworking.

International standards also have the support of most of the governments of Western Europe as well as the support of standards organizations. These factors, coupled with the richer functionality and more extensive protocol stack of the international standards, has led U.S. governmental organizations, including the Department of Defense, to announce that they too will move to OSI over the next decade.

In the interim, however, more products are available for TCP/IP than for OSI. Moreover, the installed base of TCP/IP networks is still far greater than for OSI standard networks. All this means is that the migration from TCP/IP-based networks to OSI-based networks will take several years and for some purposes there may be room for both. A consequence of the need for migration, however, has been a significant spurt of literature discussing the problem of mapping TCP/IP to OSI. Some networks, such as the high-speed scientific network funded by the U.S. National Science Foundation (NSF) in early 1987, was designed to allow reasonably easy migration from one set of standards to the other. Until full migration is complete we will see products for gateways and protocol converters between TCP/IP and OSI networks.[14]

TCP/IP and the ANSI/IEEE 802 LAN Standards

TCP/IP itself is independent of the physical layer. The most commonly used protocol suites below TCP/IP, however, are IEEE 802.3 (commonly called Ethernet) and X.25. The United States Air Force has recently been working on the definition of a Unified Local Area Network Architecture (ULANA) that seeks to formalize the relationship between the two protocol suites for the purpose of providing user-transparent communications, especially for linking dedicated workstations and shared database capabilities.[15] ULANA is, therefore, one specification of the way in which TCP/IP and IEEE 802.3 can work together. In the ULANA scheme the IEEE MAC sublayer and the IEEE physical layer underlie the Internet Protocol without making use of the IEEE Logical Link Control. IP, of course, feeds TCP and TCP, in turn, supplies services to TELNET, FTP, and SMTP. This formal use of IEEE standards will, ultimately, enhance the ability of the Air Force to migrate to OSI standards.

An Introduction to TCP/IP

It is unfortunate that some authors occasionally mislead the unwary reader into the belief that there is some automatic relationship among certain standard protocol stacks. This is especially apparent in discussions of LANs. I will, therefore, reiterate again, that although TCP/IP has been frequently implemented on 802.3 standard LANs, TCP/IP is a set of protocols unrelated to the physical and data link layers as described in the OSI reference model. TCP/IP can be implemented on top of virtually any physical data communications medium and related physical and data link layer protocols.

One other caveat should be noted. The classification of TCP and IP into different network layers is not accidental. TCP can reside on a single, integrated network and not require IP. That is, if node A on network Y wishes to communicate with node B on network Y, routing functions that exist within IP are typically not required. If network Y is an IEEE 802.3 LAN, for example, the 802.3 standard implementation will take care of getting a frame from node A to node B. If, however, node A on network Y wishes to send a message to node C on network X, and network X is, perhaps, an X.25 network, then IP is required. TCP provides the packet sequencing, error control, and other services required to provide reliable end-to-end communications while IP will take the packet from TCP, pass it through whatever gateways are needed, for delivery to the remote TCP layer through the remote IP layer.[16] Some networks may, in fact, use IP, but not TCP, preferring instead to use some alternative protocol at the transport layer.

Although we will continue to use the hybrid term *TCP/IP* to refer to several different protocols, the set of protocols is often called the "Internet protocol suite" or the "Internet protocol stack." At this writing, the term *protocol stack* seems to be the catchall of choice of the data communications industry and we will continue to use it here. The internet stack consists, as implied above, not only of TCP and IP, but also of some application layer protocols. We will also continue to use "TCP/IP" to refer to the entire internet stack.[17]

Much of the impetus for the development of TCP/IP was the need for internetworking services—the ability of an end user to communicate through a local machine to some remote machine or remote end user. The traditional TCP/IP services are supported by the appropriate protocols, which are described in this chapter. Those protocols are as follows:

- The File Transfer Protocol (FTP) allows the transfer of files from one computer on the Internet to any other computer on the Internet.

- The Network Terminal Protocol (TELNET) provides a means for allowing a user on the Internet to log onto any other computer on the network.
- Simple Mail Transfer Protocol (SMTP) allows users to send messages to one another on the Internet.

Each of the services implied by these protocols should generally be present in any implementation of TCP/IP, although SMTP is not always supported by microcomputer-based systems.

TCP/IP was originally designed before the widespread deployment of microcomputers and high-performance workstations. It was conceived in an era when users communicated through minicomputers and mainframes. With the changing nature of both computer technology and data communications technology, however, a need has developed for some computers on the Internet to perform specialized services, leading to a *client/server* model for the delivery of services. A server system provides specific services for network users, while a client system is a user of those services. Server and client may be on the same or different computers. Additional services provided within the scope of TCP/IP are:[18]

- Network file systems
- Remote printing
- Remote execution
- Name servers
- Terminal servers
- Network-oriented window systems

Not all the protocols that support these services, however, are a part of the official TCP/IP protocol stack.

The way in which information is transferred from one node to another in a TCP/IP network is illustrated in Figure 1.5. TCP communicates with applications through specific *ports* and each port has its own local number or address. If a process on node A, associated with port 1, must send a message to port 2, node B, that process transmits the message to its own service layer TCP with appropriate instructions to get it to its intended destination (node and port). TCP hands the message to IP with instructions to get it to the appropriate node. IP, in turn, transmits to the physical layer with instructions to get the message to the gateway, which is the first *hop* to

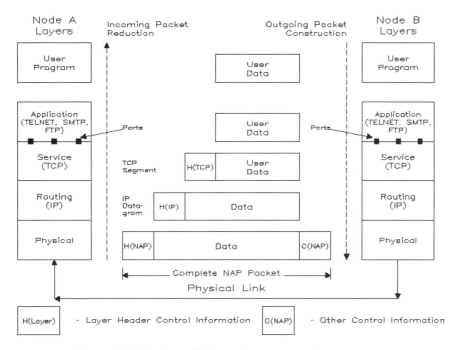

▰▰▰▰▰▰ **Figure 1.5** Nesting of Internet layer protocols.

node B. This sequence of events is regulated by adding control information to user data at the various layers:

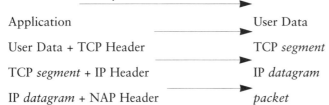

Application	User Data
User Data + TCP Header	TCP *segment*
TCP *segment* + IP Header	IP *datagram*
IP *datagram* + NAP Header	*packet*

TCP segments user data into manageable units, then appends a TCP header that includes the *destination port*, *segment sequence number*, and *checksum* to test for errors in transmission. This unit is called a *TCP segment*. Note that in Figure 1.5 H(Layer) denotes layer header control information, while H(TCP), H(IP), and H(NAP) refer to the specific layer header information and C(NAP) symbolizes other control information.

Various applications have been conventionally assigned specific ports. The assignment of ports at a particular installation is often contained in a file called *services*. A typical small *services* file sometimes appears as follows:

```
#          @(#)services    1.16 (Berkeley) 86/04/20
#
# Network services, Internet style
#
#name          port/protocol    aliases
#
echo          7/tcp
echo          7/udp
discard       9/tcp            sink null
discard       9/udp            sink null
systat        11/tcp           users
daytime       13/tcp
daytime       13/udp
netstat       15/tcp
qotd          17/tcp           quote
chargen       19/tcp           ttytst source
chargen       19/udp           ttytst source
ftp           21/tcp
telnet        23/tcp
SMTP          25/tcp           mail
time          37/tcp           timserver
time          37/udp           timserver
rlp           39/udp           resource         # resource location
nameserver    42/tcp           name             # IEN 116
whois         43/tcp           nicname
domain        53/tcp           nameserver       # name-domain server
domain        53/udp           nameserver
mtp           57/tcp                            # deprecated
tftp          69/udp
rje           77/tcp           netrjs
finger        79/tcp
link          87/tcp           ttylink
supdup        95/tcp
hostnames     101/tcp          hostname         # usually from sri-nic
```

```
ns              105/tcp                                 # ph name server
pop2            109/tcp         postoffice2
pop3            110/tcp         postoffice
sunrpc          111/tcp         portmapper
sunrpc          111/udp         portmapper
auth            113/tcp         authentication
sftp            115/tcp
uucp-path       117/tcp
nntp            119/tcp         readnews untp           # USENET News Trans. Protocol
#
# UNIX specific services
#
exec            512/tcp
biff            512/udp         comsat
login           513/tcp
who             513/udp         whod
shell           514/tcp         cmd                     # no passwords used
syslog          514/udp
printer         515/tcp         spooler                 # line printer spooler
talk            517/udp
ntalk           518/udp
efs             520/tcp                                 # for LucasFilm
route           520/udp         router routed
timed           525/udp         timeserver
tempo           526/tcp         newdate
courier         530/tcp         pc
conference      531/tcp         chat
netnews         532/tcp         readnews
netwall         533/udp                                 # -for emergency broadcasts
uucp            540/tcp         uucpd                   # uucp daemon
remotefs        556/tcp         rfs_server rfs          # Brunhoff remote filesystem
ingreslock      1524/tcp
```

Port definitions can be changed but then the application in question might not be able to communicate with similar applications on other systems unless their port designations had been adjusted for the change. In other words, don't change your *services* file.

Once the TCP segment has been assembled, it is passed to IP where an IP header is appended. A major item stored in the IP header is the destination host/node address. The resulting unit is an *IP datagram*. Generally, a datagram may be defined as a finite-length packet with sufficient information to be independently routed from source to destination without reliance on previous transmissions. Datagram transmission typically does not involve end-to-end session establishment and may or may not entail delivery confirmation acknowledgment. The IP data-gram is then given to the physical layer where the network access protocol appends its own control information, thus creating a *packet* or *frame*. The packet is then sent out on the physical medium. The packet header contains sufficient information to get the entire packet from node A to at least the gateway and perhaps beyond. In the case of an IEEE 802.3 network, for example, the packet would be an 802.3 frame that encapsulates the TCP/IP data and control information. Note that error correction is likely to take place at several levels. IEEE 802.3, 802.4, and 802.5 protocols do their own error correction. The IP header also contains a checksum, as does the TCP header. At the receiving end, the reverse process takes place.

In Figure 1.5, the layer labeled *Physical* is intended to contain the functions of both the OSI data link and physical layers. All nodes of a TCP/IP network might reside on a single LAN, such as an Ethernet. In such a case, TCP/IP would be operating as a LAN NOS. The original concept behind TCP/IP, however, was that it would pro-vide a common standard for linking many remote machines, and more recently, many remote networks, together. Consequently, some sort of system of router/gate-way/bridge must be used.

Addresses on the Internet

In order to contact other people or computers over the Internet it is necessary to have an address, just as it is necessary to have a phone number if you want to use the telephone. There are three types of addresses in common use within the Internet. They are email addresses; IP, internet, or Internet addresses; and hardware or MAC addresses. Software handles the conversion of an internet address into the corresponding physical address. This process is called *address resolution*. An email address consists of a user name and a domain name separated by an "at" (@) sign: **username@domainname**. A typical email address is my own: **tmadron@ewc-inc.com**.

The domain name is a mnemonic device that is easier to remember than a numeric IP address, although the one must be resolved into the other. The Internet Domain Name System (DNS) is the formal name of the scheme that consists of a hierarchical sequence of names, from the most specific to the most general (left to right), separated by dots, for example, **nic.ddn.mil**. An IP address is the numeric address of a computer connected to the Internet consisting of 32 bits but usually used in the format n1.n2.n3.n4. Each of these four numbers may range from zero to 255. We will discuss these addresses and how to get them later in the book. The IP address is still at a relatively high level, although it does specify a particular machine. It must still be related to a hardware address and this is the function of the Address Resolution Protocol (ARP). ARP is used to dynamically discover the low-level physical network hardware address that corresponds to the high-level IP address for a given host. ARP is limited to physical network systems that support broad-cast packets that can be heard by all hosts on the network.[19] Dealing with addressing is one of the more arduous parts of setting up a link to the Internet.

Assembling the Resources

The purpose of this chapter has been to provide a context for subsequent discussions, to provide you with a minimal network vocabulary, and to introduce some of the issues we will have to resolve as we proceed to set up your link to the Internet. This chapter will not make you an expert, but it will enable you to understand much of the material we will be confronting. Most of the remaining chapters take a more explicitly how-to approach. To make the connection, however, here is a list of services, software, and hardware you will need to add to your LAN:

1. Select an Internet services provider. See Appendix A for a list of such providers, bearing in mind that it changes frequently.

2. Select, purchase (when necessary), and configure a router. See Chapter 2 for a discussion of issues and needs. Other chapters deal with specific solutions.

3. Select, purchase, and install TCP/IP software for each of your workstations. See Chapter 3 for a review of the options.

4. Put the Internet to work in your business or organization!

Notes

1. UUCP is an older form of dial-access networking using machines equipped with an operating system named *Unix*. This approach is still widely used, however. For an extensive discussion of using UUCP as the basis for email, see Thomas Wm. Madron, *Low-Cost Email Using UUCP* (New York: VNR, 1994).

2. Frank Derfler, Jr. and William Stallings, *A Manager's Guide of Local Networks* (Englewood Cliffs, NJ: Prentice-Hall, 1983), p. 79.

3. The actual text of standards is sometimes difficult to obtain. An easily accessible compilation of many of the more important standards can be found in Harold C. Folts, ed., *McGraw-Hill's Compilation of Data Communications Standards*, Edition III (New York: McGraw-Hill, 1986), 3 volumes. The ISO 7498 standard (OSI) was adopted from CITT Recommendation X.200. X.200 has been used as the basis for the discussion in this chapter and references are made to that document, designated as *Fascicle VIII.5—Rec. X.200*. In references following the identification of the actual standard, volume and page references to the standard are found in *McGraw-Hill's Compilation of Data Communications Standard*s, *Fascicle VIII.5—Rec. X.200*, p. 3 (vol. 2, p. 2235).

4. *McGraw-Hill's Compilation of Data Communications Standard*s.

5. *McGraw-Hill's Compilation of Data Communications Standard*s, p. 3 (vol. 2, p. 2235).

6. *McGraw-Hill's Compilation of Data Communications Standard*s, p. 4 (vol. 2, p. 2236).

7. The concepts of a layered architecture are given in *McGraw-Hill's Compilation of Data Communications Standard*s, p. 40, pp. 6ff (vol. 2, pp. 2238ff), section 5.

8. National Research Council, *Transport Protocols for Department of Defense Data Networks*, February 1985.

9. As summarized by William Stallings, et al., *Handbook of Computer-Communications Standards*, vol. 3, "Department of Defense (DOD) Protocol Standards" (New York: Macmillan, 1988), p. 22.

10. Note Gregory Ennis, "Routing tables locate resources in bridged broadband networks," *Systems & Software*, March 1983.

11. The state of OSI development can be followed in various places. See, for example, Jean Bartik, "OSI: From model to prototype as commerce tries to keep pace," *Data Communications*, March 1984, pp. 307–319; Jerrold S. Foley, "The status and direction of open systems interconnection," Data Communications, February 1985, pp. 177–193; Sunil Joshi and Venkatraman Iyer, "New standards for local networks push upper limits for lightwave data," *Data Communications*, July 1984, pp. 127–138; and Kevin L. Mills, "Testing OSI protocols: NBS advances the state of the art," *Data Communications*, March 1984, pp. 277–285.

12. Alan Reinhold, "TCP/IP," *Communications Systems Bulletin* (Raleigh, NC: IBM Telecommunications Marketing Center, February 1988), p. 7. Other authors have named

these layers somewhat differently, for example, William Stallings, et al., *Handbook of Computer-Communications Standards*, vol. 3, "Department of Defense (DOD) Protocol Standards" (New York: Macmillan, 1988), p. 21. The formal definitions for the TCP/IP standards are found in the U.S. Military standards documents and in requests for comments (RFCs) available over the Internet or from the DDN Network Information Center, SRI International, 333 Ravenswood Avenue, Menlo Park, CA 94025.

13. Stallings, et al., p. 21, have compared TCP/IP (DOD) and OSI reference layering somewhat differently and have named the four layers *process*, *host-to-host*, *internet*, and *network access*. RFC: 793 (1981), which is one of the formal documents detailing TCP, labels the layers *application*, *host*, *gateway*, and *network*. My labeling is a modification of that found in Reinhold, p. 33. For a recent overview of TCP/IP see William Stallings, "Tuning into TCP/IP," *Telecommunications*, September 1988, vol. 22, no. 9, pp. 23ff. Note also, Michael Hurwicz, "TCP/IP: Temporary glue or long-term alternative?" *ComputerWorld*, September 26, 1988, pp. 73ff.

14. H. Kim Lew and Cyndi Jung, "Getting there from here: Mapping from TCP/IP to OSI," *Data Communications*, August 1988, vol. 17, no. 8, pp. 161ff.

15. Jerry Cashin, "ULANA: New name in networking," *Software Magazine*, October 1988, vol. 8, no. 12, pp. 91–94.

16. For a brief description, see Bill Hancock, "TCP/IP for network services," *DEC Professional*, July 1988, pp. 102ff.

17. Defense Communications Agency, *Military Standard Transmission Control Protocol*, MIL-STD-1780, May 10, 1984. It is also reprinted in Defense Communications Agency, *DDN Protocol Handbook* (Menlo Park, CA: DDN Network Information Center, SRI International, December, 1985). See also RFC: 793 (1981), "Transmission Control Protocol." One introduction to TCP/IP is Charles L. Hedrick, "Introduction to the Internet Protocols," Computer Science Facilities Group, Rutgers, the State University of New Jersey, Center for Computers and Information Services, Laboratory for Computer Science Research, September 22, 1988, unpublished paper.

18. Hedrick, pp. 2–3.

19. ARP is defined in RFC 826.

2

PROTOCOLS,

ROUTERS,

AND GATEWAYS

Protocols and routers were briefly discussed in Chapter 1. In this chapter we look at the various ways that we might connect a LAN to the Internet and what we need to be successful in our task. Although there are many networking protocols, the two we are interested in for connecting to the Internet are the Transmission Control Protocol (TCP) and the Internet Protocol (IP). A *protocol* is not particularly mysterious. It is simply a formal set of conventions governing the format and relative timing of message exchange in a communications network. Several protocols, such as TCP and IP, along with application protocols, such as TELNET or FTP, form a protocol suite. A *protocol suite* is a collection of networking protocols that provides the communications and services needed to enable computers to exchange messages and other information, typically by managing physical connections, communications services, and application support.

Once we start connecting networks together, such as hooking our LAN to a wide area network (WAN), one of the things we need to do is to route our protocol of choice from one network to another, and finally to a particular machine. *Routing* is the assignment of the path by which a message will reach its destination. A *router* consists of the hardware and software necessary to link two subnetworks of the same network together; the hardware and software necessary to link two subnetworks at the network layer of the OSI reference model; or any machine responsible for making decisions regarding which of several paths network traffic will follow. In the Internet, each IP gateway is a router because it uses IP destination addresses to choose routes. Not all routers are gateways, however. In order to connect a LAN to the Internet, some kind of router is required as illustrated in Figure 2.1.

The word *gateway* is used in a number of contexts in discussions of the Internet, but in general, a gateway consists of the hardware and software necessary to make two technologically different networks communicate with one another; a gateway provides protocol conversion from one network architecture to another and may, therefore, use all seven layers of the OSI reference model. A gateway may also be a special-purpose, dedicated computer that provides a linkage between disparate protocols or networks. Electronic mail (email) systems also rely on a suite of mail-related protocols. We frequently hear the term *mail gateway* in connection with software that translates email from one protocol suite to another. This issue will be discussed at length in Chapter 3.

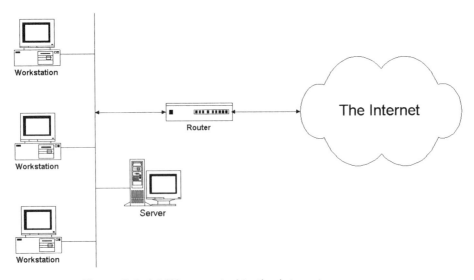

■■■■■■ **Figure 2.1** A LAN connected to the Internet.

LAN Protocols and the Internet

When you bought your LAN, you probably talked about the network operating system (NOS) more than anything else. A NOS is a control program that resides in a file server within a local area network or on every workstation or a combination of these two. It handles the requests for data from all the users (workstations) on the network; on a peer-to-peer LAN the NOS may be distributed across all the attached workstations. The NOS also provides the protocol suite for the LAN. Regardless of your NOS, however, today it will most likely use either Ethernet or Token Ring protocols at the data link layer. Here *layer* refers to the OSI network layers discussed in Chapter 1. The vast majority of the market has been captured by Ethernet in large part because Token Ring network interface cards (NICs) cost up to ten times as much as Ethernet NICs.

Ethernet and Token Ring

Ethernet is a network cable and access protocol scheme originally developed by Xerox, then further developed by DEC, Intel, and Xerox. It is now superseded by IEEE 802.3 (ISO 8802/3) standards. The basis for this protocol is a grouping of data called a *frame*. The difference between the original *Ethernet* and the 802.3 standard lies in the way the data in the frame are organized. The word Ethernet has become so ubiquitous, however, that today it is frequently used to refer primarily (albeit incorrectly) to the 802.3 standard. Early in the history of the PC, IBM started developing its own data link protocol, called Token Ring. IBM's Token Ring became the IEEE 802.5 (ISO 8802/5) standard. A key to understanding the difference between Ethernet and Token Ring relates to the way each avoids the collision of packets once the packets get out on the cable. Token Ring technology uses token passing, a collision avoidance technique in which each station is polled and must pass the poll along. Within the context of IEEE 802 standards, the token is a specialized frame that regulates the right of access in a token passing bus or ring. Ethernet, by way of contrast, uses a probabilistic method for avoiding collisions called Carrier Sense Multiple Access/Collision Detection (CSMA/CD).

Higher-Layer Network Protocols

If we had to work at the data link layer most of the time, it would become tedious, difficult, and time consuming. The result of this is that additional protocols have been developed that provide various kinds of LAN services from the network layer through the presentation layer. This book does not discuss these issues in depth. For that, you might take a look at my *Local Area Networks: New Technologies, Emerging Standards*.[1] It is important, however, that you develop a clear picture about how these things work together. The primary protocols that most installed LANs use today employ one or a combination of NetBIOS/NetBEUI, IPX/SPX, and TCP/IP.

Microsoft/IBM NetBIOS/NetBEUI

Back in the late 1970s and early 1980s, when all these transport protocols were first being developed, microcomputers had just been unleashed on the marketplace. In order to support early networking of personal computers, Microsoft and IBM developed NetBIOS (Network Basic Input/Output System) and later, NetBEUI (NetBIOS Extended User Interface). NetBIOS is a programmable entry into the network that allows systems to communicate over network hardware using a generic networking API (application programming interface) that can run over multiple transports or media. NetBIOS was later extended into the NetBIOS Extended User Interface, or NetBEUI. NetBEUI is the primary network transport system used in Microsoft and IBM LANs. It is a programming interface that allows I/O requests to be sent to and received from a remote computer. It hides networking hardware from applications. NetBIOS/NetBEUI is not a protocol in the same sense that IPX/SPX and TCP/IP are protocols, but the term protocol is now commonly applied to it even by Microsoft.[2] Microsoft actually refers to NetBEUI as a protocol and to NetBIOS as a programming interface. However, NetBIOS is today a subset of NetBEUI, so these distinctions become blurred.

Novell IPX/SPX

Back in the 1970s, Xerox was the corporation that first started seriously marketing LAN technology. It developed a transport protocol called the Xerox Network System (XNS) in addition to its development of Ethernet. In the mid-1980s, after the advent of the IBM PC, Novell was the company that developed some of the LAN NOS technologies most aggressively. At the heart of Novell's transport technology was IPX/SPX, which originally owed at least an intellectual nod to XNS. The Internetwork Packet Exchange (IPX) is, generally, a protocol that allows the exchange of message packets on an internetwork. Novell's version was originally a proprietary version of IPX, although today, like NetBIOS/NetBEUI, it is available to anyone who wants to develop protocol suites for LANs. IPX is paired, in Novell's NetWare NOS, with the Sequenced Packet Exchange (SPX) protocol by which two workstations or applications communicate across the network. SPX uses NetWare IPX to deliver the messages, but SPX guarantees delivery of the messages and maintains the order of messages on the packet stream. IPX is analogous to IP in TCP/IP, while SPX shares some functions with TCP.

TCP/IP

Both NetBIOS/NetBEUI and IPX/SPX were developed specifically to support LANs. By way of contrast, TCP/IP was developed first for WANs. Because of the importance of TCP/IP to the Internet, it was treated more extensively in Chapter 1. When LANs became popular, however, TCP/IP was readily adaptable to the new media in large part because TCP/IP lies above the physical and data link layers. It had to be interfaced to the hardware, however, and the two solutions for that involved using NetBIOS on the one hand or IEEE 802.2 Logical Link Control (LLC) on the other hand. In the context of the IEEE 802 standards the data link layer is divided into two sublayers: LLC and Media Access Control (MAC). It is LLC that is the direct link to upper layers of the protocol stack and MAC that interfaces directly with the hardware. Regardless of whether our base technology is Ethernet or Token Ring, the MAC sublayer provides a common interface to LLC, which, in turn, provides a standard interface to the network layer. NetBIOS provides a similar functionality.

SLIP/PPP

All of the foregoing is helpful in understanding the link between two or more LANs directly connected via a high-speed dedicated line to a WAN. What do we do, however, if all we can afford is a standard dialup line between our LAN and a WAN that is part of the Internet? What we need is a protocol that can transport an IP packet over a connection between point *A* and point *B* across a simple serial line (see Glossary). We have special problems on such lines because they are relatively slow, are subject to noise (static), and generally exhibit behaviors that IP and other protocols do not understand. This problem was initially attacked through the development first of the Serial Line Internet Protocol (SLIP) and then of the Point-to-Point

Protocol (PPP). These protocols are extremely important because you will likely be using them along with TCP/IP.

SLIP is a simple protocol used to transmit datagrams across a serial line. It was a predecessor to the point-to-point protocol. It is simple in that it is limited in its scope. It will process an IP packet at one end and deliver it intact to the other end of the serial link. Although it is being superseded by PPP, you may decide to use an Internet provider that offers only SLIP connections. The primary alternative to SLIP is PPP, which is an industry-standard protocol for data transfer across serial links. It allows for several protocols to be multiplexed across the link. It is successor to the serial line Internet Protocol. Which one you should use depends on your own situation and the services offered by your Internet provider.

One client of mine, for example, needs to pass both IP packets directed to the Internet, and IPX packets directed to their Novell NetWare LAN from remote offices and from people in the field. In that environment, PPP would be the appropriate protocol to use for dialup connections. In any case, if you are dialing into somewhere else, the remote end must have a SLIP or PPP server that will allow you to connect over the serial line. Although there are still many providers that use SLIP, PPP is currently the protocol of choice to replace SLIP for dial access to the Internet, largely due to the robustness of PPP and the fact that multiple protocols can be passed along a PPP connection. When you connect to the Internet you will, in all likelihood, have to run TCP/IP along with some other protocol (NetBIOS/NetBEUI or IPX/SPX) and this can be accomplished with moderate ease.

■■■■■■ **TIP**

NetBIOS/NetBEUI, IPX/SPX, and TCP/IP can all exist concurrently on the same LAN.

■■■■■

Routing and Routers

Now that we know what we have to route (IP packets), we need to understand how and where we do the routing. Remember, routing is the assignment of the path by which a message will reach its destination. In linking our LAN to the Internet the primary thing we need to be concerned with is routing, rather than protocol conversion, which usually takes place with some sort of gateway. At the physical layer there may also be the need to convert from one medium to another as, for example, when two LANs are linked over a phone line. Today, if protocol or media conversions are necessary, there are off-the-shelf devices that make it relatively simple to accomplish. A dialup router, for example, normally accomplishes medium conversion as well, in that it may be connected to an Ethernet LAN on one side and through a modem to the phone line on the other side.

The device that does the routing is called a *router*. A router is a software and hardware connection between two or more networks, *usually of similar design* (in this case, TCP/IP-based networks), that permits traffic to be routed from one network to another on the basis of the intended destinations of that traffic. In general there are two classes of routers: dedicated devices (which are small computers) called *routers*, and routing software that runs on a more general-purpose computer. The latter approach can be either a machine that is used only for routing or one that does routing among other things. The approach that you will eventually elect to use will be a function of existing resources, ease-of-use, and the level of access to the Internet that you desire. These functions will in large part determine the real cost of your connection to the Internet. If your LAN already uses a dedicated file server, then you may already have enough resource to add a software routing system to your LAN. If, however, you are using a peer-to-peer LAN, such as Microsoft's Windows for Workgroups (or Win95), Novell's Personal NetWare, or Artisoft's LANtastic, then you will likely have to add either a dedicated router or an additional PC dedicated largely to email and router functions.

Existing Resources

Let's step back for a moment and take a look at your existing LAN and what you have on it. In fact, you might wish to use a form something like the one in Figure 2.2.

Network Operating System (NOS)

The NOS you are using can make your task easier or more complicated. Possible options (not an exhaustive list) you might have installed are Microsoft's Windows for Workgroups (or WIN95), Microsoft's Windows NT networking (using a

Current LAN Resources and Configuration

Network Operating System (NOS): _____ Version:_____

Do you have a Dedicated File Server?___yes; ___no.

    If "yes," then type of file server:

        CPU (386, 486, Pentium, etc.):_____ DX or ____SX? Speed?_____

        Amount of Memory (RAM) in Megabytes:_____

        Total Amount of Disk Storage in Megabytes:_____;   Free Disk Storage:_____

        Operating System (NetWare, Windows, DOS, Unix, etc.):_____Ver._____

        Briefly describe how your file server is used: _____

        _____

        _____

Do you have any other Dedicated Servers (for Communications, for example)?___yes; ___no.

    If "yes," then type of file server:

        CPU (386, 486, Pentium, etc.):_____ DX or ____SX? Speed?_____

        Amount of Memory (RAM) in Megabytes:_____

        Total Amount of Disk Storage in Megabytes:_____;   Free Disk Storage:_____

        Operating System (NetWare, Windows, DOS, Unix, etc.):_____Ver._____

        Briefly describe how your file server is used: _____

        _____

        _____

Do you have someone on staff responsible for your LAN? ___yes; _____no.

    If "no," then:

    Do you have a regular consultant that assists with your LAN?: ___yes; ___no

What do you want to do with your Internet connection? (Check all that apply)

    ____Email (Electronic Mail).

    ____Obtaining information from others to assist in your business.

    ____Provide information you generate to others.

■■■■■ **Figure 2.2** Current LAN resources and configuration.

Windows NT Server), Novell's Personal NetWare, Novell's NetWare 3.1x or 4.x, or something else of a similar nature. While we use these products as examples, most of the commentary will apply to other NOSs as well. You will, however, have to research the capabilities of other NOSs more extensively. If you are using Windows for Workgroups (or WIN95) or Personal NetWare you may or may not have one or more dedicated servers. These NOSs use peer-to-peer networking.[3] A client of mine, for example, has a Windows for Workgroups LAN with a dedicated print server (a 386 DX33 with 4 Mb of RAM) that is inadequate to perform its present functions *and* other communications activities.

The version of the NOS you are using is also important. If you happen to have Windows for Workgroups 3.1 then you cannot use the Microsoft TCP/IP software available (without charge) for WFW 3.11. In later chapters we will assume that you have upgraded to at least WFW 3.11 or to WIN95. If you haven't, you should (must?). Although I don't have specific marketing estimates at hand, my guess is that today the lion's share of the peer-to-peer LAN market has been captured by Windows for Workgroups and this will migrate over the next year or two to WIN95. Even on WFW or Personal NetWare LANs, however, you may have installed a higher-powered machine to act as a dedicated file server that may have sufficient capacity to function as your gateway to the Internet.

LANs with Servers

Instead of a peer-to-peer LAN, you may already have a server-based NOS such as Novell's NetWare or Windows NT. There are many small LANs belonging to organizations that have opted for a somewhat more expensive NOS, but one with considerably more capabilities. If that is the case, then you should look carefully at how the server (usually called a *file server)* is used and whether there is capacity to add functions to it. For server-based LANs there is no question who has the greater market share: Novell. Both Novell and Microsoft, however, provide additional modules that can be installed on their servers to provide TCP/IP communications and various forms of access to your Internet provider. On a Novell NetWare 3.1x or 4.x server you can buy, as an add-on, a NetWare Loadable Module (NLM) that will provide the necessary gateway/routing services to the Internet. With the Windows NT Server 3.5 software, the appropriate modules come with the distribution or with the optional *Windows NT Resource Kit*.

What is a dedicated server? It is a computer in a network that is shared by multiple users such as a file server, print server, or communications server; a computer in a network designated to provide a specific service as distinct from a general-purpose, centralized, multiuser computer system; a computer system that provides services for another. Put somewhat differently, a server is a computer on the network capable of recognizing and responding to client requests for services. These services can range from basic file and print services to support for complex, distributed applications. For example, a distributed database management system can create a single logical database across multiple servers. A NetWare router, for example, can connect networks that use different network adapters or transmission media as long as both sides of the connection use the same protocols. If a router is located in a server, it is called an *internal router*; if located in a workstation, it is called an *external router*.

Much of the organization of the Internet is structured around machines that use an operating system known as Unix (developed originally by AT&T and now owned by Novell). It is possible to place a small Unix machine, running on a 486 or Pentium processor (or even a 386, for that matter), on LANs using any of the NOSs discussed in this section, and program it to be an email server and/or TCP/IP gateway/router. This approach can be either more expensive or less expensive than other approaches. There is one very good low-cost Unix-like operating system, call Linux, that has virtually all the capabilities of standard Unix distributions, and is available for less than $100 (U.S.). This option will be discussed at length in Chapter 5. Novell developed an Intel-based Unix called UnixWare, which is an alternative, as well. There are also other PC-based Unix variants available (recently sold to SCO). Using *nix (Unix or Linux or some other *nix) allows you access to a very broad range of networking tools but may require a rather steep learning curve on your part. It is possible, however, that you already have a *nix system available to you on your LAN. If so, that system can be configured to be your link to the Internet.

Who Will Do All This?

The answer to this question will vary from organization to organization. If your organization is large enough to already have one or more people who take care of your LAN (and related computer equipment), then they would be the appropriate choice. If, however, you do not have such a staff, you have probably installed your LAN yourself or used a consultant. If your LAN is a do-it-yourself (DIY) project, or if you have used a consultant, those are likely your options for setting up and maintaining your link to the Internet. If you are on the edge of recruiting someone to look after your computing facilities, now may be the time to do so. The problem is not that this whole process is so complicated (although sometimes it can be), but that it definitely has personnel implications and you should certainly identify who will be looking after your Internet connection. Sometimes this could be an appropriate argument for maintaining multiple individual accounts with a provider rather than using a direct link from your LAN. (That is a business decision you will have to make after reading this book.)

One caveat is in order here. Depending on the Internet Services Provider (ISP) you choose, they *may* be able to provide you with consulting services to help out with the connection. Investigate carefully before you buy a service. Find out the costs for on-site and remote consulting services. Find out whether they will acquire a domain name and IP addresses for your organization, and whether they will configure and manage your router for you and how much that service will cost.

Ease of Use

There are actually two components to the ease-of-use issue: (1) how easy it is to install and maintain the link; and (2) how easy it is for your average employee to use in day-to-day activities. The answer to the second question is more or less the same for any router option. With the appropriate software installed on each workstation, Internet resources will be relatively easy for everyone to use and that software will look about the same. As we have already implied, the answer to the first question is more complicated and is dependent on the level of access to the Internet you desire and how much you can afford to spend on the project. In general, the more expansive your Internet service requirements, the more expensive and complicated will be your server/gateway/routing needs.

Email-only installations can be set up at very little cost and effort, and are relatively easy to maintain. Expanding your access to include other Internet services accessible by your employees takes the complexity up a couple of notches. Providing information to others can significantly expand the complexity of your system.

What Internet Services Do You Need?

When you answer this question you will have a resource that will determine the answer to some of the previous issues raised in this section. If all you need is email, then you may wish to try the setup entirely on your own regardless of whether or not you have an Information Technology staff. If you want a complete set of services, then your configuration will have to be considerably more complete and this has all the implications already alluded to. You will normally have email services regardless of whatever else you checked in the little questionnaire presented above. If, however, you checked only the email option, then you will not have the other services noted. It might be helpful to look again at the information that we introduced in Chapter 1, reproduced here and in Figure 2.3:

- Option A: Provide your employees or members the resources to surf the Internet for information important for your business, plus email, but do not allow external access to your LAN.

- Option B: Provide your customers or other people external to your location an information resource regarding your activities, but allow no one in your organization to use other Internet resources, plus (perhaps) email.

- Option C: Provide both your employees and your customers complete access to Internet resources both internal and external to your LAN.

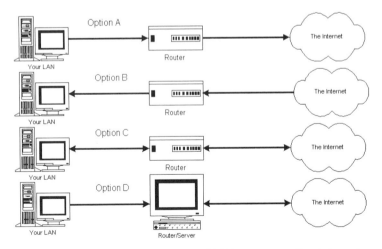

Figure 2.3 Varieties of LAN access to the Internet.

- Option D: Provide your employees surfing capabilities, provide your customers access to your information, but do not allow customers or others access to your LAN. This option requires a somewhat more elaborate configuration of the router than do the previous options and that router may need to be a computer running a more powerful operating system, such as Unix.

Putting it Together: Your Router/Server Needs

So what do you need? You probably do not want to answer this question definitively until you read the rest of this book, but the general outline should be clearer. Let's take this step-by-step, based on your Internet service requirements: email only; access to Internet resources by your employees but no external access to your LAN; and full two-way access.

Email Services Only

Many ISPs (Internet Service Providers) will have what is called a POP3 email service available for you to buy.

Introducing email

Electronic mail (email) is a system to send messages between or among users of a computer network and the programs necessary to support such message transfers. In order for email to work, however, there must be a Mail Transport Agent (MTA) and a Mail User Agent (MUA). The MTA is the software responsible for transporting mail from source to destination—possibly transforming protocols, addresses, and routing the mail. An MUA is the user interface to the mail system—the software that the user needs to read, store, and send mail. There are (or may be) other elements of a mail system. A mail exploder, for example, is part of an electronic mail delivery system that allows a message to be delivered to a list of addressees. Mail exploders are used to implement mailing lists. Users send messages to a single address (e.g., hacks@somehost.edu) and the mail exploder takes care of delivery to the individual mailboxes in the list. And, as we will see, you may have need for a mail gateway on your LAN. A mail gateway is a machine that connects two or more electronic mail systems (especially dissimilar mail systems on two different networks) and transfers messages between them. Sometimes the mapping and translation can be quite complex, and generally it requires a store-and-forward scheme whereby the message is received from one system completely before it is transmitted to the next system after suitable translations. The mail transfer is typically organized using the Simple Mail Transfer Protocol (SMTP), an application protocol within the aegis of TCP/IP.

One method widely used on the Internet by providers of email services is the Post Office Protocol (POP), with the current version being POP3. This is important to our discussion because a POP account can provide you with the lowest-cost access to the Internet mail services.

Post Office Protocol (POP3)

The Post Office Protocol was intended to allow a user's workstation to access mail *from* a mailbox server. Mail is posted *from* the workstation to the mailbox server via the Simple Mail Transfer Protocol. This protocol assumes a reliable data stream such as provided by TCP or any similar protocol. If you will go back to Chapter 1 and take a look at the *services* file listing you will find that when TCP is used, a POP2 server listens on port 109 and a POP3 server on port 110. POP mail servers typically reside on *nix systems, although today such servers can be found on other operating systems as well. The key to the operation of POP is that it resides on a system where the user has a user ID and password. A POP mail client, on the user's workstation, then logs into the host machine, gets the mail from the server and transfers it to the workstation. It takes place in a very short period of time. The connection between the client and the server is usually a TPC/IP link either directly on a network or over a SLIP/PPP dialup connection. There are a few products that will allow collection of mail over a standard telephone link without the use of SLIP/PPP. POP was introduced in order to simplify the transfer of mail received by a server to the client workstation.

A workstation on the Internet is viewed as an Internet host in the sense that it implements IP. If the computer we were using was a standard Unix system, and we were attached to it with a terminal, our mailbox would reside on the Unix machine. With a workstation, however, we do not necessarily expect the workstation to contain the user's mailbox. Particularly when using POP the expectation is that the mailbox will continue to reside on the server machine. A major reason for this is that your workstation may not always be available to the network (you might have turned it off to go to lunch, for example). An Internet mail receiver needs to be on all the time. POP was designed for an environment of workstations and servers on local area networks.

To give an example, suppose your real name is John Smith. You have a user ID and password on a Unix machine somewhere and the name of the machine is FIDO. In the simplest case, if a POP server is running on FIDO, your email address might be something like **jsmith@fido.com**, assuming that the domain name for the machine was **fido.com**. If the domain of which FIDO is a part were something else, such as **doghouse.com**, then your email address would be **jsmith@fido.doghouse.com**.[4] If this were the situation you could just connect to FIDO with a terminal, type **mail**, and read your mail on-line. You might, however, have a workstation connected to FIDO via an Ethernet LAN. If that were the case you could instruct your POP mail client software to retrieve your mail. Your workstation might be named COCKER so your fully qualified domain name would be cocker.doghouse.com. Your mailbox is still on FIDO, however, so your *mail address* is still **jsmith@fido.doghouse.com** (*not* **jsmith@cocker.doghouse.com**). Your POP client software would log into your account on FIDO, find your mail, and transfer it to your workstation.

If doghouse.com is the name of your ISP, and FIDO has been assigned only to you as an alias for the ISP's mail server, then you can actually receive mail on FIDO addressed to anyone (people in addition to jsmith). All the mail that comes to any-one at **fido.doghouse.com** will be transferred to your workstation when your POP client logs in. I have a similar situation with one of my ISPs, for example, but, in addition, I have my own domain name: **ewc-inc.com** (to signify my corporation, Enterprise-Wide Computing, Inc.). The ISP has made **ewc-inc.com** an alias for their fully qualified domain name assigned to me so that now I can be reached at **tmadron@ewc-inc.com**. The ISP does not care about the user ID, so I can transfer all mail intended for **ewc-inc.com** with a single machine. On my end my machines are on a LAN. With the right kind of POP client software, when the mail is trans-ferred from FIDO I can have it automatically distributed to workstations (and users) on my LAN. The precise methodology and software for this is described in Chapter 3.

As was noted in RFC1081, "On certain types of smaller nodes in the Internet it is often impractical to maintain a message transport system (MTS)." A local workstation may not have sufficient resources to permit an SMTP server and associated local mail delivery system to be kept resident and continuously running. Similarly, especially if the only route to your ISP is a dialup line, it may be expensive to keep a personal computer interconnected to an IP-style network for long periods of time. The Post Office Protocol version 3 (POP3) is intended to permit a workstation to dynamically access a maildrop on a server host in a useful fashion. Usually, this means that the POP3 is used to allow a workstation to retrieve mail that the server is holding for it. In Chapter 3 we will explore ways of having our local mail server (which is, in part, a POP client) retrieve mail from a POP server, then place it in an environment where it can be redistributed to the appropriate local users. The alternative to using POP is to set up a complete SMTP mail system on your local LAN. This is more complicated and requires greater maintenance, but is probably appropriate in some cases. However, the latter approach does not work well in a dialup environment.

Email Plus Outbound Internet Access

Once you have a SLIP/PPP connection between your LAN and your ISP, you should be able to access all of the available Internet services provided you have the appropriate workstation software. The difference between this level of service and the use of a POP mail service is that you do not need a router for the POP mail service and could, in fact, put the distribution software on a local workstation (although this would probably not be a good idea). In the case of redistributing full Internet access to all the workstations on your LAN, however, the only way that can be done is through a formal routing mechanism. That formal routing mechanism may be a standalone dial access router, a *nix machine, a Windows NTServer, a Novell NetWare Server, or possibly something else. The key issue here is that you will have to install either an external or an internal router (the latter being a software solution running on one of the operating systems just mentioned). This extends the cost and complexity of acquisition, installation, and maintenance, although the costs are still very reasonable. Chapters 4 through 7 will discuss each of these alternatives.

Email Plus Outbound and Inbound Internet Access

For you to provide information to other Internet users there is one additional requirement: a connection that is open for a substantial period of time each day. This is illustrated in Figure 2.3 by options C and D. I suggested in Chapter 1 that to implement options C and D a permanent (leased line) connection was required. In point of fact, that was an oversimplification. Such services could be made available over a SLIP/PPP connection, but maintaining a dialup connection 24 hours a day would be as costly as getting a higher-speed leased line to your ISP. The initial investment would be lower, however. You might select a compromise depending on the pricing your ISP gives you. If you kept your link up, say, 12 hours a day rather than 24, you could still cover most of your customers' needs, but if that would be half the cost of running 24 hours a day, it would be considerably less than a leased line and with a lower initial investment. The problem with dial access however, is that it is very much slower than with a leased line, although using ISDN services (from your telephone company) might somewhat mitigate that situation.

Conclusion

As we have seen, routers are at the heart of full Internet LAN access. The one caveat to that statement is the condition of an email-only access that may be handled with a POP service. In that instance there would have to be a machine on the local LAN that would receive and redistribute the mail to other LAN users, but that machine would not be configured as a full-scale router. It would, however, be used as a mail server/gateway. If the ISP provides the service it would even be possible to retrieve the mail with a standard asynchronous serial connection rather than having to use even SLIP/PPP. It is not difficult to set up the SLIP/PPP connection and we will discuss in subsequent chapters software that can be used for that purpose.

The point that I hope has come across in this chapter is that you can connect your LAN to the Internet in ways that are very cost effective. In the chapters that follow we will cover ways of actually setting up to do all the things discussed here.

NOTES

1. Thomas Wm. Madron, *Local Area Networks: New Technologies, Emerging Standards* (New York: Wiley, 1994).

2. See, for example, the definition in the *Microsoft Windows NT Resource Guide* (Richmond, WA: Microsoft Press, 1995), p. 807.

3. For an extensive treatment of peer-to-peer networking, see Thomas Wm. Madron, *Peer-to-Peer LANs: Networking Two to Ten PCs* (New York: Wiley, 1993).

4. This illustration is modified from a similar one in RFC938. This discussion is based on RFC938 (POP2) and RFC1081 (POP3).

3

SOFTWARE
AND HARDWARE
REQUIREMENTS

Specifically, what do you need to connect your LAN to the Internet? You need, of course, both software and hardware. In this chapter I will suggest an economical approach, not necessarily the cheapest approach. "Cheapest" in this context applies only to the acquisition of software and hardware since a cheap approach may end up costing you more in lost time than a slightly more expensive, but immensely better way to proceed. Bear in mind that for every suggestion I make here, someone elsewhere will undoubtedly have a different approach.

In order to connect your LAN to the Internet you need several items. In this chapter I am assuming that your workstations (PCs) are running Microsoft Windows. What is said here, however, has parallels for the Apple MacIntosh, for Unix, for the Amiga, and for a wide variety of other platforms. For ease of operation, I would strongly recommend that you upgrade to Windows 95. In a moment you will see why this is so. For successful operation, if you do not upgrade immediately to Win 95, then you should at least upgrade to Windows (for Workgroups) 3.11. The requirements for a successful link, then, are the following:

1. Latest or near-latest version of your workstation operating environment (Windows 3.11 or Win 95).

2. An established and working local area network (Ethernet is the easiest and least expensive with which to deal).

3. For each workstation, software that supports TCP/IP under Windows. This is usually called winsock or winsock.dll for the full name of the program. Versions of winsock.dll are available from a number of different vendors (see below).

4. One PC connected to your LAN, running Windows, that will act as a server/gateway/router.

5. An (optional) on-demand dialup router.

Let's look at each of these issues in turn.

The Operating System and Workstation Software

It is not always necessary, and sometimes not even desirable, to have the latest version of operating system software. Sometimes, however, the value of new services exceeds any problems that may ensue from installing more recent versions of the operating system. Such is the case with Windows. Microsoft has a stable version of TCP/IP (in *winsock.dll*) available for Windows 3.11. Earlier versions were neither as stable nor as easy to install. In the case of Windows 95 it comes with TCP/IP (in *winsock.dll*) and can be automatically installed at setup time. If you have Windows 3.11 you will need to acquire two additional sets of software from Microsoft: win32s.exe and pw1118.exe. The former allows the running of selected 32-bit software (the standard in Win 95) and the latter is the latest update of Microsoft TCP/IP (winsock) for Windows 3.11. This version of TCP/IP requires the 32-bit win32s installation.

There are many other implementations of winsock.dll and TCP/IP for Windows on the market. Each has its own advantages and disadvantages. Some versions are shareware, others are standard commercial products. In general, the commercial products cost in the range of $150 to $250 (U.S.) per workstation while the shareware products range from $30 to $50 (U.S.). One of the disadvantages with the Microsoft TCP/IP stack is the lack of built-in SLIP/PPP dialup networking. That has been remedied in Win 95, but Win 95 cannot act as a server because of limitations in routing TCP/IP. Windows NT version 3.5, however, does come with both TCP/IP and SLIP/PPP and it does have extensive routing capabilities. Thus, while you will probably want Win 95 for workstations, you probably will not want to use it on your server. More will be said of this in subsequent chapters. If you want to look forward to full-scale access to the Internet, you will need a winsock TCP/IP package on each local workstation, plus a server or router that can handle TCP/IP routing and dial into your Internet Service Provider (ISP) using SLIP/PPP. If you want to have the capability of independently dialing out from selected workstations, or if you want that capability on laptop machines, then an alternative TCP/IP-winsock implementation will be necessary. A good alternative from the many available is Trumpet Winsock, currently at the version level of 2.1, revision B.

There is one important caveat to be taken into consideration. Only a single version of *winsock.dll* can run on a workstation at one time. If, for example, you were to get the CompuServe SLIP/PPP software, it comes with a *winsock.dll*. Likewise, if you were to subscribe to Network MCI, its software also includes a *winsock.dll*. Each of the multitude of Internet packages that you might buy at your local computer store will include someone's version of winsock and TCP/IP. Before you load one version you must unload other versions. The application software that comes with many of these packages, however, like gopher, FTP, TELNET, or a World Wide Web browser, can usually be used with any variety of *winsock.dll*.

Microsoft Winsock (and TCP/IP)

The *win32s.ZIP* (or *win32s.exe*) file contains Win32S 1.2x. This version also provides support for OLE 32s. Win32s is redistributable software from Microsoft. Win32s requires Windows or Windows/Workgroup 3.1 or 3.11 running in 386 enhanced mode with 4 Mb of memory, and a swap file (temporary or permanent). Installation is relatively easy and the user need only run SETUP.EXE under Windows, with no other Windows application running. Win32s can be found on CompuServe by typing **GO MICROSOFT**, then searching for the file. It can also be obtained directly from Microsoft by anonymous FTP to **ftp.microsoft.com** or via World Wide Web at **http://www.microsoft.com**. Acquisition of such software is one of the reasons why I suggested earlier that it is essential to have some Internet connection before you start the project to connect your LAN to the Internet. That can be done through such services as CompuServe or America Online.

Pw1118.exe contains the setup files for Microsoft winsock and TCP/IP for Windows for Workgroups 3.11. This file can be obtained from the same sources noted earlier for win32s. What is winsock? More properly, *winsock* is an implementation of the Windows Socket specification, or, alternatively, the actually software module, *winsock.dll*. The Windows Sockets specification defines a network programming interface for Microsoft Windows that is based on the *socket* paradigm popularized in the Berkeley Software Distribution (BSD) from the University of California at Berkeley. It encompasses both familiar Berkeley socket-style routines and a set of Windows-specific extensions designed to allow the programmer to take advantage of the message-driven nature of Windows. The Windows Sockets specification is intended to provide a single API to which application developers can program and multiple network software vendors can conform. Network software that conforms to this Windows Sockets specification is considered *Windows Sockets Compliant.*[1] The TCP/IP protocol suite is a standard subset of winsock.dll. The advantage of moving to Win 95 is that all of the foregoing comes as a standard part of that system and is automatically installed during setup. There are other ways to add TCP/IP to a Windows system, but the use of win32s and winsock are among the easiest.

Trumpet Winsock (and TCP/IP)

The Trumpet Winsock is a Windows Sockets 1.1–compatible TCP/IP stack that provides a standard networking layer for many Windows networking applications to use, and has itself been a major vehicle in achieving widespread use of Windows Sockets 1.1. From the perspective of this book Trumpet Winsock has some very useful characteristics. First, it is inexpensive ($25/workstation). Second, it has the following capabilities:

1. Dialup SLIP and PPP connections.
   - Demand load dialing. This important capability means that when an Internet service is requested, Trumpet Winsock wakes up and dials your ISP.
   - A scripting language for automatically logging in and out of your SLIP/PPP server.
   - Dynamic IP address assignment.

2. Connection to a local area network by way of a packet driver and WINPKT under enhanced mode or with *winsock*.

- BOOTP and RARP.

3. Ethernet and SLIP packet driver types.

Trumpet can be configured for use with Novell NetWare and Windows for Workgroups (WFW), among LAN configurations. An automatic installation procedure is available for WFW from the Trumpet FTP server:

```
ftp://ftp.trumpet.com.au/pub/winsock/wfwsetup/twswfwg.zip/
```

You will also need to pick up a copy of the DIS_PKT9 program. It currently supports only NDIS2, not NDIS3. If the automatic installation procedure is used with WFW the process is relatively straightforward. There is a *readme.txt* file that specifies the installation process.

If you have a NetWare-based LAN, you will need to have your workstations configured to use ODI and you will need ODIPKT for Trumpet. It is important that ODIPKT reference the correct protocol for IP access. This can be specified as the first parameter to ODIPKT (0 = 1st, 1 = 2nd, etc.). A sample network attach batch file taken from one version of the Trumpet documentation is the following fragment used either as a standalone batch file called from *autoexec.bat* or entirely coded into *autoexec.bat*. For the ODI installation of workstation NetWare services, this is usually in a file called *net.bat*.

```
@echo off
cd \
lh lsl
lh \odi\ne2000
cd \net
lh ipxodi
lh odipkt
lh WINPKT 0x69
lh netx
path c:\dos;c:\net\win31
f:
echo on
login
```

You will also have a small file called *net.cfg*, and it must be suitably configured. Here are the relevant excerpts from one *net.cfg* file:

```
Link Support
     Buffers 8 1586
     MemPool 16384


Link Driver NE2000 varies depending on your NIC.
     Port #1 300 20
     Int #1 2
     Frame Ethernet_II
     Frame Ethernet_802.3
     Protocol IPX 0 Ethernet_802.3
```

The ordering of the frame protocols is important for the default setup of ODIPKT and must match the command line sequence number noted above. You should be aware that there are two versions of ODIPKT, one released by FTP Software, and the other in the public domain. This example refers to the public domain version. Also note that there are *two* programs named ne2000.com. One is a packet driver and is referred to in an earlier section. The one referred to in this section is actually an ODI driver and won't function as a packet driver at all. The most likely source for this driver is the diskette that came with your Ethernet network interface card.

Several times during this discussion we have mentioned packet drivers. If you need a packet driver for your installation it will most likely be found in the crynwr packet driver collection. This collection contains packet drivers for a large number of Ethernet boards, for limited support of token ring cards, and specialty drivers like winpkt.com. The entire collection is available by mail, by FTP, by email, by UUCP, and by modem. The drivers are distributed in three files: *drivers.zip*, which contains executables and documentation, *drivers1.zip*, which contains the first half of the .ASM files, and *drivers2.zip*, which contains the second half of the .ASM files. Copies of the crynwr collection are available from a number of sites, including CompuServe (use the PC File Finder to find where they are on CompuServe), and America Online. The ODIPKT is also available at these locations as well as at the Trumpet anonymous FTP site noted above. In general, the use of this *winsock* version of Trumpet supercedes the use of packet drivers.

One distinct advantage of Trumpet is that when using its built-in SLIP/PPP (it supports both) there is a good scripting language to support automated logons to your ISP. We will have cause to return to this issue in Chapter 4 when we discuss ways of automating Internet mail with LAN distributions.

Related Software

As you will be able to see from Appendix B, there are a number of applications that make use of winsock and TCP/IP. Again, there are both shareware and standard commercial products. If you plan on using only email, then you will need an email system for your LAN, plus a mail gateway, plus a methodology for collecting your mail (for you and your employees) from your ISP. One system we will discuss in detail in Chapter 4 uses Microsoft Mail as it comes with Windows for Workgroups plus an inexpensive mail gateway, plus a SLIP/PPP connection. In that configuration the gateway machine need only run WFW with TCP/IP as an operating environment. None of the workstations would need TCP/IP (winsock) installed.

If you are going for a more comprehensive set of Internet services, then you will probably need winsock and some support software. A basic configuration might include FTP, TELNET, and a World Wide Web browser such as Netscape or Mosaic:

- FTP: File Transfer Protocol allows a user to transfer files electronically from remote computers back to the user's computer. Part of the TCP/IP/TELNET software suite. *Anonymous* FTP is a procedure for connecting to a remote computer, as an anonymous or guest user, in order to transfer public files back to your local computer. (See also: FTP and Protocols.) Anonymous FTP allows a user to retrieve documents, files, programs, and other archived data from anywhere in the Internet without having to establish a user ID and password. By using the special user ID *anonymous*, the network user will bypass local security checks and will have access to publicly accessible files on the remote system. (See also: archive site, File Transfer Protocol.)

- TELNET: The Internet standard protocol for remote terminal connection service. It is defined in STD 8, RFC 854 and extended with options by many other RFCs. TELNET is a portion of the TCP/IP suite of software protocols that handles terminals. Among other functions, it allows a user to log in to a remote computer from the user's local computer.

- World Wide Web (WWW or W3): A hypertext-based, distributed information system created by researchers at CERN in Switzerland. Users may create, edit, or browse hypertext documents. The clients and servers are freely available. WWW clients are often called *Web browsers* and include such products as Netscape and Mosaic. Other browsers are available that contain various bells and whistles.

New software supporting Internet access, both shareware and standard commercial, is coming on the market almost daily. When you are ready for such software, check with your local computer stores. Many of the Internet packages now sold will have a selection of useful software even though you may not use the winsock that comes with that package. You may occasionally find software that will not work with your version of winsock, however. For shareware, you should explore at least the following FTP sites:

wuarchive.wustl.edu	Washington University, St. Louis, MO, USA
oak.oakland.edu	UC at Oakland, Oakland, CA, USA
ftp.cica.indiana.edu	University of Indiana, USA
ftp.cdrom.com	Mirror site for **ftp.cica.indiana.edu**

Several of these archives are also published regularly on CDROM by several companies. One easy way to get a head start on collecting appropriate software is to buy several such collections. The most useful are the *cica* archives and the *simtel* archives. The former are all Windows-based, while the latter contain DOS programs as well.[2] Many of these programs will be undergoing updates to conform to Win 95. The following is a recent index of several of the shareware offerings available from the cica winsock archive:

```
**
** Index of:
**   Windows Sockets (Winsock) Compliant TCP/IP Networking Applications
**   and Other Windows Internet-working Utilities
**
** In Directory: ~ftp/pub/pc/win3/winsock
**   On Archive: ftp.cica.indiana.edu [129.79.26.27]
** Last Updated: Wed Sep 06 1995 at 12:49:16 AM EST
**
```

anzl102f.zip	950502	Anzio Lite 10.2f is a Winsock TELNET client
atisml03.zip	950418	Atismail Winsock Mail Agent sends/receives email [1.6m]
autown16.zip	950627	Automated Internet for Windows 1.6
cello.zip	940711	Cello WWW Browser Release 1.01a
cfing11.zip	950321	CFinger 1.1 Winsock Finger/echo/ping/daemon
col_12b1.zip	940311	NCSA Collage for Winsock [203k]
comt.zip	950630	COMt, the Telnet Modem for Windows
cooksock.zip	931002	Cookie server for windows sockets interface
cuteftp1.zip	950501	CuteFTP is a GUI/Winsock-based FTP client
email099.zip	950417	Beta version of E-Mail Notify for Win 95/Winsock
eudor143.exe	941102	Eudora 1.4.3 WinSockAPI 1.1 POP3/SMTP mail client
ewais200.zip	940517	EINet WAIS client application for Winsock [1.5m]
ewan105.zip	941222	EWAN a free Winsock 1.2 Telnet with VT100
facto1.zip	950504	Factotum for Word note-taking add-in for v6.0
fagent10.zip	950711	Forte Free Agent News Reader v1.0 release
fingd100.zip	940801	Windows Finger Daemon v1.0.0
finger31.zip	930810	Windows Sockets Finger Client
fp10.zip	950417	FTP a text file with your IP address to UNIX host
fp2_0b4.zip	950627	FingerPlan 2.0 Beta 4 for Windows
fsp4win.zip	950702	The Winsock based FSP client
ftp4w22j.zip	950629	FTP4W.DLL: an interface for FTP based programs V2.2
ftpsrv11.zip	950312	Serv-U v1.1 - FTP Server (Daemon) for WinSock
gcp_24.exe	940402	REMOVED BY REQUEST OF DART COMMUNICATIONS
gophbk11.zip	930713	GopherBook, ToolBook based Gopher Client for WinSock
goslip2.zip	941002	GoSlip: A Winsock SLIP dialer (VB app) [1.23mb]
hgoph24.zip	940117	H gopher 2.4 is a Winsock compliant gopher client
icc119.zip	950710	Internet Control Center 1.19, 7/02/95
iefng097.zip	950410	Finger client for Winsock 1.1 Internet connection
indxer11.zip	950501	makes an Index of your Netscape cache
inetv22.zip	950323	Internet-Connect, Version 2.2 [957k]
iphlp.zip	941031	.HLP files for TCP/IP protocol & management
ircii2-6.zip	950130	IRC 2.6 for Winsock
ivc11.zip	941222	REMOVED: PROGRAM HAS GONE COMMERCIAL
kalive.zip	940824	App (w/src) keeps Winsock connect alive by pinging it

mirc34.zip	950710	Internet Relay Chat v3.4
mircfq13.zip	950710	FAQ about mIRC version: 3.4
mmwwwpc1.zip	941008	MultiMedia World Wide Web PC
mosaic.exe	950628	Spry Mosaic with Internet Account
msntcn16.zip	950703	Convert Mosaic mosaic.ini to bookmark.htm for Netscape
nd250s.zip	941208	NetDial v2.5 Internet Dialer with many features
nslookup.zip	950305	NSLOOKUP - name server lookup for Winsock v1.1
nsmed23.zip	950505	Netscape Bookmark Editor Version 2.3
nx10b4.zip	950630	News Xpress Version 1.0 Beta for Winsock
powwow13.exe	950422	PowWow: Internet chat, file transfer and Web Browser
prontoip.zip	950418	Pronto/IP is an advanced Windows Internet mail client
qvtw3989.zip	950107	Windows-Sockets compliant version of TCP/IP WinQVT/Net
qws3270.zip	950731	qws3270 winsock tn3270 emulator
serweb03.zip	931209	World Wide Web Server for Windows 3.1 and NT
sextnt10.zip	950703	Manages Netscape Navigator bookmarks
sl1001.zip	950222	SlipStream Jet 1.001: Import Usenet into QWK Readers
slip11p.exe	950710	Slip.Net Internet Launcher - Version P
slipdb10.zip	941022	Records SLIP connect and disconnect times/calc cost
smosaic.zip	940919	Simple configuration utility for Mosaic for Windows
smtsrf11.zip	950627	SmartSurf V1.1 Windows Online Costs Monitor
sticky07.zip	950110	Sticky POST-IT(TM) Notes allow inter-pc talk (Winsock)
syslogd.zip	950116	Syslog-daemon for MS-Windows and Windows-NT (Winsock)
tardis2a.zip	950108	Windows time synchronization utility that uses winsock
tchess11.zip	950318	TeleChess 1.1 for Winsock Chinese Chess Game
tcp32.zip	950114	MS TCP/IP 32 Release for Windows/Workgroup 3.11
trmptel.zip	940311	Trumpet TELNET (VT100) Terminal for Winsock
tronfs10.zip	941219	Tropic NFS Server v1.0: NFS server via Winsock
trp110.zip	950406	offline news/mail reader, NNTP, SMTP, POP3,fingerd
trtcp11b.zip	941206	Tropic TCP/IP v1.1b TCP/IP Stack for Windows
tsync1_8.zip	940819	Winsock app sets your PC's clock to match a remote host
twnsck12.zip	941203	TwinSock free implementation of proxy sockets for Win
twsk20b.zip	941106	Trumpet Winsock.DLL Version 2.0 Rev B (11/3/94)
twsk21e.zip	950718	Trumpet Winsock.DLL Version 2.1 Rev E
txtsrv.zip	931002	ext server for Winsock API; speaks finger protocol

wanvas10.zip	950627	Winsock based computer network whiteboard
wftpd196.zip	950130	Windows FTP daemon 1.96 for Winsock 1.1
wgopher.zip	940201	Gopher for Windows Version 2.2
winapps2.zip	941031	Winsock apps that were prev bundled with winsock.zip
winelm.zip	940319	WinElm E-mail reader for Winsock
winfsp12.zip	930810	FSP download application which uses WINSOCK.DLL
winftp.zip	940111	WinSock FTP program executables for Windows NT
wingp.zip	940311	Green Pages for Window Sockets 1.1 Winsock [951k]
winpanda.zip	940311	Panda:gopher, FTP, email & news clients for Winsock
winsock.zip	940202	Peter Tattam's Trumpet Winsock ver 1.0
wintelb3.zip	931202	NCSA Telnet for MS Windows (unsupported beta 3)
winter14.zip	950702	Listing of Winsock based Shareware/Freeware clients
winvn926.zip	941009	NNTP newsreader for Microsoft Windows 3.1 or Windows/NT
winweb.zip	940810	WinWeb Version 1.0 A2: Web Browser
wlpr20.zip	950220	WinLPR 2.0, a Windows Sockets based LPR client
wlprs40c.zip	950220	WLPRSPL v4.0c, a Windows Sockets based print spooler
wmaster2.zip	950722	WebMaster v2.0 - World Wide Web Address Book
wnvndc92.zip	941007	WinWord Doc for WinVN Topic Based Client Newsreader
ws_cha30.zip	950722	Chat program for Windows (winsock)
ws_ftp.zip	950424	Windows Sockets FTP Client Application v95.04.24
ws_ftp.zip	950628	Windows Sockets FTP Client App Version 94.10.18
ws_ftp32.zip	950628	Windows Sockets FTP Client Application v95.04.24
ws_ping.zip	931020	Windows Sockets PING Client App Rel 1 Version 94.10.20
ws_watch.zip	950311	Windows Sockets Net Watch - Alpha version 17 95.03.11
wsarch08.zip	950720	ALPHA (V0.8) of a Winsock archie client
wsatest.zip	940311	WSA Test Program for Winsock
wschesb1.zip	940318	Multiplayer Winsock Chess Beta 1
wsck-nfs.zip	931029	Allow PC-NFS v5.0 to handle any Winsock compliant app
wsfngr15.zip	950501	Winsock Finger Client Version 1.5
wsftp32.zip	950107	Windows Sockets FTP Client for NT
wsftp32.zip	950701	WinNT Sockets FTP Client
wsg-11.exe	941015	WinSock WSGopher v1.1 (350k)
wshost11.zip	941012	Windows Sockets Host V1.00 (IP number to hostname)
wsircc20.zip	950703	WinSock IRC Client Ver 2.00

wsircv20.zip	950703	WinSock Video IRC Client Ver 2.00
wslpd.zip	931002	Winsock Line Printer Daemon LPD for Windows
wsmtpd16.zip	931027	Windows 3.1 and NT SimpleMailTransProtocol Daemon
wsntp15f.zip	941107	WINSNTP - A Simple NTP client for Windows
wsock1b2.zip	930728	WinSock: Socket-DLLs for NCSA Telnet for Windows
wsping32.zip	950305	WSPING32 for Winsock and Win32s
wstbar25.zip	950711	Toolbar for Internet winsock apps
wstim101.zip	940817	Windows Time (RFC 868) Client for Winsock
wtalk124.zip	950429	Wintalk Version 1.24
wtwsk10a.zip	931002	Trumpet Newsreader NNTP for Windows Sockets API
wvnsc926.zip	941007	Sources for WinVN Topic Based Client Newsreader [1.1m]
wwebst07.zip	950320	Windows Socket Webster client v0.7
xfing025.zip	950627	XFinger v0.2 Winsock finger client
xfs191.zip	950404	NFS client for use with packet drivers
xfs32120.zip	950404	NFS client for WfW and MS-TCP/IP-32
xplan03.zip	950627	Update .plan file through winsock
xraywi12.zip	940825	X-Ray/Winsock - Winsock API trace/debugger for Win 3.1
yawtel07.zip	950721	Yet Another Windows socket Telnet v0.7 Beta

This list is presented not to suggest that it is in any way comprehensive, but to give you a sense of the variety of good, low-cost software currently available. By the time you read it, this list will undoubtedly be outdated. A Win 95 list is in the process of growing and it is likely that many of the foregoing items will be modified for consistency with Win 95. The Win 95 list, at the time I downloaded it, also from the cica archive, was:

```
**
** Index of:
**    Network Utilities: Windows Sockets (Winsock) Compliant TCP/IP
**    Networking Applications and Other Windows95 network Utilities.
**
** In Directory: ~ftp/pub/pc/win95/netutil
**    On Archive: ftp.cica.indiana.edu [129.79.26.27]
** Last Updated: Wed Aug 30 1995 at 02:29:46 AM EST
**
```

atalkw95.zip	950730	Version 2.0.0.100 Beta of A-Talk Comm App
e9911w95.zip	950818	email Notify retrieves mail headers from POP3 server
e997w95.zip	50704	The Fingerer/32 v0.31b finger client and more
hostinfo.zip	950817	Shows IP address information (host names and numbers)
mirc35.zip	950808	mIRC v3.5: IRC client with user-friendly interface
ntsntp22.zip	950801	Simple Network Time Protocol for Win95
popmon01a.zip	950710	POP your mail from multiple emailboxes
qvtnt398.zip	950801	TCP/IP for Windows 95 and NT
rdun61.zip	950730	RoboDUN: Dial-Up Network Script Utility V0.61
recon.zip	950820	Recon 1.0: Redial a lost netork connection
stst07b4.zip	950801	32-Bit SMTP/POP3 Daemon for Windows 95
ttcfing.zip	950709	TTC Finger Custom Control v2.00a
ttcftp.zip	950709	TTC FTP Custom Control v2.00a
ttcghst.zip	950709	TTC GetHost Custom Control v2.00a
ttctime.zip	950709	TTC Time Custom Control v2.00a
ttcwho.zip	950709	TTC Whois Custom Control v2.00a
w4serv21.zip		W4-Server 2.1 is a HTTPD server
watch95.zip	950628	Win 95 Sockets Net Watch v95.05.28
winvn_99.zip	950801	32-Bit Usenet News Reading/Posting program
ws_ftp32.zip	950628	Win 95 Sockets FTP Client App for Win95

Hardware Requirements

There are no special hardware requirements for use of the software noted above other than a machine that will properly run Windows in a networking environment. Each of the workstations must, therefore, be equipped with a network interface card, adequate memory and disk storage, and have a 386/486/Pentium processor. In general, for a business environment, this means a machine with 8 Mb of memory and probably 500 Mb+ of disk storage; 16 Mb of memory would be better, especially if you are considering Win 95.

A Server/Gateway/Router

Several of the configurations suggested in subsequent chapters require a PC set aside for use as an Internet server, a gateway, or a router. Much of the substance of those chapters revolves around a detailed look at the software necessary for these tasks. Keep in mind what each of these terms means:

- Server—a computer in a network that is shared by multiple users, such as a file server, print server, or communications server; a computer in a network designated to provide a specific service as distinct from a general-purpose, centralized, multiuser computer system; a computer system that provides services for another. A computer on the network capable of recognizing and responding to client requests for services. These services can range from basic file and print services to support for complex distributed applications.

- Gateway—the hardware and software necessary to make two technologically different networks communicate with one another; a gateway provides protocol conversion from one network architecture to another and may, therefore, use all seven layers of the OSI reference model; a special-purpose, dedicated computer that attaches to two or more networks and routes packets from one to the other. The term is loosely applied to any machine that transfers information from one network to another, as in mail gateway. A hardware/software package that runs on the OSI application layer and allows incompatible protocols to communicate.

- Router—A software and hardware connection between two or more networks, usually of similar design, that permits traffic to be routed from one network to another on the basis of the intended destinations of that traffic. If a router is located in a server, it is called an internal router; if located in a workstation, it is called an external router. The hardware and software necessary to link two subnetworks of the same network together; the hardware and software necessary to link two subnetworks at the network layer of the OSI reference model; any machine responsible for making decisions about which of several paths network traffic will follow. In the Internet, each IP gateway is a router because it uses IP destination addresses to choose routes. Routing is the assignment of the path by which a message will reach its destination.

The most generic of these terms is *server*. Throughout this book we will talk about mail servers or internet servers or something similar. The intent is merely to convey the idea that it is often useful to take a PC, put it on your LAN, and dedicate it to providing the communications between your LAN and the Internet, no matter how we design those communications. Sometimes, however, such servers can provide more functionality than communications. You might, for example, be able to put the communications processes on your file server or on a print server or all these functions might coexist on the same machine. A basic rule is, however, that the more functions you place on a machine, the more powerful the machine must be in terms of speed, memory, and disk resources. It is also sometimes advisable to use separate machines for two or more of these functions in order to have the entire LAN run more smoothly. Even if yours is a peer-to-peer LAN that does not formally require a dedicated server, dedicated servers can be set up and will provide more stable operations.

As we will use the term here, *Internet server* implies a PC with an appropriate operating system that can handle all Internet access, including on-demand dialing of the ISP, routing of IP packets to and from workstations on your local LAN, and assorted email and news chores. In this configuration all your local workstation users must go through the Internet server to obtain Internet services. Appropriate operating systems would include *nix (Unix, Linux, etc.), Novell NetWare 3.1x or 4.x, or Windows NT Server version 3.5. Conversely, if you use a standalone router (see below), then you might still opt to have an Internet server, but it is not necessary. In this scenario, while all workstations must access the Internet through the router, the router provides no services other than routing. If any additional services are offered, that must happen on individual workstations. Even in this iteration of possible configurations, therefore, you might opt to also set up an Internet sever, but one without the router capabilities. By way of contrast, if all you need are mail services, then you might opt for only a *mail server*, or *mail gateway*. In this context these terms are more-or-less interchangeable.

The mail server/gateway has the more limited task of finding Internet mail intended for your LAN users, downloading it, and redistributing it. From Chapter 2 you may recall that the two basic methods for transferring mail is with a POP client on your LAN plus some gateway software for redistributing the mail, and providing full SMTP services on your LAN, which requires a level of management in which you may not wish to engage. There are techniques available that can allow a POP client to operate over a standard asynchronous dialup line, but your ISP may not be set up to make use of such features. For that reason we'll bypass that option. Let's just assume that you will have a SLIP/PPP connection to the ISP. If you do the full SMTP service, you will still need to distribute the mail, and that may include setting up a POP server on your mail server with POP clients on each workstation. This is a level of complexity you might wish to avoid. Fortunately, there is email gateway software available that will take the Internet mail obtained through a POP client, reformat it, and redistribute it through the version of MS-Mail that comes with Windows for Workgroups (WFW). It is that option that we will describe in some detail in Chapter 4. Although there are no special server requirements other than a machine that can successfully operate with WFW, a separate machine dedicated to this, or a limited number of services is desirable.

The hardware required for the server applications varies depending on what you are doing. For a mail-only server you can refer to the suggestions for workstations, discussed earlier. If you have a Novell NetWare LAN, then you have probably already followed the recommendations of Novell for servers. Windows NT Server 3.5 and *nix systems do not require special considerations over the workstation suggestions other than memory. Microsoft recommends no less than 16 Mb of memory for the NT server and most versions of *nix work better with more memory. Depending on whether you plan to use the machine as a file server as well will dictate the amount of disk storage. In general, a faster machine (a fast 486 or a Pentium) will do better in these applications than an old 386 that you may have lying around. Although both Novell and Microsoft have a variety of software available to do some of the tasks mentioned in this book, you may also want to look at third-party software from the standpoint of both cost and functionality.

An On-Demand Dialup Router

We discussed earlier what routers are supposed to do. As we have already noted, one of the attributes needed to make a low-cost connection to the Internet work effectively is on-demand dialing, whether the routing is to be accomplished by a server doing routing or by a standalone device. *On-demand dialing* simply means the ability of the router to dial your ISP when someone on your local network wants a connection to the Internet. What this usually means in terms of setting up your own LAN is that the router defaults to dialing the ISP when it receives a request for connection to an address that does not exist on the local network.

Dedicated Routers

Several such routers were reviewed for this book and will be discussed separately and in some detail. Such routers can operate to provide dial access to your LAN as well as dialup capabilities from your LAN. Some of the routers support more than a single asynchronous port (to be connected to a modem), and some have built-in modems. A few are designed primarily for connection with related equipment made by the same manufacturer while others should be able to connect to virtually any appropriate SLIP/PPP service. In its simplest form the router will have a single asynchronous port to be connected to a modem or an RJ11 modular outlet from a built-in modem to be connected to the telephone line. In addition, it will have a connector for your LAN. Some of the routers come with the capability of connecting to either a 10BASE-T (twisted pair) or a thin wire (RG50 Coax) Ethernet cable; with others the kind of connection must be specified. The range of prices for single port units runs from about $1,300 to about $1,700. The units, when connected, must be configured for your LAN.

PCs as Routers

In addition to dedicated routers, we have already noted that personal computers, running the appropriate operating system, can also be used as routers. The operating systems we will review in subsequent chapters, used for purposes of routing, will be Linux (a Unix clone) and Windows NT Server 3.5. The example of Linux should be considered as a more or less generic discussion of using almost any *nix system for routing. Chapters 5 and 6 are devoted to each of these operating environments, and will detail what is necessary on the router side. The remainder of this chapter will note some issues relating to workstation setup when using a router.

Workstation Issues When Using a Router

If you intend to use a router, whether a dedicated router or a personal computer configured with an appropriate operating system, then you should make some initial decisions concerning your configuration on each workstation on your LAN:

1. You will need a winsock system that will provide you with the ability to manipulate a *routing table* on each local workstation. Although Trumpet can be configured to be used with a router, you may find the Microsoft winsock to be more flexible. You might also wish to look into commercial third-party TCP/IP stacks. The advantage of the Microsoft subsystem is that it offers several additional tools that you may find useful. The TCP/IP utilities offer network connections to non-Microsoft hosts such as UNIX workstations. You must have the TCP/IP network protocol installed to use the TCP/IP utilities. These standard utilities are:

   arp—Displays and modifies the IP-to-Ethernet or token ring address translation tables used by Address Resolution Protocol (ARP). This command is available only if the TCP/IP protocol has been installed.

   ftp—Transfers files to and from a computer running an FTP server service (sometimes called a *daemon*). FTP can be used interactively or with ASCII text files. The FTP application is found in the Accessories program group if you install the TCP/IP connectivity utilities.

   ipconfig—This diagnostic command displays all current TCP/IP network configuration values. This utility is of particular use on systems running DHCP for automatic TCP/IP configuration that do not have user-specified values, but this command can be used on any computer that has Microsoft TCP/IP-32 installed.

   nbtstat—Displays protocol statistics and current TCP/IP connections using NBT (NetBIOS over TCP/IP). This command is available only if the TCP/IP protocol has been installed.

   netstat—Displays protocol statistics and current TCP/IP network connections. This command is available only if the TCP/IP protocol has been installed.

   ping—Verifies connections to a remote host or hosts. This command is available only if the TCP/IP protocol has been installed.

   route—Manipulates network routing tables. This command is available only if the TCP/IP protocol has been installed.

   telnet—This connectivity command starts terminal emulation with a remote system running a TELNET service. The TELNET application is found in the Accessories program group if you install the TCP/IP connectivity utilities. TELNET is a Windows Sockets–based application that simplifies TCP/IP terminal emulation.

tracert—This diagnostic utility determines the route taken to a destination by sending Internet Control Message Protocol (ICMP) echo packets with varying time-to-live (TTL) values to the destination. Each router along the path is required to decrement the TTL on a packet by at least 1 before forwarding it, so the TTL is effectively a hop count. When the TTL on a packet reaches zero, the router is supposed to send back an ICMP Time Exceeded message to the source system. Tracert determines the route by sending the first echo packet with a TTL of 1 and incrementing the TTL by 1 on each subsequent transmission until the target responds or the maximum TTL is reached. The route is determined by examining the ICMP Time Exceeded messages sent back by intermediate routers. Notice that some routers silently drop packets with expired TTLs and will be invisible to tracert.

Under Windows for Workgroups 3.11 there is a help file called *mtcpip32.hlp*. Each of the commands given above are described in detail in that help file. For Windows 95 these commands are detailed in the Windows 95 Resource Kit manual, pp. 1136ff. Windows NT Server 3.5 has a help file named *tcpip.hlp*.

2. If you are using Microsoft TCP/IP, along with a router, then you must place an entry in your routing table with the route.exe command:

```
route add yyy.yyy.yyy.yyy xxx.xxx.xxx.xxx
```

where yyy... = ip address of the router/gateway at your ISP, and xxx... = ip address of the router on your local LAN. To successfully access the Internet through your ISP, this route must be present on each of your workstations. Most notably, you must have a route from each workstation to your router/gateway:

```
route add zzz.zzz.zzz.zzz xxx.xxx.xxx.xxx
```

where zzz... = the ip address of a given workstation, and xxx... = the ip address of your local router.

It is not always apparent that these commands need to be issued. They can be issued only after TCP/IP is loaded. You might place them in a batch file that is executed from a pif file with an icon in your startup program group, for example. In order to see what your routing table looks like, from a DOS command prompt (under Windows) issue the command **netstat -r<Enter>**. The result will be a listing of your routing table.

Conclusion

In this chapter I have attempted to provide an overview of the software and hardware necessary for setting up your connection to the Internet. Some of the software discussed or mentioned above will be described in greater detail in subsequent chapters. In fact, most of the remaining chapters will be given over to specifying particular solutions for attaching your LAN to the Internet. No book can cover all possible solutions, but those you find here are premised on the notion that there are relatively inexpensive solutions. As you may have inferred from comments given above, the emphasis should probably be on the word *relatively*. If you decide to go with both a server and a router, which in some ways is the easiest way to set up your connection, you will spend (assuming you buy everything new) something in the following neighborhood:

Server hardware and software:	$1,500 to $2,000
Router:	$1,300 to $1,700
Telephone line:	$240 to $300/year
Internet Service Provider:	Depends on service offerings
Total:	$3,040 to $4,000/first year

This does not include the value of your time or anything you might spend to have someone else set up the connection. For these expenditures, however, you will get easy access to the Internet.

The figures given above are approximate and hardware and software prices generally decline each year. Likewise, with greater numbers of ISPs coming to the market, service prices are also coming down. These numbers are to be compared with figures in the $15,000 to $25,000 range for first-year operation of a connection with a leased line. They also need to be compared with multiple individual subscriptions to services such as CompuServe, America Online, or local ISPs. If all you need is email for a small group, these latter alternatives may be the least expensive.

Notes

1. The material in this paragraph is drawn largely from: *WINSOCK FAQ* (Sept. 1994), Frequently Asked Questions About Windows Sockets Version 1.1, 6 Sept. 1994. This file lives at: **ftp://SunSite.UNC.EDU/pub/micro/pc-stuff/ms-windows/winsock/FAQ** and **ftp://papa.indstate.edu/winsock-l/faq+txt/winsock.faq**. This FAQ has been put together by Mark Towfiq, with much-appreciated assistance from Jay Allard, Bruce Backman, Paul Brooks, Mark Fisher, Martin Hall, Simon Hewison, Lynn Larrow, Mike Morse, Bob Quinn, Ed Schwalenberg, J. Daniel Smith, Bill Tang, Dave Treadwell, and Fred Whiteside. If you have any modifications to this FAQ, send them to **towfiq@East.Sun.Co**.

2. One of the better CDROM collections, and one that is updated periodically, is that from InfoMagic. They may be contacted at 602-526-9565 (voice); 602-526-9573 (fax); and by email at **info@infomagic.com**.

ALL WE WANT

IS MAIL

(AND MAYBE NEWS)

When email is the primary service of interest, there are three methods that can be employed: the use of UUCP (Unix-to-Unix CoPy), SMTP (either through dial access or through high-speed lines), and the Post Office Protocol (POP). The advantages and disadvantages of these three approaches, and how to set them up, are the subjects of this chapter. One of the first things to keep in mind is that electronic mail is simply a system to send messages between or among users of a computer network and the programs necessary to support such message transfers. It is, in other words, a system a computer user can employ to exchange messages with other computer users (or groups of users) via a communications network. Electronic mail is one of the most popular features of the Internet.

Email Issues

Unix-to-Unix CoPy (UUCP) was originally (and still is) a program run under the Unix operating system that allows one Unix system to send files to another Unix system via dialup phone lines. Today, the term is often (inappropriately) used to describe the large international network, called Usenet, which uses the UUCP protocol (among others) to pass news and electronic mail.[1] It is a system of closely integrated programs providing file transfer capabilities; it originated in the Unix world, but has expanded to many other operating environments. UUCP can also apply to the UUCP command, which is part of the UUCP system, thus resulting in some confusion.

The Simple Mail Transfer Protocol (SMTP), defined in STD 10, RFC 821, is used to transfer electronic mail between computers. It is a *server-to-server protocol*, so other protocols are used to access the messages. The Post Office Protocol (POP) is originally designed to allow single-user hosts, using early PCs, to read mail from a server. There are three versions: POP, POP2, and POP3. Later versions are *not* compatible with earlier versions, although POP3 has become the primary variant. The use of POP requires a host machine that runs both SMTP and POP since POP receives messages from SMTP (from the Internet) or from local email systems. On your LAN, what you need is a POP mail client that can collect mail from the remote POP server.

Each of the methods just referred to are in widespread use on the Internet today. The thing that they have in common is not the method of transportation so much as it is the common formatting of the email messages. An email message, as defined by RFC#822, consists of header fields and, optionally, a body. The body is simply a sequence of lines containing ASCII characters. It is separated from the headers by a null line [i.e., a line with nothing preceding the CRLF (carriage return/line feed characters)]. The key to the email message is that the header fields are standardized and readable by both people and machines. Therefore, it is relatively easy to produce new programs that manipulate email in a network environment.

There are other mail protocols in widespread use, although they were originally developed for proprietary and competitive marketing purposes. There is, for example, the messaging application program interface (MAPI), which is a set of calls developed by Microsoft used to add mail-enabled features to Microsoft Windows applications. Similarly, Novell supports MHS (Message Handling Service), an electronic mail system developed by Action Technologies, Inc., and licensed by Novell for its NetWare operating systems. It allows for the transfer and routing of messages between users and provides store-and-forward capabilities. MHS also provides gateways into IBM's PROFS, Digital's All-in-1 office automation system, and X.400 message systems. The use of the acronym *MHS* is sometimes confusing in that it also refers to the more generic concept of *Message Handling System*. MHS often refers to mail systems that conform to the OSI (Open Systems Interconnect) model, which are based on CCITT's X.400 international message protocol.

Unfortunately, email systems that have their origins in proprietary marketing activities frequently have addressing schemes, as well as headers, that make simple transferral of their email messages to and from the Internet difficult. Within the context of the Internet an email address has the general form *userid@domainname*. The older UUCP-oriented addressing, of the form *machinename!userid*, is also recognized where *domainname* becomes a part of the *machinename* or where *domainename* is substituted for *machinename*. Thus, my Internet address, *tmadron@ewc-inc.com*, can also be written, for some purposes, as *ewc-inc.com!tmadron*. Thus, an email address can be defined as the domain-based or UUCP address that is used to send electronic mail to a specified destination. There are three types of addresses in common use within the Internet. They are email address, IP (or Internet) address, and hardware or MAC address.

When an exclamation point (!) is used in an address it is called a *bang*. It is used to separate machine names in an extended UUCP path. When a file or email message is traversing a long distance via UUCP it may have to go through several machines. Thus, a *bang path* is a series of machine names used to direct electronic mail from one user to another, typically by specifying an explicit UUCP path through which the mail is to be routed. Today, over the Internet, it is rarely necessary for you to use a bang path. When mail is not properly addressed it can bounce back to you. *Bounce* is the return of a piece of mail because of an error in its delivery. It is caused, more often than not, by incorrect addressing by the sender.

When setting up your email system, whether as part of broader access to the Internet or as your sole method of using Internet services, you will want to make the system as friendly as possible to your employees. "Friendly" means, among other things, to have a single point of contact for email. Many users of small LANs, be they Novell or Microsoft or something else, use email systems. Microsoft's current Windows offerings all come equipped with a version of Microsoft Mail, for example, and you may already be using it. If you can avoid it, it would be best not to have to use another Mail User Agent (MUA). An MUA is the user interface to the mail system—the software that the user uses to read, store, and send mail. The MUA passes the email message off to the Mail Transport Agent (MTA), which is the software responsible for transporting mail from source to destination, possibly transforming protocols and addresses, and routing the mail.

When we're trying to get messages from Microsoft Mail, or an MHS-based mail system, to the Internet, however, we're more likely to need a more comprehensive mail gateway. A gateway, you will recall, is the hardware and software necessary to make two technologically different networks communicate with one another; a gateway provides protocol conversion from one network architecture to another and may, therefore, use all seven layers of the OSI reference model. The term *mail gateway* is loosely applied to any machine that transfers information from one email system to another. Here we use it in the sense of protocol conversion as well as the transferral of messages.

There are other things to think about once you start using Internet email. These are largely issues of convention and taste. It is common, for example, to provide a *signature block* at the bottom of an email or newsgroup message. The signature consists of a three- or four-line message at the bottom of a piece of email or a Usenet article that identifies the sender. Large signatures (over five lines) are generally frowned upon. The information you may wish to include in such a signature might be your full name, your company name, your physical address, phone number, fax number, and Internet email address. Why include the email address when your address should come along with the email message in the first place? There are several ways in which a sender's email address might end up being reformatted or otherwise changed, which would make it difficult to do a simple reply. It is good practice, therefore, to add your email address to your signature block.

Internet Newsgroups

Newsgroups provide a method for groups of people to correspond in a discussion group about a particular topic. Newsgroup technology is essentially an extension of email, so you can usually arrange for subscriptions (which tend to be free) to

newsgroups from your Internet Service Provider (ISP) and receive and reply to
newsgroup messages with the same software you use for email. Although there are
literally thousands of newsgroups accessible via the Internet, one of the more popular classes of newsgroups are those that provide support for specific computer-
related products. Newsgroups came into being with the development of Usenet (not
the Internet). Usenet is a collection of thousands of newsgroups, the computers that
run the protocols, and the people who read and submit Usenet news. Not all
Internet hosts subscribe to Usenet and not all Usenet hosts are on the Internet.
Usenet came into being when the only available method of communication was
UUCP. A newsgroup host on the Internet must use the Network News Transfer
Protocol (NNTP), defined in RFC 977, for the distribution, inquiry, retrieval, and
posting of news articles.

Some newsgroups are moderated, some are not. The moderator of a newsgroup is a
person, or a small group of people, who manages moderated mailing lists and
newsgroups. Moderators are responsible for determining which email submissions
are passed on to list. You may have noticed that I slipped in a new term, *mailing
lists*. Some discussion groups do not use newsgroup software. Rather, they are literally operated over the email system. They operate from a *listserve*. Listserve lists (or
listservers) are, like Usenet newsgroups, electronic discussions of technical and nontechnical issues conducted by electronic mail originally over BITNET using LIST-
SERV protocols. BITNET, one of the precursors to the Internet, can now be
considered a subset of the Internet. Similar lists, often using the Unix readnews or
rn facility, are available exclusively on the Internet. Internet users may subscribe to
BITNET listservers. Participants subscribe via a central service, and lists often have
a moderator who manages the information flow and content.

As with email itself, some conventions have grown up in the use of newsgroups.
Newsgroups can be very helpful, although the resulting volume of email can be
enormous. Many of the contributions to newsgroups tend to be sophomoric in their
content. A result of this is that beginners are often encouraged to just listen to discussions before becoming active participants. An Internet-specific definition of the
word *lurking* has been concocted to apply to such activity. Lurking happens when
there is no active participation on the part of a subscriber to a mailing list or
Usenet newsgroup.

How Do We Do It?

Within a single chapter there is no room to provide detailed notes on how to set up on your LAN all the variants of email described earlier. The approach we will take, therefore, is to provide you with an overview concerning the general way in which you might deal with this issue using UUCP and SMTP, and a detailed look at how to do this with a POP service. There are several reasons for this approach: (1) the relative simplicity of the POP approach; (2) the relatively low cost of POP service; (3) the complexities of handling UUCP and SMTP; and (4) the general undesirability within a low-volume, not-always-on-line SMTP server. If you want to go in either of these directions for any reason, then you should, after reading this chapter, be able to find appropriate software and explanatory materials.

First, a note about costs. Email software comes in three price ranges: cheap, moderate, and expensive. These categories do not necessarily correlate with poor, middling, and good products. In fact, depending on what you wish to do, some of the more expensive systems may not provide a good solution for you. The solution I have chosen to present here is based on the use of mail gateway software from netApp Systems.[2] The cost of the server software, called *Office Version for MS Mail*, was, at this writing, $89 per user on your LAN (there are multiple price breaks, all the way up to $2,200 for an unlimited number of users per server).

The client product was originally designed to run on Microsoft's Windows for Workgroups, although support is now available for Windows NT Workstation and Win 95 (Microsoft Exchange, the '95 version of MS Mail). The server software runs nicely on Windows NT Server 3.5 and will work on WFW 3.11 as well. The key here is that this is a relatively low-cost gateway solution allowing you to use MS Mail, which comes with WFW, and other Windows products. The product installs very easily and quickly. A primary advantage of this product is that you can get a trial copy and use it with five users for 30 days before you decide to buy.

Internet Service Requirements

You will need to acquire a SLIP/PPP Internet service. It should be with a service provider that delivers mail via POP. It should also be with an ISP that will assist you in obtaining your own domain name and is willing to associate with your real Internet address. Not all ISPs extend these services, but those that cater to businesses will almost always provide them.

Hardware/Software Requirements

Although netApp Systems says that you need only Windows 3.1 or greater, you should probably upgrade to at least Windows for Workgroups 3.11, and for purposes of networking, Win 95 is much better. On the server you will need Winsock 1.1 or greater. If you want to use this product, and you want to move to Win 95 or Windows NT on your workstations, you might wish to place a call to netApp Systems and check the status of their support for Win 95. At the moment, a reasonably configured 386/486/Pentium will handle the task—use whatever is easily and cheaply available. It would make sense to configure MS Mail to have its post office (a directory called *wgpo*) on the mail server. If you configure to use Windows 3.11, I suggest the use of Trumpet Winsock because of the ease of setting up its dialer and the fact that it supports both SLIP and PPP so you do not have to be concerned about what your ISP offers. It will also do on-demand dialing. Of course, you will need a network interface card in the server to access your LAN. Win 95 and Windows NT are delivered with extensive networking capabilities.

Software Installation

One of the most irritating things about software is incomplete instructions telling how to install it, or having it spread across a number of different documents. The installation of this particular email system requires the following software components on your mail server/gateway:

A. If using WFW 3.11:

1. Microsoft Windows for Workgroups 3.11, standard LAN installation. Three system files are of particular importance: *autoexec.bat*, *protocol.ini*, and *system.ini*. There will be some modification of these files when installing this software. For the installation of WFW 3.11, however, follow Microsoft's instructions.

2. Trumpet Winsock (try to get the latest version, which at this writing was 2.1 and the zipped file was called *twsk2lb.zip*). When you obtain Trumpet,

also get the separate installation procedure, a zipped file entitled *twswfwg.zip*. They both may be obtained by anonymous FTP from **ftp.trumpet.com.au**.

B. Or Windows NT Server 3.5, or Win 95.

C. netApp Systems *Internet Offiice for MS Mail*. A similar, though currently unsupported gateway is available from Microsoft and on various archives for WINNT, but it requires an upgrade to the MS Mail post office that may constitute an additional expenditure. A 30-day evaluation copy may be obtained by connecting to **http://www.netapps.com/download.htm/**. From this page you can directly download the current version via FTP.

Trumpet Winsock

For purposes of this demo setup, Trumpet Winsock is probably the easiest winsock to set up. Trumpet can be set up for either SLIP/PPP or for TCP/IP on a LAN. You may need to use both at some point and this can be accomplished with a single installation of the programs by setting up two icons in your program manager group that contains Trumpet pointing to different versions of *trumpwsk.ini*. For local use, unzip *twswfwg.zip* in a suitable temporary directory on your hard disk, or to a floppy, then follow the instructions given. This section will focus on an installation to support the netApp System Office Version for MS Mail. There are ten critical files that must be unzipped from the Trumpet archive: *winsock.dll*, *tcpman.exe*, hosts, services, protocol, *sendreg.exe*, *setup.cmd*, *login.cmd*, *bye,.cmd*, and *trumpwsk.hlp*. Installation instructions, beginning with version 2.1, are contained in *trumpwsk.hlp*, so this is also a critical file. These notes are based on the information provided in that help file.

Preparing for Installation

These notes, like *trumpwsk.hlp*, do not assume much, if any, knowledge concerning the Internet, although we do assume that you know your way around Windows. Most users of Trumpet use it in a manner similar to the procedures described here: for dealing with TCP/IP over a SLIP/PPP connection. In order to install Trumpet successfully you will need adequate memory (about 300–400 k RAM), about 1 Mb of disk storage, and the ability to enter some data for the setup screen (which we'll get to shortly).

You will probably acquire Trumpet in an archive file called *twsk21f.zip* or something similar. You will need a copy of *pkunzip.exe* or *unzip.exe* to unzip the files listed above and contained in the archive. Shareware versions of *pkunzip.exe* are readily available on virtually all on-line services and bulletin boards. To place all the files in the appropriate directory, at your DOS prompt, type the following (suitably modified for your environment):

```
md c:\trumpet
pkunzip twsk21f c:\trumpet
```

This will put all the listed files into a directory called *c:\trumpet*. You can, of course, change the *c:* to any appropriate drive letter.

The files that will be unzipped into *c:\trumpet* will include all those noted above, plus some utilities. After setup you will also have one additional important file: *trmpwsk.ini*. The files in the system as distributed at the time of this writing were:

- *winsock.dll*. Some version of *winsock.dll* is required for a standard operation of TCP/IP under Windows since it contains the TCP/IP protocol stack. You must be careful not to have multiple copies of *winsock.dll* lying around on your computer or none of them will work. If you acquire winsock-based software from several different sources, you can end up with this situation.

- *tcpman.exe*. With Trumpet, an additional program, *tcpman.exe*, is required to control the way in which *winsock.dll* communicates with the Internet. Many versions of *winsock.dll* do not have an equivalent management program, although the functions must be available, especially if both SLIP/PPP services and local LAN TCP/IP services are provided. The settings for *tcpman.exe* are stored in *trumpwsk.ini*.

- *trumpwsk.ini*. Although many *.ini* files reside in your Windows directory, you will normally want *trumpwsk.ini* to remain in *c:\trumpet*. This placement facilitates setting up the Winsock in a networked environment. If you are using Trumpet for both SLIPP/PPP and local LAN TCP/IP purposes, you will have to implement alternate *.ini* files. This can be done from the *tcpman.exe* command line that can be set by using alternate Icons in a Trumpet program group. Alternately, you can type everything in each time by clicking /File/Run in Program Manager.

  Alternate *.ini* files can be set on the command line by using the **inipath** command line option. A typical command line for use with SLIP/PPP might be the following:

  ```
  tcpman -inipath=C:\winsock\dialup.ini
  ```

  where *dialup.ini* is your Trumpet *.ini* configured for SLIP/PPP. The file can be called anything, but the entire pathname must be given. You can change the command line for an icon in a Program Manager program group by highlighting the icon and selecting File/Properties from the menu.

The Trumpet documentation discourages directly editing the *.ini* file settings, since most of the parameters can be changed from *tcpman.exe*. Experienced users may find it helpful, however, to understand the following parameters:

ip_buffers	The number of buffers for internet frames
pkt_buffers	The number of buffers specifically for the packet driver
slip_logging	Takes a log of a dialup SLIP/PPP session, and saves it as *usage.log*
font	Sets the font of the Tcpman displays
lip_rcvbuf	Size of the outgoing comms ring buffer
slip_sndbuf	Size of the incoming comms ring buffer

Some network parameters can be overridden by environment variables. They have the same names as the saved parameters in *trumpwsk.ini*.

- *sendreg.exe*. When you get ready to register your copy of the Trumpet system, you can use this automatic registration program. You are strongly encouraged to register the software.

- *hosts*. A list of host names to which you will be connecting. Because you will be using several programs that make use of *hosts*, this file is probably best placed in your Windows directory. It follows the format of standard Unix *hosts* files.

  I use essentially the same *hosts* file on my WFW machines, a Unix machine, Win 95 machines, and Windows NT Server 3.5 machine with *winsock.dll* from a variety of publishers. A *hosts* file might look something like the following:

```
# Sample HOSTS file:
#
# This file contains the mappings of IP addresses to host names. Each
# entry should be kept on an individual line. The IP address should
# be placed in the first column followed by the corresponding host name.
# The IP address and the host name should be separated by at least one
# space. Aliases to the basic host name can usually be inserted by separating
```

```
# the aliases on the same line by at least one space or tab character. For
# many winsock-based programs the hosts file does two things: First, it
# allows you to get an IP address without going through a name server. Second,
# it allows your winsock-based programs to use a shorthand form of the fully
# qualified domain name (FDQN) for some remote host.
#
# Additionally, comments (such as these) may be inserted on individual
# lines or following the machine name denoted by a '#' symbol.
#
127.0.0.1       localhost       #Universally required, do not change.


# The first entry following the 'localhost' line is usually your own local address.
# If you are using TCP/IP on a LAN, you would also add the IP addresses and
# names of other systems on your LAN at this point. My own workstation
#       is (this will not work for you), for example:
198.139.158.3 arms1             arms1.ewc-inc.com


# Other systems you frequently access are then listed here. Typical entries might
# be the following:
203.5.199.51    trumpet         ftp.trumpet.com.au


198.105.232.1   microsoft       ftp.microsoft.com


137.65.1.3      novell          ftp.novell.com


# You may also want to have the addresses of you ISP's mailserver, DNS
# hosts, and gateways listed here. Real IP addresses and FDQNs are required
# at this point:
aaa.bbb.ccc.ddd         isp.mailreader.network.net
aaa.bbb.ccc.ddd         isp1.network.net
aaa.bbb.ccc.ddd         isp2.network.net
```

- *services*. List of Internet services. This almost never needs to be edited.

- *protocol*. List of Internet protocols. This almost never needs to be edited.

- *trumpwsk.hlp*. The general Trumpet Winsock help file in Windows helpfile format.

- *login.cmd*. A sample login script. Since everyone's login sequence will be specific to your own ISP, it will probably be necessary for you to modify this sample script. See "Automating Your Login Sequence" in *trumpwsk.hlp* for some tips from Trumpet on how to do this quickly.

- *setup.cmd*. A short script that allows you to update your login phone number, username, and password. This information is saved in your *trumpwsk.ini* file.

- *bye.cmd*. A sample bye script. All modem initialization strings are written with the assumption that you will be using a Hayes or Hayes-compatible modem.

Miscellaneous utilities distributed with Trumpet Winsock include the following:

- *tcpmeter.exe*. Displays the network bandwidth. Incoming traffic is displayed across the top of the screen in green, and outgoing is across the bottom in red.

- *trumphop.exe*. Provides a list of the gateways that are traversed by a packet on its way to a destination address.

- *trumpdig.exe*. Provides information on a domain or address.

- *trumping.exe*. Trumpet Ping is a diagnostic program that allows you to send test packets to a known host on the Internet. It is useful for checking your TCP/IP connection.

Installing the Trumpet Winsock Over SLIP/PP

You must modify the path line in your *autoexec.bat* to contain a reference to your Trumpet directory. For example, the path statement in *autoexec.bat* might be modified to look like the following:

```
path c:\dos;c:\windows;c:\trumpet
```

You can make this path statement active by rebooting your computer, executing your autoexec.bat, or by typing the foregoing line when in DOS (not in a DOS window from within Windows), and hitting the <Enter> key. You can check that the path is set correctly by starting *tcpman.exe* from the File Manager. To do this select File/Run from Program Manager and enter **tcpman**, then click **OK**.

For simplicity of operation you should create a program group for your Trumpet files: Select File/New from Program Manager, and choose Program Group. If you do not know how to do this, see the installation instructions in *trumpwsk.hlp* for a detailed, step-by-step procedure for getting this accomplished. We're now ready to set up Trumpet Winsock for SLIP/PPP.

The setup screen for SLIP/PPP is found in *tcpman.exe*. Open *tcpman.exe* by double clicking the Tcpman icon, then select /File/Setup to open the Setup dialog. Depending on the service your ISP offers, you will need to check either Internal SLIP or Internal PPP. These options can be seen in Figure 4.1. This is a real setup, so yours *must* change. Some details will be grayed out now. You cannot fill them in. If you have a preassigned IP address, enter it; otherwise, if your ISP allocates IP addresses dynamically, enter 0.0.0.0 as your IP address. Set the SLIP (or PPP) port to the number of the communications port to which you've connected your modem (COM1, COM2, COM3, or COM4). If you are using COM2, enter 2. Set the Baud rate for your modem. For a fast, smart modem, enter something like **38400** or **57600** (check your modem manual for a recommendation). Set hardware handshake and Van Jacobson CSLIP compression as required. Your ISP can tell you about the Van Jacobson parameter. Select the kind of on-line status detection your modem supports (or leave it at "none" for the moment). Make sure that your modem has a default power on setting of AT&C1 for DCD detection to function. You may also need to set &D2 or &D3 as well. By default, all dialing is done with 8 bits, no parity. This may not work for you, depending on what your ISP requires. If your ISP does not use 8 bits with no parity, you will need to go to Dialer/Options and select Use Control Panel settings for parity and word size. When you are done, click on **OK** and if all goes well, the Trumpet Winsock will be initialized, although you will probably get a message to quit *tcpman* and restart it. These setup options may be seen in Figure 4.1.

The next step in a successful automated logon to your ISP is to determine the precise login requirements. It is possible that your ISP has provided you such information. Frequently, however, that is not the case, particularly when the ISP delivers its own software package. You can log onto your ISP using a terminal emulator package. The easiest thing to do is to use a package that will record the entire session to a file. You will then not be able to use that file to build your *login.cmd* script.

To obtain all the information necessary for a successful login script you may still have to ask your ISP for some specific information, but recording a logon session will help you identify what you need. A typical and real (though fictitious user IDs

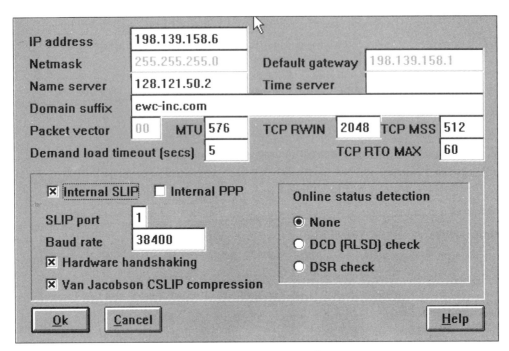

◼◼◼◼◼◼◼ **Figure 4.1** Trumpet Winsock (*tcpman.exe*) setup screen.

and passwords are given) login for a PPP connection with a preassigned IP address is the following (I typed the material in **bold** type; the computer generated all other information):

```
CONNECT 38400

<cr>

<cr>

<cr>

The system's name is hwmin.

Welcome to USL Unix System V Release 4.2 Version 1

login: pppuser

Password: mypasswd

Unix System V/386 Release 4.2 Version 1.1.3

hwmin

Copyright (c) 1992 Unix System Laboratories, Inc.

Copyright (c) 1987, 1988 Microsoft Corp. All rights reserved.
```

```
Last login: Sun Sep 10 22:58:35 on term/i1A
~}#@!}!7} }4}!}$}%\}"}&} } } } }%}&P*r<R~
~}#@!}!8} }4}!}$}%\}"}&} } } } }%}&P*~
~}#@!}!9} }4}!}$}%\}"}&} } } } }%}&P*r5};~
~}#@!}!:} }4}!}$}%\}"}&} } } } }%}&P*r&~
~}#@!}!;} }4}!}$}%\}"}&} } } } }%}&P*r65~
```

For this system there are three items or sets of items of importance: 1. the first three
<cr>s following the CONNECT message; 2. the line starting with **login:**; and 3. the
line starting with **Password:**. The CONNECT message is sent by your modem to
your computer to indicate that your machine is connected to your remote host.
Once that CONNECT message has been received you must wait for the login:
request. Some machines, however, require you to send one or more carriage returns
(**<cr>**, the **<Enter>** key) before it returns anything and the number of **<cr>**s required
may vary with your phone system, noise on the line, and similar issues. The login
procedure recorded above translates into the following login script:

```
#
# initialize modem
#
output atz\13
input 10 OK\n
#
# send phone number
#
output atdt1-800-555-1212\13
#
# now we are connected.
#
input 30 CARRIER
input 30 CONNECT
#
# wait for the username prompt
output \13
output \13
```

```
output \13

output \13

#

input 30 ogin:

output pppuser

output \13

#

# and the password

#

input 30 word:

output mypassword

#

# we are now logged in

#
```

Similarly, the following session is recorded from a login to a SLIP provider:

```
CONNECT 38400

****************************************************************************

*                                                                          *

*                     Welcome to Ringo Terminal Server                     *

*                                                                          *

*                          $Revision: 1.68 $                               *

****************************************************************************

User Access Verification

Username: myuserid

Password: mypasswd

Ringo>slip default

Entering SLIP mode.

Your IP address is aaa.bbb.ccc.ddd.  MTU is 1500 bytes

Header compression will match your system.
```

The SLIP provider doesn't require any carriage returns to get the initial prompt, which, in this case, is not **login:** but **Username:**. This provider also generates IP addresses dynamically, so what I have given as **aaa.bbb.ccc.ddd** will be a real IP address but will change with every login.

```
#
# initialize modem
#
output atz\13
input 10 OK\n
#
# send phone number
#
output atdt555-1212\13
#
# now we are connected.
#                        .
input 30 CONNECT
#
# wait for the username prompt
#
input 30 name:
username myuserid
output \u\13
#
# and the password
#input 30 word:
password mypassword
output \p\13
#
# we are now logged in
#input 30 >
output slip default\13
#
# wait for the address string
#
input 30 address is
#
# parse address
```

```
#
address 30
input 30 \n
#
# we are now connected, logged in and in slip mode.
#
display \n
display Connected. Your IP address is \i.\n
```

Both these illustrative login scripts do something that is probably not a generally wise idea: They hardcode the user ID and password. Variables can be used for this purpose. The use of the backslash (\) tells the script processor to send special characters symbolized by the numbers or letters that follow (\13 is a carriage return, for example). For a complete description of the scripting language, see "Scripting Language" in *trumpwsk.hlp*.

Before modifying or writing your own script take a look at the sample *login.cmd* file that comes with the Trumpet distribution. Second, find out if your ISP has a preconfigured Trumpet Winsock login script. Many Internet providers have prepared scripts for connecting to their systems; it may be worth contacting yours to see if they have a suitable script. And make sure that that you've got logging in manually under control.

Next, try running the sample *login.cmd* without any modifications. The first time it is launched you will be asked to enter phone number, username, and password. You can change these later by running *setup.cmd*. If you receive a message saying that either SLIP or PPP has been established and that the script was completed, then your script may require no further work. It is possible that you will receive "script aborted" (possibly preceded by another error message). If that happens, go back to *trumpwsk.hlp*.

Finally, after you have tested out the software, register it.

Internet Series for MS Mail[3]

"Internet Series for MS Mail" is a product of netApp Systems, providers of messaging systems for the Windows environment. netApp's Internet Series of products for MS Mail provides individuals with mail and news services commonly found within the Internet or corporate network under the familiar graphical interface of Microsoft's Mail product (standard edition or WFWG add-on). All user interaction to these network facilities are performed within MS Mail in the same fashion that local mail is processed. In other words, sending and receiving mail to the network is identical to sending and receiving a message locally. No special encoding of recipient names is required and all received mail is properly tagged for easy replying. Attachments may be added for mail targeted to the network and any attachments received from the network are contained within the body of the received message as an icon. Signatures, a feature commonly found in general Internet mail user agents, are provided as well. There are actually three closely related gateway products.

- Internet Personal for MS Mail

  Internet Personal for MS Mail is the right solution for individuals and small offices looking for access to global mail facilities, and who are unwilling to pay the high costs of installing a gateway, acquiring a dedicated communications line(s) and setup of a private domain. As most (if not all) Internet service providers already have a POP3 or shell mail server, why reinvent the wheel? By using your existing MS Mail client and Internet Personal for MS Mail you will have full mail and news service capabilities at your disposal whether in a dedicated or dialup arrangement.

- Office Version for MS Mail

  Office Version for MS Mail is a true gateway solution, and is most likely used in situations where the added costs outweigh the administrative or network learning curve issues. In addition to the SMTP interface, Office Version can manage multiple remote POP3 mailboxes, forwarding mail to the particular owner of the mailbox or determining the local MS Mail owner of each mail message within a shared POP mailbox. Only one Office Version is required and this need not be a dedicated machine. However, for performance and availability reasons a dedicated machine is recommended.

  Internet Remote is an option to Office Version and creates a POP3 server interface to the MS Mail post office. When enabled, POP3 mail programs like Eudora or Internet Personal for MS Mail can be given access to local MS Mail mailboxes from anywhere on the Internet, making this a good solution for out-of-office employees. For Internet Personal users, this lets them manage all mail from within the MS Mail client whether they are in the office or on the road.

- Internet Middleware

  The Internet family of products for MS Mail are built on top of netApp's Internet Middleware toolkit which provides full mail and news facilities to C and VB programs, and DDE- and MAPI-aware applications (like Word, WP, Excel). Internet Middleware is an option to the Internet Series for MS Mail products or may be purchased separately.

The Internet Series products are licensed on a per user basis to maintain a low up-front investment, although unlimited versions of the Office Version functionality are available. Through a simple on-line reconfiguration the Personal product can take on the Office functionality (and vice versa), allowing installations to start with the Personal product and grow into the Office product.

Office Version

Of these products, it is Office Version that has primary applicability for this chapter. The features of the product include the following:

- Simple Mail Transfer Protocol (SMTP) support for inbound and outbound mail.
- Post Office Protocol v3 (POP3) support for inbound mail retrieval for selected users.
- Network News Transfer Protocol (NNTP) support for receiving and posting Usenet news.
- Can service multiple MS Mail users from a single gateway machine.
- Redirection to multiple MS Mail local users from a single shared POP mailbox.
- Can be used in multiple post office configurations.
- Inbound distribution list support (i.e., **all@abc.com**).
- Admin./Postmaster support for nondelivery reports (NDR).
- Automated client s/w distribution mechanism to ease roll-out of functionality to end users.
- User selectable encoding scheme (mime or UUencode).
- User defined signatures.
- Internet menu item on the MS Mail menu bar for easy access to options.
- MAPI/SMI support for seamless email operations from mail enabled applications like Word, Excel, WordPerfect, and so on.

- Internet Remote add-on. Post Office Protocol v3 (POP3) gateway support for retrieval of local MS Mail messages from a POP3 mail client (like Eudora).

Messaging Services

- Mime and UUencode aware (inbound and outbound).

- Automatic detaching of UUencode and MIME file attachments.

- Security to control auto detaching of files attached to a mail message (no, yes, prompt).

- Queued outgoing mail for SLIP/PPP connections (off-line mode).

- Signature capability for outgoing mail.

Server Facilities (available to all services)

- Event driven to allow other applications to continue processing while mail is being uploaded/download from the internet.

- No blocking calls, which provides the optimum access to the winsock interface.

- Multi-tasked to support multiple concurrent sessions.

- Standalone task to ensure performance with other applications.

- User reconfigurable to Office (gateway) functionality from the Personal model and vice versa.

Requirements

- Windows 3.1 or greater, Windows NT 3.5 or greater, or Windows 95.

- Winsock 1.1 or greater is only required for the Internet Server machine.

- **msmail.exe** and its associated components for Windows, or Windows 95, and **msmail32.exe** and its associated components for Windows NT.

The following is not required:

- MS Mail Gateway.

- Post Office upgrade. The standard Post Office that comes with Windows for Workgroups or Windows NT is sufficient.

Installation and Setup

The installation and setup of the server is quite simple. First, on the machine you intend to use as a mail server, unzip the zipped archive file (probably something like *inet_120.zip*) in which you received the software onto a floppy disk or a temporary hard disk directory. Then, from Program Manager, click on File/Run and run **install.exe** from the directory that contains your setup files. Log on as the MS Mail postmaster (whoever originally set up MS Mail on your LAN) and create a new MS Mail user for the gateway. The name should be "Inet GW," with a mailbox of "inetgw." These are the *required* names. At this point we can start the server and configure it:

The three main configuration steps are:

1. Install the software from the distribution disk or directory.
2. Configure the Internet Server component.
3. Configure the Internet Spooler component

The full set of installation steps are the following:

Step 1—Installation of the software

1. Run the installation program INSTALL.EXE out of the distribution directory.

Step 2—Configuration of the Internet Server

1. Create a new MS Mail user for the Internet Server. This is performed by MS Mail postmaster, using general administration utilities. The name should be "Inet GW," with a mailbox of "InetGW" (case insensitive).

2. Start the server by executing the Internet Server icon from the newly created Internet Series Program Manager group or by executing TM_SERVE.EXE out of your installed directory (*c:\inet*).

3. Enter your registration number if you have one through the About box (File Menu).

4. Select Config/Internet Default from the menu.
   - Enter your SMTP relay server name (smart host). This is the SMTP main gateway provided by your service provider.
   - Enter your NNTP server name (Usenet server). This is the News server provided by your service provider.
   - The other information is not required for an Office Version configuration.
   - Press OK.

5. Select Config/Attachment Options
   - Select the desired action to be performed when an attached file is received.

Not Enabled: The special encoding of any attached files will remain in the body of the message and will not show up in MS Mail as an attachment

Enabled: The special encoding of any attachments will be removed and the attachment will show up in MS Mail as an icon.

Prompt: Should not be selected while in Office mode.

Enter the default directory in which to temporarily store any attached files before they are transferred into the MS Mail system.

- Press OK.

6. Select Config/Office Version

- Enter the MS Mail login id (mailbox name) and password for the Inet Gateway user defined in step 1 above. This will be the mailbox id of the "Inet GW" user (i.e., InetGW).

- Enter the full friendly name of the MS Mail user who will act as the system administrator for the Office Version system (postmaster in SMTP terms). This may be left blank. If configured, any mail which Office Version cannot determine an owner for will be forwarded to this MS Mail user.

- Select Active in the Mail section.

- Enter the desired interval to check for outbound mail.

- Unselect Active (for now) in the Mail section.

- Press OK.

7. Press the User Aliases button to define the association between local MS Mail users and the network. This brings up the Local Name Associations dialog. For each user to be defined to the system the following steps must be followed.

- Press Add Name and enter the full friendly name of the MS Mail user.

- Press Add Assoc. and add the network name for that user. The network name is the portion of an Internet address to the left of the @. Any number of network associations may be added for each MS Mail user. The first entry for each MS Mail user will be used as the return address (from address) for any outgoing mail.

  For example:

  John Smith
     jsmith
     john
  Jane Doe
     jane

Any incoming mail for **jsmith@domainName** or **john@domainName** will be forwarded to MS Mail user John Smith. Any outgoing mail from John Smith will have a network address of **jsmith@domainName**.

Notes:

Changes are dynamic and are acted upon immediately. There is no need to recycle the product after an update has been made.

MS Mail names may be a distribution list. In this case any mail received from the network alias will be forwarded to all members of the distribution list. Distribution lists are defined while in MS Mail.

8. POP Server Access (optional)

Office Version can connect to one or more POP servers and pull down the mail, distributing it to specified users. When accessing a remote POP server, Office Version can forward the POP mailbox to a single MS Mail user (one to one association) or can scan the headers of each mail message with the POP mailbox to determine the local MS Mail recipients (POP redirection).

POP redirection mode uses the associations defined in step 7 above to determine which local user(s) receive the mail. Any mail which has no corresponding MS Mail recipient will be forwarded to the administrator/user if defined in step 6 above.

To define POP accounts, press the POP Accounts button to access the POP Accounts dialog.

For each POP server to be accessed the following steps must be followed.

- Press Add.
- Fill in the server, account name, and password for the remote POP account in the Remote POP Account Information section.
- Select the desired direction method to be performed for this POP account in the Direct Mail To section. One to One redirection requires the MS Mail friendly name of the recipient to be entered.
- Select OK.

Notes:

Changes are dynamic and are acted upon immediately. There is no need to recycle the product after an update has been made. To initiate the connection sequence (provided one is not already in progress), press the Check Mail button.

Mailing lists received via the POP Redirection interface need special handling. See Receiving Mailing Lists below.

By default POP mail will remain on the remote POP server once downloaded. To delete the mail once it has been successfully downloaded into MS Mail follow these steps:

Select the Services button from the Office Version main dialog.

- Click the "Delete Mail" checkbox.

- Select OK.

9. Usenet Access (optional).

Office Version can connect to Usenet servers (NNTP servers) and download news articles from various news groups. Once downloaded they will be distributed to MS Mail user(s) or distribution list(s). In addition, news can be posted to the Usenet system.

To define the news groups to be downloaded, press the News Groups button to access the News Groups dialog.

For each News Group to be accessed the following steps must be taken.

- Press Add.

- Enter the name of a news group and select OK.

- Press Subscriber.

- Enter the MS Mail name of a user (or distribution list) who is to receive the news articles and press OK. Repeat this step for all subscribers of this news group.

- Press OK.

Note:

The MS Mail Spooler "check for mail" setting for the InetGW user should be modified through MS Mail to be less than that of the Internet Server to ensure timely delivery of outgoing mail. This dialog is available from the MS Mail menu Mail/Options.

Step 3—Quick check of the server

- Connect your Winsock to the network if you are not already connected.

- Get into the Config\Office Version Dialog.

- Click the Mail and/or News checkboxes Active.

- Check the status window. A started message and mail logon message should be visible.

Step 4—Distribution of the Internet Spooler to the MS Mail users

- Run the Internet Spooler Client Configuration utility INETCCFG.EXE from the installation directory (C:\INET).

- Address the distribution of the Internet Spooler Client Kit to the appropriate users.

- Press Send.

The client kit has now been distributed to those users. Eventually a mail message will be received in the MS Mail Inbox of those users (you can help this along by doing a "View New Messages" on the MS Mail menu of the client machine).

Note:

Windows users:

A manual copy of *inetspl.exe*, *inetmsm.dll*, *inetmsn.dll*, *inetrmt.exe*, and *inetmsr.dll* to the Windows directory of the client machine or to a shared directory which everyone has access to can replace the above operation. Once copied, each user must run *inetspl.exe* once to perform the initial configuration of the Internet Spooler.

Windows NT users:

A manual copy of *intspl32.exe*, *intmsm32.dll*, and *intmsn32.dll* to the WinNT/System32 directory of the client machine or to a shared directory which everyone has access to can replace the above operation. Once copied, each user must run INTSPL32.EXE once to perform the initial configuration of the Internet Spooler.

Step 5—Configuration of the Internet Spooler on the MS Mail clients

- Open the mail message with a subject of Internet Series for Microsoft Mail Client Installation.
- Double-click on the Internet Spooler Client Installation Program Icon.

MS Mail will be exited while the Internet Spooler is configuring itself. Once completed, MS Mail will be restarted with the Internet support enabled.

Step 6—Quick Check of the Internet Spooler

- Two folders will have been created (Windows users only); Inet Out and Inet In. These are holding areas for the Internet Spooler.
- An Internet menu item will be available on the MS Mail menu bar.
- Compose a new note.
- Address it to your network mail account (e.g., **jsmith@abc.com**) and enclose the name in square brackets. Also add your MS Mail id.
- Send it.
- The note should also end up in your standard Inbox (only your local MS name), while the networked message has been sent to the gateway.
- Your message will eventually come back in and find its way to your standard MS Mail Inbox.

- The mail should look like a standard mail message. That is, the envelope icon should be to the left and the message should be bold (as it is currently unread).

Return Addresses When mail is forwarded to an Internet address, a return address (or From address) is generated so that the receiving end may reply to the mail message. The return address is a combination of a local mailbox name and the domain name for the gateway (i.e., **localName@domainName**). The local name is determined by a lookup of the originator's real MS Mail name (not mailbox name) from the associations defined previously. If multiple entries are present for the originator's real MS Mail name, then the first entry within the definition is used.

The domain name is automatically taken from the configuration parameters of the Winsock interface. If the PC has been configured for a domain name other than desired, the domain name can then be overridden by getting into the Services dialog available from the Config/Office Version dialog. Some Winsocks (Trumpet being one) assign the domain name when the connection is made. In these cases it is best to define the domain name through the Services dialog. When Office Version starts, check the "SMTP Gateway active . . ." message to ensure the domain name is correct.

There are a number of finer points that the system is capable of handling. An example is the use of distribution lists. Another is the ability to set an idle time-out. With Idle time-out enabled, when the server has been idle for the specified amount of time, either it can be terminated completely or it can disconnect itself from the Winsock interface. Depending on the Winsock interface this may cause the connection (dialup) to be broken. This used in conjunction with "check mail every x minutes" can provide a cost-effective means of sending and receiving mail, as the server can dialup, connect into the network, download any mail and then disconnect. This is not recommended when the SMTP gateway function is required, as other SMTP gateways will not be able to communicate with the Office Version server, possibly resulting in lost mail.

This chapter is not a substitute for reading the documentation that is supplied with the product. Before implementing such a system it is incumbent on you to fully understand the product's installation and operation procedures. In any event, the actual distribution you receive may vary from the notes given above as a result of changes applied to the product. netApp Systems can be contacted at **infoinet@netapps.com**, **http:www.netapps.com**, or by telephone at 613-823-3839.

Conclusion

What we have presented in this chapter is a low-cost, third-party solution to setting up an Internet-to-MS Mail gateway. Its advantage is that it is low-cost. It is also relatively easy to implement. It requires only a SLIP/PPP account with an Internet Service Provider and a POP mail box. If your ISP will also associate your own domain name with your basic service, and help you get your own domain name, then you will have a service that will be economical and easy to operate. Your employees will not have to learn a new mail system and you will not have to buy addons from Microsoft.

Be aware, however, that you can achieve similar (though not identical) results through the use of Microsoft's own gateway products. They do not, so far as I have been able to ascertain, support POP accounts. Moreover, they can be a bit pricey. Finally, they may not fully or easily support on-demand dialing of your ISP. We will, however, return to some of the Microsoft solutions in later chapters. Similar results can also be achieved by using a Unix style operating system on a server that is dedicated to collecting and distributing email. While this specific issue is not addressed in Chapter 5, there should be enough detail in that chapter to provide some ideas about how you might go about configuring Linux (a Unix derivative) for that purpose.

Notes

1. For a fairly complete treatment of the use of UUCP as the basis for an email system, see Thomas Wm. Madron, *Low-Cost email Using UUCP: Integrating Unix, DOS, Mac, and Windows* (New York: Van Nostrand Reinhold, 1994).

2. netApp Systems, 95 Pheasant Run Dr., Nepean, Ontario, Canada, K2J-2R3, (613) 823-3839.

3. The notes given here for the installation of this software closely follow the instructions given in the appropriate files in the distribution archive. *You should also read those instructions as a supplement to this chapter.* This material is used with the permission of netApp Systems.

DO WE DARE

USE UNIX?

No solution to the server issue is without its pitfalls. How complicated it gets depends on what is being used and part of this revolves around the volume and the variety of ways that Internet access is desired. In Chapter 4 we outlined a methodology for setting up an inexpensive email-only system. We will now start to consider techniques for more expansive use of the Internet. As we have emphasized previously, the key to the use of the Internet by a group of people (as distinct from a solitary individual) is the use of a router. The router can take the form of a special-purpose standalone device, or a PC equipped with an appropriate operating system. The Internet itself was more or less founded on the use of machines running the Unix operating system.

In recent years, Unix-like operating systems, in addition to Unix itself, have come on the market and a standard for operating systems, Posix, has been developed. Posix is, in some ways, Unix without proprietary control. The result has been the development of other systems, such as Linux, that have most or all the capabilities of Unix, but are based on the Posix standard or have been developed independently.

The word *Unix* itself is not a generic term. Rather, it is a specific trademarked word (originally by AT&T, and now owned by Novell), that refers to a specific multitasking, multiuser operating system based on specific proprietary code. For this reason we have used the term **nix*, which is widely bandied about the Internet, to refer to our discussion of Unix and Unix-like operating systems. We will, in fact, concentrate on a Posix-compliant, Unix-like operating system called Linux, since it is designed for use on Intel-based technology (386, 486, Pentium, etc.). Regardless of what approach you finally take to setting up a router/gateway, I would encourage you to read this chapter, especially the section on routing.

Unix is a multitasking, multiuser operating system developed by Ken Thompson, Dennis Ritchie, and coworkers at Bell Laboratories (AT&T) in the 1970s. It is a powerful operating system implemented on a wide variety of computers from mainframes to microcomputers. During the early 1990s Unix was purchased by Novell and it is that corporation to which the code now belongs. A number of Unix variations have evolved, although most required the licensing of code, first from AT&T and now from Novell. Linux, by way of contrast to the corporate development of most popular operating systems, was originated by Linus Torvals, mostly as a hobby, while he was a student at the University of Helsinki in Finland. Torvals still retains the right to develop and maintain the Linux kernel, which is the foundation of the system. For the most part, however, Linux has found an important place in the marketplace because it has been developed and designed by hundreds or thousands of programmers around the world contributing their time and effort to its development. It can now be found in various versions in almost any large bookstore.

For our purposes, you need only know that Linux works pretty much like Unix and what is true of Unix is also usually true of Linux. This point is important because the networking tools available under *nix allow *nix systems to be configured as routers to the Internet. One reason why you might choose Linux is its low cost. Linux can be purchased for under $60 and is able to run on a 386 with 8 Mb of memory without much of a problem. The target hardware should have a CDROM drive (for installation) and adequate hard disk space (as little as 200 Mb can be used, but like any other OS, more is better). This chapter, then, focuses on Unix as a solution, and particularly on Linux as a low-cost Unix-like solution.

Advantages of Using Unix

There are, of course, both advantages and disadvantages in using any particular configuration of software, and using *nix is no different. There are several advantages of using a *nix system, and, assuming that *nix system will be Linux, they include the following:

1. Primary hardware and software can be obtained for relatively modest cost. Linux will run adequately on a 386 and quite well on a 486 machine. It will certainly run very well on a Pentium.

    a. Disk space requirements are very moderate and a 500+ Mb IDE disk drive will probably be adequate for the applications we discuss in this book.

    b. As with other contempoary operating systems, the more memory the better, but you can certainly start with 8 Mb.

    c. A CDROM drive is desirable for installation (and, I would say, well worth the expenditure).

    d. Linux is available on CDROMs in many books in the Computer sections of large book stores and may be ordered by U.S. Mail, by email, and through the WWW. It is available from any of these sources for under $75 and a subscription to updates can be obtained for $200–$300 depending on the frequency of updating.

2. Unix-based systems are *very* rich in the tools to make the processes discussed in this book work. What isn't available can often be written in shell scripts (the Unix equivalent of MS-DOS batch files).

3. Email and networking software comes standard with many *nix systems, and is always a part of Linux distributions. In other words, no additional software expenditures are needed.

Disadvantages of Using Unix

Part of the problem with using a *nix system is that some of the disadvantages turn out to be identical with the advantages:

1. *nix (Unix, Linux, whatever) is a complete operating system designed to provide an environment for significant production computing rather than individual workstations, as with MS-DOS and Windows. This means, that while it can do great things, it is also a nontrivial task to learn it well. If you start this

as a DIY project, and you do not already know *nix, then you are in for a very steep learning curve.

2. Because a large number of tools for dealing with *nix are available, some of the specific items you may need for this particular project to work smoothly may have to be written as local utilities. This approach is not very significant if you have a large information technology installation with several highly technical programmers (systems programmers), but a small business with no staff may find this problematic.

3. Although there is a growing amount of support service for Linux, and while commercial versions of Unix may be well supported, at least in theory, getting technical support via telephone is very problematic with a complex operating system and the quality of that support may not be very good. In other words, if you do this as DIY, then plan on literally doing it *yourself*. The alternative is to hire a *nix consultant for a short period of time to set up the system for you, although that has its problems as well.

There are other advantages and disadvantages that we will note throughout this chapter, but these, I think, are important to understand up front. Having made these comments, we now need to take a look at some of the primary issues to which we will have to pay attention in order to use a *nix system as our doorway to the Internet.

Common Design Issues

When you design your connection to the Internet there are some design issues that are common to all the solutions presented in this book. Some of those issues revolve around your gateway/router, and some around workstation requirements. In this section we will address those issues and refer back to them in other chapters. It will not be possible to provide you with definitive and categoric answers to all the issues simply because most can be resolved in a number of different ways. You may have to delve more deeply into some of the subjects and certainly you will have to read documentation that comes with your software. An example of documentation that comes with Linux is "A small treatise on the use of ProxyARP," by Al Longyear <longyear@netcom.com> (December 5, 1994). ProxyARP is one of the routing techniques often used with LANs connected to the Internet. As Longyear notes, proxyARP is used when you have a server, for it "will allow the dynamic connection of remote systems without the need for the update of the routing tables on [any] other system [than] the one associated as the 'server.'" Another problem common to setting up your gateway/router involves serial and modem connections. Generally, when dealing with serial/modem issues, using a dedicated router or Windows NT Server is somewhat easier than dealing with a *nix system. If you elect to use Linux, please read the Serial-HOWTO that will come with your system. The HOWTOs are a series of relatively detailed articles, updated with some frequency, that are available via anonymous FTP and on most Linux CDs. Crucial HOWTOs are also available in printed form in a book called *DRx Linux*, reprinted by several publishers. [1]

As we have done elsewhere, the term *server* is used here in a somewhat generic sense rather than in a technical client/server context. TCP/IP is essentially a peer-to-peer networking system. It is sometimes convenient, however, to call the system through which the Internet is accessed a server. The trick in any *nix system used as a router/gateway/server is to make certain that an IP packet is able to get from your LAN to the Internet and, when necessary, to receive a reply back from the Internet. There are several ways of accomplishing this feat, including the use of proxyARP, mentioned earlier. In Figure 5.1 you will see a LAN connected to the Internet. There are IP and Ethernet addresses attached to each of the LAN's devices. Likewise, there will be an IP address attached to the ISP's router and it will probably be attached to an Ethernet so it, too, will have an Ethernet address. The basic problem in routing IP packets stems from how the ISP's IP address is related to those of your LAN. First things first, however, so we will spend a short time on the Linux serial/modem questions, implied by the two telephones in Figure 5.1 and the line between them.

When you install Linux you will need to tell the installation program what components you need. In addition to the base system, select all the networking and communications options, regardless of what else you install.

The Serial/Modem Interface

First read the Serial-HOWTO distributed with Linux. This will give you information that is most consistent with the version of Linux you have purchased. Linux itself, and many of its components, are updated so frequently that what is said in

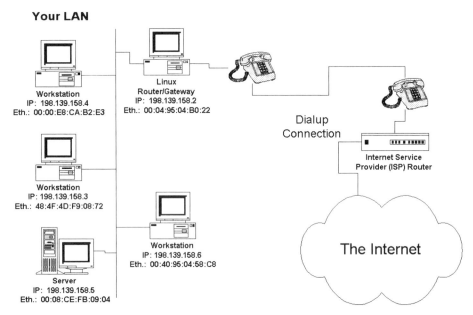

Your LAN

Figure 5.1 LAN connected to the Internet via dial access.

any book may be outdated by the time the book is published. The assumption I am making is that you will most likely buy version 1.2.x or later. The examples given in this book are based on kernel version 1.2.11. Much of what is said in this subsection is applicable, in principle (if not in detail), to other *nix systems.

Hardware Requirements

You may need only two serial ports, under MS-DOS referred to as COM1 and COM2, and under Linux as tty0 (COM1) and tty1 (COM2), for directly connected serial devices, such as a mouse or dedicated terminal, ttyS0 (COM1) and ttyS1 (COM2) for incoming modem-connected calls, and/or cua0 (COM1) and cua2 (COM2) for outgoing modem-connected calls. When this is the case, since any hardware you have will probably already be equipped with two serial ports, then the standard installation will take care of your needs. tty0 will be used for a mouse and ttyS1 and cua1 will be used for modem connections. Note, however, that with most *nix systems, while you can use the same port (in this example, the equivalent of COM2) for both incoming and outgoing modem connections, life is considerably simplified by using separate ports for incoming and outgoing purposes. Some versions of *nix may even require this.

As a side note, your computer may be equipped with four serial ports (COM1–COM4). These ports work through interrupts to communicate with the central processing unit. Unfortunately, COM1 and COM3 share interrupt 3 while COM2 and COM4 share interrupt 4. This makes it difficult to use *both* COM1 and COM3 and/or COM2 and COM4. Even when all four of these ports can be successfully configured, speed, reliability, or other communications attributes may suffer. If you need more than two ports, for whatever reason, you will be better off to acquire and install a multiport serial controller. There are several available. [2]

You will, of course, also need one or more modems. I would suggest the use of *external* modems rather than internal modems. They should be the fastest you can afford. We will assume 14.4 Kb modems in this discussion although you may wish to move to 28.8 Kb modems. Your modem requires a straight through cable, with no pins crossed. Any computer store should have these. Make sure you get the correct gender. If you are using the DB25 serial port, it will always be the male DB25. Do not confuse it with the parallel port, which is the female DB25. Hook up your modem to one of your serial ports. Consult your modem manual on how to do this if you need help.

Software Issues

The suggestions in this section may vary somewhat from those you will find in the appropriate HOWTOs. They are based on a working Linux system: a 386/DX40, 8 Mb of memory, 200 Mb disk storage, two standard PC serial ports, and a Cyclade Cyclom-8o 8-port serial board. Setup is often contingent on your particular hardware, so any suggestions, here or elsewhere, provide guides rather than categoric instructions. I am assuming that for purposes of this book you will be dialing out (not accepting incoming calls). The Serial-HOWTO explains how to set up for incoming calls.[3]

All of the CDROM distributions I have seen recently come with a full set of network and serial communications software, so you shouldn't have to go looking for anything else. The relevant programs/subsystems and their definitions are:

SLIP—Serial Line Internet Protocol. A predecessor to the point-to-point protocol. SLIP is used primarily when your ISP does not offer PPP connections. PPP is the more modern protocol used for sending IP packets across serial lines. Because both SLIP and PPP have built-in kernel support in Linux it is usually not necessary to do any special installation.

PPP—Point-to-Point Protocol. An industry standard protocol for data transfer across serial links. It allows for several protocols to be multiplexed across the link. PPP is a successor to the serial line internet protocol. Once you have installed Linux, the relevant files will be found in your */etc/ppp* and */usr/lib/ppp* directories. The PPP program is actually called **pppd**, and can be run as a daemon.

A *daemon* is a Unix program that is invisible to users but provides important system services. Daemons manage everything from paging to networking to notification of incoming mail. BSD Unix has many different daemons: without counting precisely, there are something like two dozen. Daemons normally spend most of their time sleeping or waiting for something to do, so they do not account for a lot of CPU load.

diald—On-demand dialup daemon used for facilitating transparent dial-access to the Internet. See pp. 168ff. for a detailed treatment.

DIP—Dialup IP Protocol Driver (v3.3.7n-uri [17 Apr 95] or later). **dip** handles dialup connections needed for dialup IP links, like SLIP or PPP. It can handle both incoming and outgoing connections, using password security for incoming connections.

chat—Automated conversational script with a modem. The **chat** program defines a conversational exchange between the computer and the modem. Its primary purpose is to establish the connection between the Point-to-Point Protocol Daemon (**pppd**) and the remote's pppd process. **chat** is part of the the standard Linux PPP distribution, although **dip** can now be used as well to automate the dialing of a remote system. You should need to use only **dip** or **chat**, not both.

getty/uugetty—Contained in the package getty_ps. **getty** is a program that handles the login process when you log onto a Unix box. There are three versions that are commonly used with Linux: agetty, getty_ps, and mgetty. 2.0.7e is the latest version of the getty_ps package, and supersedes any older versions. Most distributions come with the getty_ps package installed as */sbin/getty*. The getty_ps package contains two getties: **getty**, used for console, and terminal devices, and **uugetty**, which is used for modems.

setserial—**setserial** is a program that allows you to look at and change various attributes of a serial device, including its port address, its interrupt, and other serial port options.

stty—A program to change and print terminal line settings. If given no arguments, **stty** prints the baud rate, line discipline number (on systems that support it), and line settings that have been changed.

minicom—Friendly serial communication program. **minicom** is a communication program that somewhat resembles the shareware program TELIX but is free with source code and runs under most unices. Distributed with all recent versions of Linux.

The programs *setserial*, *stty*, and *minicom* are used to configure or test your serial/modem configurations.

Setting Up Your Modem   Only ttyS{0–3} are configured when you first bring up Linux. Those ports use the default IRQs of 4 and 3, just as is the case with COM1–COM4 on MS-DOS systems. If you have any other serial ports provided by other boards or if ttyS{0-3} have a nonstandard IRQ, you must use *setserial* in order to configure those serial ports. The full listing of options can be found in the man page.

First off, make sure your modem is working. Use **minicom** (or some other terminal program) to ensure that everything is working. It comes with Linux preconfigured for (ttyS1/cua1 [COM2]). It should work out of the box by typing:

```
minicom<Enter>
```

If all goes well, it will automatically configure the serial port and modem for its own use and you should see something like the following:

```
Minicom 1.70 Copyright (c) Miquel van Smoorenburg
Press CTRL-A Z for help on special keys
AT S7=45 S0=0 L1 V1 X4 &c1 E1 Q0
OK
```

The line beginning with "AT" are commands sent by *minicom* to your modem, and the modem responded with **OK**. If you type **AT<Enter>**, the modem should respond with **OK**. While you are in the program you may want to configure the modem completely for use by *uugetty*.

To do a configuration you need to be logged in as **root** or as **superuser**. Then issue the **minicom** command as follows:

```
minicom -s<Enter>
```

This will put you into setup mode. Highlight the Exit option on the menu and you will get the responses noted above. Then type:

```
AT S0=0 E1 V1 Q0 &C1 &S0 S7=60 &W0<Enter>
```

The modem should respond with **OK**. If it does not, or if it responds with **ERROR**, then retype the line. See the *minicom* man page for detailed information on how to use *minicom*. If you do not understand what you have just typed, read your modem manual. Exit from *minicom*.

If all has gone well, then type **Ctrl-a, x** (hold down the control key, press *a*, let up on the control key, then press *x*). This will take you out of the program and back to the command prompt. What you have just done is to configure your modem for use with **uugetty**, you stored it as configuration zero, and you (or a program) will be able to retrieve it by by issuing the modem command **atz<Enter>**. If all of this does not work properly, read the *Serial-HOWTO* carefully and try again.

If your modem responds to AT commands, you can assume your modem is working correctly on the Linux side. Use **minicom** to call another modem. When you dial out with your modem, set the speed to the highest bps rate that your modem supports. Since there is no speed named 57,600 or 115,200 bps, you must use the **setserial** program to set your serial port to a higher speed. Then, set the speed to 38,400 bps in your comm program. A 14.4 Kbps modem can typically be set for 57,600 bps and a 28.8 Kbps modem for 115,000 bps. The reason for this is that these smart modems communicate with your local computer at one speed and over a phone line with another modem at a different speed. A 14.4 Kbps modem can communicate locally at 57,600 bps even though the highest absolute speed that can be achieved over the phone line is 14,400 bps. Under some circumstances, providing the modems on both ends support it, the data can be compressed before being sent over the phone line, thus achieving a *throughput* rate higher than 14,400 bps. Most modems default to data compression and error correction off and these features should be left off (or turned off) while testing the link and may need to be turned off permanently. It is usually best to configure the modem to a fixed speed (57,600 bps) in order to prevent mismatches between your local computer and the modem.

You will quickly note that the highest speed for most communications software, including *getty*, is 38,400 bps. For the software to run at a higher speed, first use **setserial**, which allows you to use the maximum speed for your modem by issuing the command:

```
setserial /dev/cua1 spd_hi<Return>
```

This command can be run at boot time in a file called */etc/rc.d/rc.local* and it will hold for the session. If you run the command by hand, you will need to do so at least before you try to use a speed like 57,600 bps.

If your modem supports hardware flow control (RTS/CTS), you should use it. This is particularly important for modems that support data compression. First, you have to enable RTS/CTS flow control on the serial port itself. RTS/CTS is set using **stty**:

```
stty crtscts < /dev/cua1<Enter>
```

This procedure can be accomplished at startup in */etc/rc.d/rc.local* or */etc/rc.d/rc. serial*, both of which should be run from */etc/rc.d/rc.M*. If you have more than one port that you want to have run in this manner, you need to issue the command for each port (*/dev/cua1*, */dev/cua2*, etc.). You must also enable RTS/CTS flow control on your modem. For the typical Hayes-compatible modem, issue the command

```
AT&K3&W0<Enter>
```

to your modem while in **minicom**. Be sure to save your modem configuration by also using &W0, as in the example.

Controlling the Modem Ports with uugetty

In order to actually use serial (or other) ports, there must be some control software present. This is true of MS-DOS and Windows as well as Linux. The difference between DOS/Windows and any *nix system is, however, that under *nix the software must be set up explicitly. The advantage of this is that you have a great deal of control over the configuration of the ports. The disadvantage is that the setup becomes somewhat more difficult. The ports under Linux are controlled by

getty and **uugetty**. **getty** is used to control the ports when terminals are directly attached while **uugetty** controls the ports when modems are attached. There are three files that must be written or modified in order to configure **getty** and/or **uugetty**:

```
/etc/gettydefs
/etc/inittab
/etc/conf.uugetty.ttyS1
```

uugetty can control ports that use either fixed- or variable-speed modems. If you use several modems, and they are identically configured, both the */etc/gettydefs* and */etc/inittab* files can be very simple. If, however, you have several modems and they are configured differently, the files can get a bit more complicated. My own setup is probably fairly typical for a small business environment:

/etc/gettydefs:

```
#
#   This file works only with getty_ps.
#
#   Be sure to use CLOCAL for vt's and hard-wired terminals.
#
#   default/virtual console entry:
#
vc# B9600 SANE # B9600 SANE -ISTRIP CLOCAL #@S login: #vc

#   Modem locked at 38400:
#
F38400# B38400 CS8 CRTSCTS # B38400 SANE -ISTRIP HUPCL CRTSCTS #login: #F38400

DT19200# B19200 CS8 CRTSCTS CLOCAL # B19200 SANE -ISTRIP HUPCL CRTSCTS CLOCAL
        #login: #DT19200

2400# B2400 CS8 CRTSCTS # B2400 SANE -ISTRIP HUPCL CRTSCTS #login: #2400

#   Modem that autobauds to different speeds, terminal locked at 9600, etc:
```

```
#              - SANE includes CS8 ISTRIP HUPCL

#              - DON'T USE SANE or ECHO for initial config!!!!!

#


#2400# B2400 CS8 # B2400 SANE -ISTRIP #login: #2400


#1200# B1200 CS8 # B1200 SANE -ISTRIP #login: #1200


#300# B300 CS8 # B300 SANE -ISTRIP #login: #300
```

The lines that start with a pound sign (#) are comments. *Each of the substantive lines must be separated by a blank line.* The latter requirement is not obvious so you need to pay attention to it. This *gettydefs* defines four classes of *ports*. The first field in each line (five fields are delimited with pound signs) is a label. Hence, the four labels used are "vc," "F38400," "DT19200," and "2400." The line labeled vc defines your *virtual console*, the keyboard and display directly attached to the PC running Linux. Each of the other three lines define devices accessed through serial ports.

The five fields in a *gettydefs* record are: 1. label; 2. initial-flags; 3. final-flags; 4. login-prompt; and 5. next label.

1. The label field often contains the speed of the port for purposes of documentation, but it can be anything. The label will be used later in the */etc/inittab* file.

2. initial-flags—These flags are the initial ioctl(2) settings to which the terminal is to be set if a terminal type is not specified to **getty**. **getty** understands the symbolic names specified in /usr/include/termio.h (see termio(7)). Normally only the speed flag is required in the initial-flags field. **getty** automatically sets the terminal to raw input mode and takes care of most of the other flags. The initial-flag settings remain in effect until **getty** executes login(1m). [4]

3. final-flags—These flags take the same values as the initial-flags and are set just prior to **getty** executes /bin/login. The speed flag is again required. The composite flag SANE takes care of most of the other flags that need to be set so that the processor and terminal are communicating in a rational fashion. The other two commonly specified final-flags are TAB3, so that tabs are sent to the terminal as spaces, and HUPCL, so that the line is hung up on the final close.

4. login-prompt—This entire field is printed as the login-prompt. Unlike the above fields where white space is ignored (a space, tab, or new-line), they are included in the login-prompt field.

   The login-prompt may contain various @char and \char parameters. These are described in full in the getty(1m) [man page **getty**] section PROMPT SUBSTITUTIONS.

5. next-label—This indicates the next label of the entry in the table that getty should use if the user types a <break> or the input cannot be read. Usually, a series of speeds are linked together in this fashion, into a closed set, for instance, 2400 linked to 1200, which in turn is linked to 300, which finally is linked back to 2400.

   If **getty** is called without a speed argument, then the first entry of */etc/gettydefs* is used, thus making the first entry of */etc/gettydefs* the default entry. It is also used if getty can't find the specified label. If */etc/gettydefs* itself is missing, there is one entry built into **getty** that will bring up a terminal at 9600 baud.

   It is strongly recommended that after making or modifying */etc/gettydefs* it be run through **getty** with the check (-c) option to be sure there are no errors. This is accomplished by issuing the following command:

   ```
   getty -c<Enter>
   ```

   The initial and final flags are parameters that can also be set through the use of **stty**.

It may be helpful to take a close look at the sample listing given above. The five fields in the example are:

```
label:                F38400
initial-flags:   # B38400 CS8 CRTSCTS
     Sub-fields:
              B38400 - port speed in bits per second (bps).
              CS8 - set character size to 8-bits.
              CRTSCTS - set hardware flow control.
final-flags:     # B38400 SANE -ISTRIP HUPCL CRTSCTS
     Sub-fields:
              B38400 - port speed in bits per second (bps).
              SANE - set to base defaults.
              -ISTRIP - Clear high (8th) bit of input characters.
              HUPCL - Send a hangup signal when the last process closes the
                  tty.
```

```
                     CRTSCTS - set hardware flow control.
   login-prompt:     #login: [here, only the word "login:" is sent to the terminal].
   next-label:       #F38400 [go to the label "F38400", in this case, back to itself].
```

This record defines a port for a fixed-speed modem operating at 38,400 bps or higher.

The second record defines a port for a dumb terminal operating at 19,200 bps, hence the label "DT19200." One parameter has been added: **CLOCAL** (disable modem control signals). The **CLOCAL** parameter is required since we do not have a modem connected to the port, just a terminal:

```
 DT19200# B19200 CS8 CRTSCTS CLOCAL # B19200 SANE -ISTRIP HUPCL CRTSCTS CLOCAL
      #login: #DT19200
```

The third example is for a port with a 2,400 bps modem attached. It is identical to F38400 except that the speed parameters have been changed:

```
 2400# B2400 CS8 CRTSCTS # B2400 SANE -ISTRIP HUPCL CRTSCTS #login:
      #2400
```

With the high-speed smart modems, the modem-to-modem connect automatically takes care of speed differences between the modems. With lower-speed *dumb* modems, however, you must handle *autobauding*. An example of how to do this is given in the last three lines of the sample *gettydefs* file. The lines are commented out because I don't have that particular problem. Note, however, the next-label field in those lines. They successively point to the next line, and the last one, 300, points back to the beginning in order to form a loop. Thus, if a call comes in, it will filter through the three records until it finds the correct speed.

/etc/inittab: The listing below is my current */etc/inittab* file. Most of the entries are the defaults that will be installed when you install Linux. [5] The inittab file describes which processes are started at bootup and during normal operation (e.g., */etc/rc*, gettys...). Selected entries in */etc/inittab* are critical for incoming calls into your Linux system, although it is irrelevant for controlling outgoing lines. *Init* distinguishes multiple runlevels, each of which can have its own set of processes that are started. Valid runlevels are 0–6 and A, B, and C for on-demand entries. An entry in the *inittab* file has the following four fields, each of which are separated by colons:

```
 id:runlevels:action:process
```

Lines beginning with # are ignored. In this section we are concerned with only three lines; those relating to the three lines in *gettydefs* discussed above. The fields are defined as follows:

id—a unique two-character-sequence that identifies an entry in inittab.

> Note: For gettys or other login processes, the id field should be the tty suffix of the corresponding tty, e.g., 1 for tty1. Otherwise, the login accounting will not work correctly. This is a bug in login and will be fixed.

> In the sample file below, see the lines labeled "s1", "C0", and "C1". Please read the *inittab* man page for more information on */etc/inittab*.

runlevels—describes where the specified action should be taken.

action—describes which action should be taken.

process—specifies the process to be executed. If the process field starts with a "+" character, *init* will not do *utmp* and *wtmp* accounting for that process. This is needed for *gettys* that insist on doing their own utmp/wtmp housekeeping. This is also a historic bug.

The three lines of importance are:

```
s1:456:respawn:/sbin/uugetty ttyS1 F38400 vt100


# Cyclades serial lines
C0:456:respawn:/sbin/getty ttyC0 DT19200 tvi910
C1:456:respawn:/sbin/uugetty ttyC1 2400 vt100
```

The first line, labeled "s1," helps set up the serial line ttyS1 (COM2). The other two lines, C0 and C1, set up the first two lines of an 8-port Cyclades serial board. Each of the entries use "respawn" in the action field, which simply means that the process will be restarted whenever it terminates. In this particular case, if getty or uugetty terminates, then the process (and, hence, access to the serial lines/ports) will restart automatically. If this did not happen the system would quickly get into a state where logins on these lines are not possible.

The process field is of supreme importance, of course. For lines s1 and C1 *uugetty* is started in order to control ports attached to modems. The "F38400" on line s1 relates to the record labeled "F38400" in */etc/gettydefs*, discussed above, while "2400" relates to the 2400 record in */etc/gettydefs*. Record C0 starts a *getty* process using the DT19200 record in */etc/gettydefs*, to start a link with a hardwired terminal. The final subfield in the process field specifies the terminal type that is expected when the port/line is active. In the case of s1 and C1 a Digital Equipment Corportation (DEC) vt100-type terminal is specified. Virtually any communications program on the market today will emulate a vt100 so another PC can act as if it is a vt100. The hardwired line, C0, specifies a Televideo 910 terminal. The reason for that is I happen to own an old dumb terminal that emulates a tvi910.

Several techniques have been developed for allowing programs to be written for *nix systems that do not require knowledge of specific terminals, yet can address the screen for full-screen programs. An IBM PC, for example, normally uses only a single set of screen definitions, usually called "ansi pc." IBM, on its mainframe systems, more or less requires the use of terminals that look like 3270 Display System terminals and software manufacturers write to that standard. *nix systems, on the other hand, assume that virtually any kind of terminal may be at the other end of a communications line. Even the specification of a particular terminal in */etc/inittab* can be overridden later by a user by setting the TERM= environmental variable in their own *.profile* file or interactively after they log in. One of the techniques used by Linux for defining terminals is terminfo. *Terminfo* is a database describing terminals, used by screen-oriented programs such as vi(1), rogue(1), and ncurses(3X). Terminfo describes terminals by giving a set of capabilities that they have, by specifying how to perform screen operations, and by specifying padding requirements and initialization sequences. You can define new terminals if that ever becomes desirable or necessary.

■■■■■ **TIP**

Whenever you make a change to */etc/inittab* you must have the system reread the file so that the changes will take effect. This can be done by rebooting the operating system, or, more simply, by issuing the command **init q<Enter>**.

The sample *letc/inittab* file follows:

```
#
# inittab      This file describes how the INIT process should set up
#              the system in a certain run-level.
#
# Version:     @(#)inittab        2.04    17/05/93      MvS
#
# Author:      Miquel van Smoorenburg, <miquels@drinkel.nl.mugnet.org>
#
# Default runlevel.
id:5:initdefault:

# System initialization (runs when system boots).
si:S:sysinit:/etc/rc.d/rc.S

# Script to run when going single user.
su:S:wait:/etc/rc.d/rc.K

# Script to run when going multi user.
rc:123456:wait:/etc/rc.d/rc.M

# What to do at the "Three Finger Salute".
ca::ctrlaltdel:/sbin/shutdown -t3 -rf now
# What to do when power fails (shutdown to single user).
pf::powerfail:/sbin/shutdown -f +5 "THE POWER IS FAILING"

# If power is back before shutdown, cancel the running shutdown.
#s1:45:respawn:/sbin/getty ttyS0 19200 vt100
#s2:45:respawn:/sbin/getty ttyS1 19200 vt100

# Dialup lines
#d1:45:respawn:/sbin/getty ttyS0 38400 vt100
#d2:45:respawn:/sbin/getty ttyS1 38400 vt100
s1:456:respawn:/sbin/uugetty ttys1 38400 vt100
```

```
# Cyclades serial lines
C0:456:respawn:/sbin/getty ttyC0 DT19200 tvi910
C1:456:respawn:/sbin/uugetty ttyC1 2400 vt100
#C2:45:respawn:/sbin/uugetty ttyC2 F38400 vt100
#C3:45:respawn:/sbin/uugetty ttyC3 F38400 vt100
#C4:45:respawn:/sbin/uugetty ttyC4 F38400 vt100
#C5:45:respawn:/sbin/uugetty ttyC5 F38400 vt100
#C6:45:respawn:/sbin/uugetty ttyC6 F38400 vt100
#C7:45:respawn:/sbin/uugetty ttyC7 F38400 vt100

# Runlevel 6 used to be for an X-window only system, until we discovered
# that it throws init into a loop that keeps your load avg at least 1 all
# the time. Thus, there is now one getty opened on tty6. Hopefully no one
# will notice. ;^)
# It might not be bad to have one text console anyway, in case something
# happens to X.
x1:6:wait:/etc/rc.d/rc.6

# End of /etc/inittab
```

/etc/conf.uugetty.ttyXx In order for all this to work you need to have appropriate devices defined for your ports. These devices are simply small files in *lldev*. You might consult the Serial-HOWTO for some instruction on how to define devices, but the Linux equivalents of COM1–COM4 (cua0–cua3 and ttyS0–ttyS3) are set up when Linux is installed. Likewise, if you have a multi-port serial board, the setup procedure (which may require recompiling the kernel) will usually take care of creating the device files for you. For example, if you have your modem on ttyS3 you will need the *ldev/cua3* and *ldev/ttyS3* devices. More germane to this discussion, however, is the way in which *uugetty* can be customized through specifying parameters in *letc/conf.uugetty.ttyXx*, where *Xx* refers to specific device names like S1 or C2.

Note, however, that this book is aimed at *dialing out* to the Internet, so, strictly speaking, you will not usually need to concern yourself about this file at all if getting out to the Internet is your primary concern. Where the definition and control of incoming lines might be relevant is if you are connecting to your own corporate network rather than to a public ISP. In that event, the other end of the connection can be configured to automatically call you if it has incoming messages of one sort or another for someone on your LAN. That issue is outside the scope of this book, but in that instance, you would then have to configure your port(s) for incoming as well as outgoing calls. When that is the case, then */etc/conf.uugetty.ttyXx* becomes very important.

There are several parameters you can tweak for each of your ports. In order to do this you create a file in the */etc* directory for each port that will handle incoming calls. Alternatively, if all your incoming lines are handled in the same way, you can define a single file called */etc/conf.uugetty*. This file will be used by all instances of uugetty, and */etc/conf.uugetty.ttyXx* will only be used by that one port. Sample default config files can usually be found in */etc/default* after installation. One of the configuration files I use, defining one of the ports on my Cyclades card, is */etc/conf.uugetty.ttyC1*:

```
ALTLOCK=cub1
ALTLINE=cub1
INITLINE=cub1
CLEAR = YES
HANGUP=YES
DEBUG=010
INIT="" ATz0\r
#INIT="" ATz0\r OK ATE1Q0V1s0=1&c1&s0\r OK
WAITFOR=RING
CONNECT="" ATA\r CONNECT\s\A
TIMEOUT=75
DELAY=2
```

Although this file is used for customizing the port/line for incoming calls, note that three parameters use "cub1" as values. That is because those parameters define actions involving the Linux computer in *sending* information to the port, rather than receiving from the port. During the setup of the port and the modem, therefore, the process must use */dev/cub1* rather than */dev/ttyC1*. You will not normally need all the parameters available to you and you can get additional information by running **man getty**. In early versions of Linux getty/uugetty looked for the configuration files in */etc/default*. With the advent of a more standardized approach (FSSTND compliant) these files are found in */etc*.

During its startup, *uugetty* looks for the file */etc/conf.uugetty.*line, and if it is found, reads the contents for lines of the form:

```
NAME=value
```

The use of configuration files allows **getty/uugetty** to have certain features configurable at runtime, without recompiling. The recognized NAME strings, and their corresponding values, follows: [6]

SYSTEM=name—Sets the nodename value (displayed by @S—see PROMPT SUBSTITUTIONS) to name. The default is the nodename value returned by the uname(3) call.

VERSION=string—Sets the value that is displayed by the @V parameter (see PROMPT SUBSTITUTIONS) to string. If string begins with a '/' character, it is assumed to be the full pathname of a file, and @V is set to be the contents of that file. The default is */proc/version*.

LOGIN=name—Sets the name of the login program to name. The default is /bin/login (see login(1m)). If used, name must be the full pathname of the program that getty will execute instead of /bin/login. Note that this program is called, as is /bin/login, with the user's name as its only argument.

INIT=string—If defined, string is an expect/send sequence that is used to initialize the line before getty attempts to use it. This string is in a form resembling that used in the L.sys file of UUCP(1). For more details, see LINE INITIALIZATION. By default, no initialization is done.

ISSUE=string—During startup, getty defaults to displaying, as an issue or login banner, the contents of */etc/issue* file. If ISSUE is defined to a string, that string is typed instead. If string begins a "/" character, it is assumed to be the full pathname of a file, and that file is used instead of */etc/issue*.

CLEAR=value—If value is NO, then getty will not attempt to clear the video screen before typing the issue or login prompts. The default is to clear the screen.

HANGUP=value—If value is NO, then getty will *not* hang up the during its startup. This is analogous to giving the -h argument on the command line.

WAITCHAR=value—If value is YES, then getty will wait for a character from its line before continuing. This is useful for modem connections where the modem has CD forced high at all times, to keep getty from endlessly chatting with the modem.

DELAY=seconds—Used in conjunction with WAITCHAR, this adds a time delay of seconds after the character is accepted before allowing getty to continue. Both WAITCHAR and DELAY have the same effect as specifying -rdelay on the command line. If WAITCHAR is given without a DELAY, the result is equal to having said -r0 on the command line. The default is to not wait for the character.

TIMEOUT=number—As with the -t timeout command line argument, this tells getty to exit if no user name is accepted before the number of seconds elapses after the login prompt is typed. The default is to wait indefinitely for user name.

CONNECT=string—If defined, string should be an expect/send sequence (like that for INIT) to direct getty in establishing the connection. String may be defined as DEFAULT, which will substitute the built-in string:

```
CONNECT\s\A\r\n
```

The \A escape marks the place where the digits showing the speed will be seen. See CONNECTION AND AUTOBAUDING for more details. The default is to not perform a connection *chat* sequence.

WAITFOR=string—This parameter is similar to WAITCHAR, but defines a string of characters to be waited for. getty will wait until string is received before issuing the login prompt. This parameter is best used when combined with CONNECT, as in this example:

```
WAITFOR=RING
CONNECT="" ATA\r CONNECT\s\A
```

This would cause getty to wait for the string RING, then expect nothing, send ATA followed by a carriage-return, and then wait for a string such as CONNECT 2400, in which case, getty would set itself to 2,400 baud. The default is not to wait for any string of characters.

ALTLOCK=line—Uugetty uses this parameter to lock an alternate device, in addition to the one it is attached to. This is for those systems that have two different device names that refer to the same physical port, for example, /dev/tty1A vs. /dev/tty1a, where one uses modem control and the other doesn't. See the section on UUGETTY for more details. The default is to have no alternate lockfile.

ALTLINE=line—getty uses this parameter to specify a different device to use for handling modem initialization. If the WAITFOR option is being used, WAITFOR will be done on this line also. This is necessary for systems that exercise locking between two lines.

RINGBACK=value—If value is YES, ringback call-in is enabled. This is used in conjunction with WAITFOR and CONNECT to negotiate incoming calls. The default action is to connect only if the line rings one to three times, is hung up, and is called back within 60 seconds of the first call. MINRBTIME and MAXRBTIME specify the minimum and maximum time for the second call. INTERRING specifies the maximum time between two successive rings in the same call. MINRINGS and MAXRINGS specify the minimum and maximum number of rings for the first call.

SCHED=range1 range2 range3 ... — getty uses this line to schedule times to allow logins. Each range has the form DOW:HR:MINDOW:HR:MIN. DOW is the day of the week. 0 = Sunday, 1 = Monday, ..., 6 = Saturday. HR is the hour, and MIN is the minute. If the current time falls into one of these ranges, the INIT sequence (if any) is sent and getty continues to run until the off time. Otherwise, the OFF sequence is sent, and getty sleeps until the on time.

OFF=string—This line is identical to the INIT line, except it is sent only when the line is scheduled to be OFF.

FIDO=string, EMSI=value—Used only if you are connecting to FidoNet and use a FidoNet mailer. This is not relevant to this book. If you need it, see the getty man page.

The name of the defaults file can be changed by specifying -d defaults_file on the command line. If defaults_file begins with a slash, it is assumed to be a complete pathname of the defaults file to be used. Otherwise, it is assumed to be a regular filename, causing getty to use the */etc/conf.defaults_file* when compiled with FSSTND compliance.

Using SLIP and PPP

We have previously mentioned and defined both SLIP and PPP. When you use low-cost access techniques for Internet services you must still communicate via TCP/IP. Consequently, it is necessary to get IP packets from your LAN to the Internet. When using dial access (or *voice-grade* leased lines), the basic communications approach is through the use of serial communications. That is why we have taken so much space to show how to set up your serial ports. We'll be using them extensively. Serial communications, however, is not esepecially hospitable to TCP/IP. The solution to sending IP packets over serial lines, therefore, is to encapsulate those packets using SLIP or PPP. Thus, setting up SLIP and/or PPP services becomes particularly important.

In this subsection we will deal only with the setup issues involving the use of SLIP and PPP as clients. The software that comes with current versions of Linux can also provide SLIP and PPP server functions. The server functions are outside the scope of this book, but once you are up and running you may find need to configure one or more ports for accepting incoming SLIP or PPP calls to, for example, support staff members that may travel extensively. More complete instructions on setting up comlete SLIP and/or PPP services can be found in the NET-2-HOWTO on which this discussion is based. [7]

For the most part we have assumed that your ISP will be a commercial service. It is possible, however, that you have a small outlying office within a larger corporate structure. Thus, your parent organization becomes your ISP. There is not a great deal of difference between these two approaches, although because your corporation in the latter case controls the primary gateway to the Internet, it has more control over how it can be configured. That, in turn, can provide you with some opportunities not available from an outside ISP. We will note these issues as this discussion proceeds. In either case there is some basic information you will need that can only be provided by your ISP, whoever that may be:

1. IP Address—The unique machine address, in dotted decimal notation, that your machine will use. An example is 128.253.153.54. Your ISP will provide you with this information. If you use a commercial ISP, your IP address may be *dynamically* allocated, while if you are part of a larger corporation your corporate network administrator may furnish you with a *static* IP address. It is

possible with some independent ISPs to obtain static addresses, although at a little higher monthly cost.

A *dynamic* IP address is one that is allocated on-demand each time you dial into your ISP. This means that it will probably change each time you connect to the Internet. A *static* IP address is one that is specifically allocated to you for your permanent use. When setting up a LAN connection to the Internet a *static* address is to be preferred over a *dynamic* address. In any event, regardless of how your router operates, you will need enough IP addresses for each workstation on your LAN, plus your routing device. When you select an ISP, therefore, be sure that it can provide you with sufficient addresses for each of your machines. There are some other issues you may wish to consider when obtaining IP addresses and these will be tackled in the section of this chapter on routing.

2. Network Mask (netmask)—IP addresses are divided into two segments: a network address and a host address. These addresses can be *subnetted* in a variety of ways in order to provide greater functionality and better performance. Thus, when a network is configured, a network mask is used to tell how your network is organized. Please recall that an IP address is composed of four 8-bit bytes usually expressed in decimal dot notation. This means that the address is actually a pattern of 32 bits turned on or off (sybolized by 1 = on, 0 = off). The Internet is divided into three address groups: Classes A, B, and C. This scheme is actually coming to be a problem since with the rise in popularity of the Internet the world is running out of addresses. Steps are being taken in various quarters to design a new addressing scheme that will ultimately allow everyone on the planet to have a personal address. The first byte of the address determines of which class your address is a member. The address space is subdivided as shown in Table 5.1.

Your ISP will have chosen the appropriate netmask when the network was designed, and therefore they should be able to supply you with the correct mask to use. Most networks are class-C subnetworks that use 255.255.255.0

Table 5.1 Subdivided Address Space

For addresses with the first byte:

1–127	255.0.0.0	(Class A)
128–191	255.255.0.0	(Class B)
192+	255.255.255.0	(Class C)

Table 5.2 Subnetting a Class-C Address Block

SUBNET Pro © 1995 – Guy Michaud, Halifax CANADA

NETWORK: 198.139.158.0 MASK: 255.255.255.224 Subnets=6 HostsPer= 30

No.	SUBNET_Address	SUBNET_Broadcast	SUBNET_Host_Range
0	198.139.158.32	198.139.158.63	198.139.158.33-62
1	198.139.158.64	198.139.158.95	198.139.158.65-94
2	198.139.158.96	198.139.158.127	198.139.158.97-126
3	198.139.158.128	198.139.158.159	198.139.158.129-158
4	198.139.158.160	198.139.158.191	198.139.158.161-190
5	198.139.158.192	198.139.158.223	198.139.158.193-222

as their netmask. Other larger networks use class-B netmasks (255.255.0.0). Even a class-C subnetwork can be further subnetted, however, and if you ask for a number of IP addresses less than a full block of 256, then you may receive a different netmask. Your ISP might, for example, have subdivided a contiguous block of 256 addresses into six subnets of 30 addresses each. In this case it is likely that only 180 of the 254 usable addresses in the block could be used, but that would be preferable to assigning you a block of 256 addresses of which only 30 would be used. Table 5.2 illustrates such a scheme.

Alternatively, you may find that you would like to have a full block of Class-C addresses and would, yourself, like to do subnetting. In that case some tools are available to assist you. Table 5.2 was prepared, for example, using *SUBNET Pro Version 1.0*. In this illustration the subnet mask would be 255.255.255.224 rather than the more common 255.255.255.0. The bit mask for a nonsubnetted Class-C address would appear as shown inTable 5.3. Alternatively, the bit mask for 255.255.255.224, as defined in Table 5.2 is shown in Table 5.4.

Table 5.3 Non-subnetted Class-C Subnet Mask

255	255	255	0
11111111	11111111	11111111	00000000

Table 5.4 Subnetted Class-C Subnet Mask

255	255	255	224
11111111	11111111	11111111	11100000

The 1s reflect the network part of the bit mask. The 0s reflect the host part of the address. In these illustrations I have used the Class-C network block 198.139.158.x.

3. Network Address—Out of 256 possible addresses in a Class-C block, we noted that a maximum of 254 are available for general use. Address 0 and address 255 have special uses. Your network address is your IP address masked (bitwise AND) with your netmask. For example:

```
If your netmask is:      255.255.255.0

and your IP address is:  198.139.158.3      &&

                         _____

your Network address is: 198.139.158.0      =
```

If, however, we had subnetted our block of 256 addresses, and we had the following data, then:

```
If your netmask is:      255.255.255.224

and your IP address is:  198.139.158.55     &&

                         _____

your Network address is: 198.139.158.32     =
```

This information can be seen more globally in Table 5.2.

4. Broadcast Address—For a Class-C network, with network mask 255.255.255.0, your broadcast address will be your network address, assuming that your IP address is something like 198.139.158.3, will be 255.255.255.255. Formally, this is your network address (calculated above), logically ORed with 0.0.0.255, the network mask inverted.

Although it is inappropriate to do so, you might make note that for historical reasons some networks use the network address as the broadcast address. Again, note (from Table 5.2) that the network address for a subnetted Class-C network, if your IP address is 198.139.158.55, would be 198.139.158.63. In other words, for a given subnet, the network address is ordinarily the first host address of the subnet range and the broadcast address is the last host address of the subnet range.

5. Router (Gateway) Address—In order to get out of your LAN and into the Internet you will need a gateway address. For your local router that gateway will likely be the address of the router to which it dials or is in some way attached. For workstations on your LAN this address will most likely be your local router. Conventionally, your router will have the lowest-numbered address on your network or the highest numbered host address. It can, however, have any valid address within your subnet. Your ISP should furnish you the address of its gateway for your router. If you're using PPP then you may not need a gateway address and if you use SLIP, then your gateway address will be your SLIP server address.

6. Name Server Address—A name server is a host that provides name resolution for a network. Name servers translate symbolic (human readable) names assigned to networks and hosts into the Internet (IP) addresses used by machines. This is also called a domain name server. Your ISP will probably run a domain name service and will give you that address.

Because you are linking your *LAN* to the Internet, you will probably need to use and apply all these addresses, unlike the situation where you were setting up a single-user service.

When you install Linux you will be given an opportunity to configure networking. This can lso be accomplished later as well (with */sbin/netconfig*). Much of the actual setup information is kept in */etc/rc.d/rc.inet1* and */etc/rc.d/rc.inet2*, files that are run when you boot your machine.

Configuring a SLIP Device

As we have seen, SLIP (Serial Line Internet Protocol) allows the use of TCP/IP over a serial line. The serial link may be a phone line with a dialup modem, or a leased line. To use slip you need access to a slip-server in your area. Many universities and businesses provide slip access all over the world. A recent (partial) list may be found in Appendix B. SLIP uses the serial ports on your machine to carry IP datagrams. To do this it must take control of the serial device. SLIP has device names associated with it in a manner similar to the device names used for the serial ports themselves. The SLIP devices are named */dev/sl0, /dev/sl1*, and so on. How do these correspond to your serial devices? The networking code uses an "ioctl" (i/o control) call to change the serial devices into slip devices. There are two programs supplied with Linux that can do this: **dip** and **slattach**. **Dip** is richer than the older *slattach* and for our purposes we will confine our discussion to the use of *dip*.

DIP (dialup IP) handles the connections needed for dialup IP links, like SLIP or PPP. It can handle both incoming and outgoing connections, using password security for incoming connections. **dip** is a smart program that is able to set the speed of the serial device, command your modem to dial the remote end of the link, automatically log you into the remote server, search for messages sent to you by the server, and extract information for them. The program has a powerful scripting ability, and it is this that you can exploit to automate your logon procedure. **dip** is now commonly distributed on most CD distributions of Linux.

Using a SLIP Server with a Dialup Line and DIP A dynamic SLIP server allocates an IP address from a pool of addresses each time you log on. This means you will not have any particular address. When the server receives a new incoming call, it finds the first unused address, guides the caller through the login process, and then prints a welcome message that contains the IP address it has allocated and will proceed to use that IP address for the duration of that call. The configuration for static and dynamic addressing is similar, but with dynamic addressing your local software must capture that IP address that is printed back to the user. When addressing is static you will already know what it is. **dip** does the hard work, and new versions are smart enough not only to log you in, but also to be able to automatically read the IP address printed in the welcome message and store it. This allows you to properly configure your SLIP device.

To use **dip** you will write a script that is a list of commands that **dip** understands. These commands tell **dip** how to perform each of the actions you require. A sample **dip** script is provided and the man page and *readme* document provides relatively good documentation. We will leave it to you to read the detailed documentation. For our purposes we'll look at a working **dip** script in order to gain an understanding of how it works. The example assumes you are using a dynamic SLIP server. Labels can be placed in the script as the target of goto statements. A label is a name followed by a colon on a line by itself:

```
labelname:
```

Anything following a pound sign (#) is a comment. A name that starts with a dollar sign ($) is a variable. A **dip** script is named with the extension ".dip": *myscript*.**dip**. In the example below, the script is in the left column while my comments are in the right column.

```
main:
  get $remote 198.67.236.1    #The gateway address for my ISP.

  get $mtu 1500               #Size of the maximum transfer unit.

  default                     #Tells DIP to set up the default route
                              #to the remote host it made a
                              #connection to. If this command
                              #isn't present in the command
                              #file, the route won't be set/changed.

  port cua1                   #Dialout port device name. Change if
                              #yours is different.

  speed 38400                 #Maximum speed for your modem.

  reset                       #Reset the modem. (Sends "+++" then
                              #"ATZ".)

  send Atz1\r                 #Send"Atz1\r" out the port.
                              #This is a Hayes "AT" command that
                              #initializes the modem to the stored
                              #configuration 1. The "\r" tell dip
                              #to send a following carriage return,
                              #required by Hayes modems.

  wait OK 2                   #Wait for the word "OK" to come back
                              #from the modem, but not for more
                              #than two seconds.
  if $errlvl != 0 goto error3 #If an error is generated, jump to
```

```
                              #label "error3".

                              #Note! "Standard" pre-defined

                              # "errlvl" values:

                              #    0 - OK

                              #    1 - CONNECT

                              #    2 - ERROR

                              #    3 - BUSY

                              #    4 - NO CARRIER

                              #    5 - NO DIALTONE

                              #

                              # You can change these with the

                              # chatkey command


   dial 5551212              #Dial your ISP. Change to the number

                              #for you ISP.
```

The following lines have been commented out of this script. They were part of the sample script but did not work usefully with my own ISP. The "Wait CONNECT" lines are variations on waiting for your modem to respond that it is connected. I have circumvented all these tests to wait for the prompt requiring a "Username:". I have used only the last part of that prompt (wait name: 10). The number at the end of the wait tells *dip* how long to wait for a response.

```
   # sleep 1                 #Pause for 1 second. Pauses of this

                              #sort may or *may* not be needed. You

                              #will have to experiment.

   # if $errlvl != 0 goto error3

   # wait CONNECT 60

   # wait "CONNECT 38400/REL" 60

   # if $errlvl != 0 goto error3

   # We are connected

   # print We are connected ...

 Login:

   # sleep 3

   # send \r\n

   wait name: 10             #Wait for "username:" prompt. The
```

```
                              #prompt used by your ISP may differ.

send username\n               #Send your username followed by a
                              #linefeed character.

wait word: 10                 #Wait for the "Password:" prompt.

if $errlvl != 0 goto error    #On error, jump to label "error:".

send yourpasswd\n             #Send your password followed by a
                              #linefeed.

print We are logged in ...    #Print a message.

wait ngo 30                   #Wait for some string representing
                              #the login prompt from your ISP's
                              #machine. In this case the full
                              #string is "Ringo>" and I test for
                              #just the "ngo" part of that string.

if $errlvl != 0 goto error    #Another error test.

send slip default\n           #Execute slip at the ISP's site. The
                              #parameter "default" may or may not
                              #be necessary for your ISP.

wait address is 30            #Wait for the text immediately pre-
                              #ceding the IP address ("address is").

if $errlvl !=0 goto error2    #Another error trap.

get $local remote             #Read the IP address assigned to me
                              #and place it in the variable $local.
if $errlvl != 0 goto error    #Check for errors once again.
```

The following sections simply clean up the logon process and set modes and routing. The first three lines under "done:" print a report telling the user something about the connection. Mode can be one of the following:

```
mode SLIP|CSLIP|PPP|TERM
```

The purpose of the mode command is to set the line protocol (default SLIP). Proxyarp enables proxyARP routing (see the section on routing, below).

```
done:
        print CONNECTED to $remote at $rmtip
        print GATEWAY address $rmtip        #Give me a report.
        print LOCAL address $local
        mode SLIP                           #Start SLIP on my end.
        proxyarp                            #Enable proxyARP routing.
        goto exit                           #Leave the script.

error:
        print SLIP to $remote failed
        goto exit

error2:
        print Error 2 - address is not received.
        goto exit

error3:
        print Error 3 - Connection Error

exit:
        exit
```

You should regard the foregoing script as a guide rather than as something you can use without editing. As can easily be seen, there are a few lines you *must* edit. Actual login to your ISP, however, is a function of several things: how your ISP operates; your phone lines and service; your equipment and sofware; and your modems, among other things. The **dip** man page contains another sample script showing how to set up for static IP addresses, so you might take a look at it as well. You may have to combine some of the suggestions there with those above.

Notes on SLIP over a Permanent Line For com-
pleteness, you should be aware that SLIP (and PPP) can also be used over a permanently installed serial connection. That connection can simply be your own
cable or a leased line from the telephone company. There are other, better ways of
handling such a situation but they also require higher expenditures. You might
find it necessary, for example, to link an isolated machine on a shop floor, or some
other remote area, into your TCP/IP network even though that machine is not on
your LAN and it would be difficult to get the LAN extended to that workstation.
In such a situation a dedicated SLIP or PPP connection might work out to be the
best way of handling the problem. In this case you can dispense with using **dip**
and use **slattach** which is simpler to set up.

Since your connection will be a permanent one, you will need to add some commands to your *rc.inet1* file. All you need to do for a permam*ent* connecti*on* is
ensure that you configure the serial device to the correct speed and switch the serial
device into slip mode. *slattach* allows you to do this with one command. Add lines
similar to the following to your */etc/rc.d/rc.inet1* file:

```
#
# Attach a leased line static slip connection
#
# configure /dev/cua0 for 19.2kbps and cslip
/sbin/slattach -p cslip -s 19200 /dev/cua0 &
/sbin/ifconfig sl0 IPA.IPA.IPA.IPA pointopoint IPR.IPR.IPR.IPR up
#
# End static slip.
```

Where:

      `IPA.IPA.IPA.IPA`

           `represents your IP address.`

      `IPR.IPR.IPR.IPR`

           `represents the IP address of the remote end.`

slattach, in this example, allocated the first unallocated SLIP device to the serial
device specified. **slattach** starts with sl0. Therefore, the first *slattach* command
attaches SLIP device sl0 to the serial device specified, and sl1 the next time, and so
on. **slattach** allows you to configure a number of different protocols with the -p

argument. In your case you will use either SLIP or CSLIP depending on whether or not you want to use compression. Both ends must agree on whether or not you want compression.

Point-to-Point Protocol (PPP)

The Point-to-Point Protocol is an industry standard for data transfer across serial links. It allows for several protocols to be multiplexed across the link. It is a successor to the serial line internet protocol. It offers enhanced functionality, error detection, and security options. It corrects a number of deficiencies that are found in SLIP, and is suitable for both asynchronous links and synchronous links alike. The dynamic address allocation feature in PPP is part of the system and the address is transmitted with a specially formatted frame rather than by requiring the receiving software to simply pick up and edit a string sent down the line. In this sense configuration is somewhat more straightforward than with SLIP because PPP does not require the ability to retrieve your address outside the protocol. PPP, like SLIP, is now a standard part of most distributions of Linux.

The PPP code comes in two parts. The first is a kernel module that handles the assembly and disassembly of the frames, and the second is a set of protocols called LCP, IPCP, UPAP, and CHAP, for negotiating link options, bringing the link into a functioning state, and for authentication. With the most recent distributions of Linux PPP can be automatically installed at the time Linux itself is installed. Since we are assuming that you have purchased a copy of Linux on a CDROM, it is of little use to go through manual installation procedures. Once you have installed Linux with all the networking software, try looking at the contents of */proc/net/dev*. Do this by issuing the command **cat /proc/net/dev**. This indicates that the kernel driver is correctly installed.

With the current versions of Linux (1.2.x+) you should not need to do manual installs of this software. The actual software you will use is */usr/lib/ppp/***pppd**. This software runs as a daemon, which, you will recall, is a Unix program that is invisible to users but provides important system services, such as PPP. **pppd** needs to be run as root. You can either make it suid root (this allows the program to run as root even though an ordinary user has initiated it) or you can just use it when you are logged in as root. The installation procedure should install it as suid root so it should normally be accessible by anyone.

As with SLIP, you can configure the PPP software as either a client or a server, although we will only consider its use as a client. A program called **chat**, which you will also find in *usr/lib/ppp*, performs a function similar to the **dip** program in order to automate the dialing and login procedure to the remote machine. If you are in an experimental mood, the current version of **dip** can also be used for this purpose with PPP as well as with SLIP. All of the current PPP Linux documentation, however, references *chat*, so we will stay with it. Unlike **dip** though, it does not perform the ioctl to convert the serial line into a PPP line. This is performed by the **pppd** program. **pppd** can act as either the client or the server. When used as a client, it is normally set up to invoke the **chat** program to perform the connection and log in to the remote machine. It then takes over by performing the ioctl to change the line discipline to PPP and then steps out of the way to let you operate.

As with other software discussed in this book, you should also refer to the **pppd** and **chat** man pages for more information. There are also several README files that come with the software that provide additional useful information concerning the operation of PPP. [9] There are, unfortunately, some discrepancies in the documentation that can be a bit confusing. There are several files that are used in conjunction with **pppd**. They are described in the **pppd** man page and in the NET-2-HOWTO. The man page refers to two files, */etc/ppp/***ip-up** and */etc/ppp/***ip-down** which do not exist in any of the distributions I have seen. These files are described as scripts that assist in making the PPP connection. There are, however, two other files, */etc/ppp/***ppp-on** and */etc/ppp/***ppp-off**, which seem to do the same sort of thing. Unfortunately, the **ppp-on** is incorrect in some specifics or assumes a script file that is not present or discussed anywhere (it tries, for example, to execute *ppp* rather than **pppd**). [10]

In any event, we need to look at how PPP is properly configured for the purposes of this book. When you want to establish your connection you simply have to invoke the **pppd** program with appropriate command-line arguments. Consider the following example:

```
pppd connect 'chat -v "" ATDT5551212 CONNECT "" ogin: ppp word: password'
      /dev/cua1 38400 debug crtscts modem defaultroute 192.1.1.17
```

This entire statement must be typed on a single line. The line may be broken by typing a backslash followed by <**Enter**> (assuming you are typing this at the keyboard). This may also be placed in a shell script. A shell script is something like a DOS batch file, although the shell scripting language is much more elaborate than the DOS batch file language. Before digressing too far, however, we need to look at what this statement means:

pppd   Invoke **pppd** on the command line.

connect Tell **pppd** to run another program, in this case, **chat**. The **chat** command,

      along with its command-line options, *must* be enclosed in single quotes.

    'chat   Invoke **chat** on the command line.

    -v   Execute **chat** in verbose mode so that you can see what is happening.

    [Chat script:] ""   Expect nothing.

                 ATDT5551212 Send Hayes dial commands and phone number.

                 CONNECT   Expect the word CONNECT.

                 ""   Send nothing.

                 ogin: Expect the string [l]"ogin:"

                 ppp   Send the string "ppp" to invoke PPP on the remote computer.

                 word: Expect the string [pass]"word:"

                 password'   Send your password.

/dev/cua1 Tell **pppd** the serial device being used.

38400   Tell **pppd** the speed of the connection.

debug   Tell **pppd** you want debugging information.

crtscts   Tell **pppd** to use hardware flow control.

modem   Tell **pppd** to use modem controls.

defaultroute Tell **pppd** to set up a default route.

192.1.1.17 Tell **pppd** your IP address.

This particular example shows the *concept* of how to invoke **pppd**. The actual process you use will depend on your own setup and the setup your ISP uses. In addition, although we will not discuss it here, there are methods for checking the authenticity of the user dialing in. The two common methods are PAP (Password Authentication Protocol) and CHAP (Challenge Handshake Authentication Protocol). If either of these protocols are used, a secondary set of user ID/passwords or their equivalent will be necessary.

There are other important operational differences that may occur. In the example given above, the *chat* script is used to invoke PPP on the remote end. Many installations, however, have special user IDs and passwords for PPP with PPP being invoked by the login process as the shell for the session.

It would be very painful to be required to type a long command line, such as the one illustrated above, every time we wish to run PPP. Fortunately, that is not necessary. We can cut down the arduousness of the process in several ways. First, we can simply put the line above in a file (a shell script) and run that. Second, we can put most of the command line options, for both **pppd** and for **chat** into files:

/etc/ppp/options—System default options for **pppd**, read before user default options or command-line options.

/etc/ppp/options.ttyname—System default options for the serial port being used, read after command-line options.

~/.ppprc—User default options, read before command-line options. The ~/. means the path to your home directory.

In the case of the **chat** script (the series of expect/send statements that guide the system through login or some other process), rather than placing the expect/send statements on the command line they may also be put in a file following the "-f" option:

```
chat -f parameter.file
```

All of these can be combined in a shell script that initializes the modem, starts *pppd*, and then uses **chat** to dial into a host computer. An example of a working **ppp-on** file is the following:

```
#!/bin/sh


#
#   ppp-on
#
#   Set up a PPP link
#


LOCKDIR=/var/spool/uucp
DEVICE=cub2
```

```
PHONE=5551212
USER=pppusr
PASSWORD=password
OUR_IP_ADDR=198.139.158.2
echo "Variables Initialized"

if [ -f $LOCKDIR/LCK..$DEVICE ]
then
    echo "PPP device is locked"
    exit 1
fi

/usr/lib/ppp/fix-cua $DEVICE
stty 19200 -tostop -parenb cs8 < /dev/$DEVICE > /dev/$DEVICE
setserial /dev/$DEVICE spd_hi
chat "" ATZ OK < /dev/$DEVICE > /dev/$DEVICE

(
if /usr/lib/ppp/pppd file /etc/ppp/options.old
then
    echo "You Are Connected."
    exit 0
else
    echo "PPP call failed" 1>&2
    exit 1
fi
) < /dev/$DEVICE > /dev/$DEVICE
```

To be executable, such script files need to have their mode set by **chmod** with an appropriately high value: **chmod 670 ppp-on**, for example. In the foregoing script the mode is set up and initialized, then in the "if" statement **pppd** is executed using the options in the file *etc/ppp/options.old*. If the options file were just called "options," it would not have to be explicitly stated at all. That particular *options.old* file contains the following lines:

```
connect "chat -v -l LCK..cub2 -t 90 -f /usr/lib/ppp/hwmin.chat"
-detach
198.139.158.2:198.139.157.2
netmask 255.255.255.0
name yourmachine
passive
crtscts
modem
defaultroute
proxyarp
/dev/cub2
57600
mru 1500
kdebug 2
```

The *options.old* file contains command-line options for **pppd**. Note that the "connect" option contains the command line for **chat**. The file */usr/lib/ppp/hwmin.chat*, in turn, contains the options for **chat**:

```
ABORT "NO CARRIER" ABORT BUSY
'' atdt18005551212
CONNECT ''
'' \r\r\r\d\d
ogin:-BREAk-ogin: pppewc
ssword: password
erm/ ''
```

The first line says abort the process if the modem returns NO CARRIER or BUSY. If everything is okay, then the remaining expect/send sequences are executed. The second line expects nothing, then dials the ISP's phone number. The expectation on the third line is that the modem will report a connection but in direct response to that will send nothing. Then expecting nothing after connection, it sends a series of carriage returns (\r) with a short delay (\d\d) because the system it just dialed requires some carriage returns to be sent before it will display the login: prompt. Because we don't know whether the login: prompt is capitalized, we just use the last few characters of it and do the same thing with the password prompt.

The -BREAK- sequence will try to get the login: prompt again if it somehow missed it the first time. Then the user ID (*pppusr*) is sent, followed by a wait for the password prompt. When the password prompt comes, the password is sent. In this case we use a static IP address and the login shell is PPP so we don't have to explicitly run PPP from our end. If all goes well, we are now connected.

pppd uses lock files located in */var/spool/uucp* (or */usr/spool/uucp*). Sometimes the lock files will not be erased and you must do so manually. That can be accomplished with */usr/lib/ppp/***unlock**:

```
/usr/lib/ppp/unlock devicename   (in the example, the devicename is "cua1").
```

When you finish your PPP session, you also need to kill the session, so you run */usr/lib/ppp/***ppp-off,** a small file that looks like the following:

```
#!/bin/sh


DEVICE=ppp0


#
# If the ppp0 pid file is present then the program is running. Stop it.
if [ -r /var/run/$DEVICE.pid ]; then
    kill -INT `cat /var/run/$DEVICE.pid`
#
# If unsuccessful, ensure that the pid file is removed.
#
    if [ ! "$?" = "0" ]; then
        echo "removing stale $DEVICE pid file."
        rm -f /var/run/$DEVICE.pid
        exit 1
    fi
#
# Success. Terminate with proper status.
#
    echo "$DEVICE link terminated"
    exit 0
fi
```

```
#
# The link is not active
#
echo "$DEVICE link is not active"
exit 1
```

Other files used by **pppd** may include the following:

/var/run/pppn.pid—Process-ID for **pppd** process on ppp interface unit n.

/etc/ppp/pap-secrets—Usernames, passwords, and IP addresses for PAP authentication. Used only if PAP authentication is enabled.

/etc/ppp/chap-secrets—Names, secrets, and IP addresses for CHAP authentication. Is used only when authenticating with CHAP.

A Tip on Writing Login Scripts

One of the more arduous tasks in all this is to write reliable logon scripts. The best way to get the exact information you need is to follow the instructions of your ISP, to the extent you can, but do it manually with a terminal emulator. Call into your ISP with a terminal emulator, such as ProCom Plus or equivalent, one that allows you to capture the entire session to a disk file or printer, and enter all the commands that are required to log in. You cannot get a clean SLIP or PPP login, of course, because your terminal emulator won't handle the SLIP or PPP protocols. But you should be able to capture the entire procedure short of that and then use the results in building your login script.

SLIP or PPP: Which Should I Use?

First, you probably will not have a choice. Your ISP will tell you which protocol it offers. If your ISP is your corporation, however, then there might be a choice, although even there your network manager is likely to promote a preference. Today SLIP is generally used over PPP only in those cases where that is the only protocol provided by the ISP. And there are still many installations where that is the case. From a user's perspective, I have found SLIP to be a little easier to set up, but there are also instances where it provides less reliable communications than does PPP. Finally, you may be in an environment where you need to pass not only IP packets, but also other protocols, such as Novell's IPX. SLIP can handle only IP, whereas PPP provides multiprotocol support.

Where to Obtain More Information on SLIP/PPP

We have already mentioned the NET-2-HOWTO on several occasions. A more comprehensive treatment of SLIP/PPP and related networking issues may be found in Olaf Kirch, *Linux Network Administrator's Guide* (Darmstadt, Germany: Olaf Kirch, 1994). This book, which is part of the Linux Documentation Project, is available from several sources.[11] Most discussion on PPP for Linux takes place on the PPP mailing list. To join the Linux PPP channel on the mail list server, send mail to:

```
linux-activists@niksula.hut.fi
```

with the line:

```
X-Mn-Admin: join PPP
```

at the top of the message body (not the subject line).

The relevant RFCs are 1548, 1331, 1332, 1333, and 1334. These are the definitive documents for PPP.[12]

Routing and Its Importance

Before charging into this discussion I invite you to once again look at a modified version of Figure 5.1 found in Figure 5.2. You will quickly see that IP packets need to get from your LAN to the Internet and back. The routing device or computer has two network interfaces: Ethernet and SLIP/PPP. Packets destined for the Internet must go out the SLIP/PPP interface, while all others must go via Ethernet. The routing process allows us to set up our software so that the packets can get to where they are supposed to be going.

Each host on a network has one or more network interfaces. The preceding pages of this chapter have been largely given over to describing how to configure two such interfaces: SLIP and PPP. A relatively standard networking program, **ifconfig** is used to set up (and maintain) these network interfaces. **ifconfig** is used at boot time to configure most of them to a running state. After that, it is only rarely needed. If no arguments are given, **ifconfig** just displays the status of the currently defined

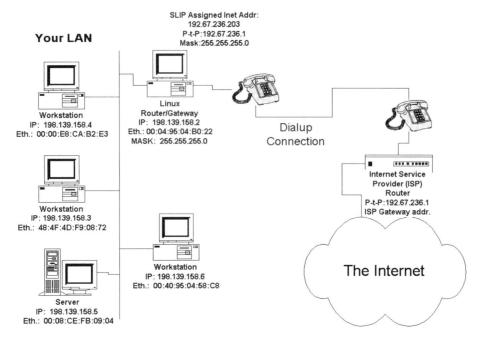

Figure 5.2 Linux system as a masquerading router.

interfaces. If the single interface argument is given, it displays the status of only the given interface. Otherwise, it assumes that the interface structure must be set up. A typical listing of the data from **ifconfig** follows, showing the local loopback, a SLIP interface, and an Ethernet interface:

```
ewcuucp:/etc/dip# ifconfig -a
lo        Link encap:Local Loopback
          inet addr:127.0.0.1  Bcast:127.255.255.255  Mask:255.0.0.0
          UP BROADCAST LOOPBACK RUNNING  MTU:2000  Metric:1
          RX packets:0 errors:0 dropped:0 overruns:0
          TX packets:814 errors:0 dropped:0 overruns:0


sl0       Link encap:Serial Line IP
          inet addr:192.67.236.203  P-t-P:192.67.236.1  Mask:255.255.255.0
          UP POINTOPOINT RUNNING  MTU:1500  Metric:1
          RX packets:352 errors:0 dropped:0 overruns:0
          TX packets:421 errors:0 dropped:0 overruns:0
```

```
eth0      Link encap:10Mbps Ethernet   HWaddr 00:40:95:04:B0:22
          inet addr:198.139.158.2  Bcast:198.139.158.255  Mask:255.255.255.0
          UP BROADCAST RUNNING MULTICAST  MTU:1500  Metric:1
          RX packets:7322 errors:0 dropped:0 overruns:0
          TX packets:7164 errors:0 dropped:0 overruns:0
          Interrupt:5 Base address:0x320
```

When you have a statically allocated IP address for your router, the likelihood is that both the SLIP/PPP device and the Ethernet device will share the same address. When your ISP assigns you an address dynamically, however, the two addresses will inevitably be different, as in the illustration above. When your ISP delivers IP addresses dynamically, or if you would rather have dynamically assigned IP addresses (the service is generally less expensive), then the only option is to have *different* IP addresses for these two devices. In such a case the eth0 device would have your locally assigned IP address and the sl0 (or ppp0) device would have the dynamically assigned IP address from your ISP. Fortunately there is a solution for this problem, at least for Linux.

A second table, called the ARP cache, translates IP addresses to MAC (Media Access Control) addresses.[13] Linux will put an entry into the ARP cache for the IP address and the associated hardware MAC address when it is to do proxy ARP. The program **arp** is used to display and manually manipulate the ARP cache. An ARP table for a small network will look like the following and is generated by typing the command, **arp -a**:

```
ewcuucp:~# arp -a
Address              HW type           HW address            Flags    Mask
198.139.158.1        10Mbps Ethernet   00:00:0C:C0:50:BF     C        *
198.139.158.3        10Mbps Ethernet   48:4F:4D:F9:08:72     C        *
198.139.158.4        10Mbps Ethernet   00:00:E8:CA:B2:E3     C        *
198.139.158.5        10Mbps Ethernet   00:08:CE:FB:09:04     C        *
198.139.158.6        10Mbps Ethernet   00:40:95:04:58:C8     C        *
```

Routing is configured with the use of files, programs, and mechanisms. The files and the programs configure the mechanisms. The files with which we must be concerned are:

```
/etc/hosts
/etc/networks
/etc/gateways
/etc/host.conf
/etc/resolv.conf
/etc/HOSTNAME
```

There are four commonly used routing techniques for Unix-oriented networking. They include static routes frequently manipulated manually with the **route** command and automatically with **routed**; ARP and proxyARP, managed with **arp**; the use of the Routing Information Protocol (RIP) managed by **gated**; and the Internet domain name service managed with **named**. **Route** and **arp** are user level (at least for user root) programs while **routed, gated**, and **named** are network daemons. A fifth technique, called IP_masquerading, is not as widely used, but addresses the specific issue noted above: the problem of connecting your LAN to the Internet when your ISP delivers a dynamically allocated IP address to you through SLIP or PPP. We will discuss this fifth option first, since it is likely to be *very* useful for small organizations.

Routing Through Masquerading

This solution is called IP_Masquerading. IP_Masquerade allows a number of hosts to pretend to be one. IP_Masquerading provides a clever solution by making all of the machines on your network look like one very active networked machine. It does this by performing real-time, on-the-fly address translations. Ken Eaves (<keves@eves.com>) maintains the latest copy at **ftp.eves.com**.

The IP_Masquerade software currently comes as a patch to the later Linux 1.2.* series kernels and a new version of the **ipfw** command. The **ipfw** program that comes as a standard part of the net-tools software releases does not yet have the masquerade option built into it. The kernel you are using must support the IP_firewalling option for IP_masquerade to work. The patch file is available from ftp.eves.com found in */pub/masq*. In this directory you will find patch files, new versions of the **ipfw** command and Ken's original *Masquerade FAQ*. See also the latest version of the *NET-2-HOWTO*. The patch file is named *masq-patch.1.2.n.* The files *ipfw* and *ipfw-for-1.3.10* are for Linux kernel version 1.2.* and 1.3.10 respectively. Pauline Middelink was primarily responsible for producing the system.

The terms *firewall* and *masquerading* are most frequently found in discussions of network and computer security. A firewall is a barrier through which broadcast or other types of packets cannot pass. Routers, not bridges, are used to set up firewalls. Masquerading is the attempt to gain access to a system by posing as an authorized client or host. When using IP_Masquerade we are, in fact, setting up a form of firewall and using masquerading for a legitimate purpose. In order to illustrate how this works, we need to look at the routing tables that are set up either automatically or through the use of **route** (see below). The three machines are those workstations with IP addresses **198.139.158.3** and **198.139.158.6** (see Figure 5.2), and the Linux system with an Ethernet IP address of **198.139.158.2**. These happen to be real addresses, so you *will not* use these on your own system.

Either get some IP addresses assigned to you by your ISP or use a block of addresses in the range 192.168.0.0-192.168.255.255. You might, for example, arbitrarily use the block 192.168.100.0-255. Remember that 192.168.100.0 and 192.168.100.255 have preassigned meanings, so do not assign these particular addresses as specific device addresses. Use the range 192.168.100.1-254 as the active range of addresses you will use for specific computers.

When you first fire up your SLIP or PPP connection (using the techniques discussed earlier in this chapter) on your Linux machine (198.139.158.2 in Figure 5.2), you should end up with a routing table much like the following:

```
ewcuucp:/etc/dip# netstat -r

Kernel routing table
```

Destination	Gateway	Genmask	Flags	Metric	Ref	Use	Iface
ewcuucp.ewc-inc	*	255.255.255.255	UH	0	0	781	eth0
ringo.jvnc.net	*****	**255.255.255.255**	**UH**	**0**		**0**	**1 sl0**
localnet	*	255.255.255.0	U	0	0	6222	eth0
loopback	*	255.0.0.0	U	0	0	33	lo
default	**ringo.jvnc.net**	**0.0.0.0**	**UG**	**0**	**0**	**14**	**sl0**

Anything else in the routing table (viewed by running **netstat -r**) can confuse the proper routing of IP packets. Another default entry, for example, can misdirect IP packets. My gateway to my ISP is named *ringo.jvnc.net*. There must be two entries in the routing table, as illustrated: one going from my machine to theirs, and one going from theirs to my machine. Mine is named *ewcuucp.ewc-inc.com*. The other three lines are the standard routes that are configured at boot time. The star in the routing table implies a route to your own local machine. Extraneous routes, if they exist, can be manually deleted with the **route** command. We can reinforce this point by looking at another connection, this time via PPP, through CompuServe, operating on the same Linux machine in my office:

```
ewcuucp:/etc/dip# netstat -r
Kernel routing table
```

Destination	Gateway	Genmask	Flags	Metric	Ref	Use	Iface
ewcuucp.ewc-inc	*	255.255.255.255	UH	0	0	1405	eth0
arl-dial-37.com		*		**255.255.255.255**		**UH**	**0**
0	**0**	**ppp0**					
localnet	*	255.255.255.0	U	0	0	19231	eth0
loopback	*	255.0.0.0	U	0	0	61	lo
default	**arl-dial-37.com**	**0.0.0.0**	**UG**	**0**	**0**	**7**	**ppp0**

Again, the two lines that are in **bold type** were automatically added. **arl-dial-37.com** is a name that is used by CompuServe. The SLIP connection was established using **dip**, and the PPP connection was set up with **pppd** and **chat**. Both of these approaches are described elsewhere in this chapter.

The workstations illustrated in Figure 5.2 can all communicate with the Internet through 198.139.158.2. On each of the workstations the TCP/IP software must be configured so that 198.139.158.2 is the default gateway. These workstations effectively exist behind a security firewall. That is, the Internet knows nothing of their existence and they cannot broadcast their addresses to the Internet. That is essentially how firewall mechanisms work. This one is not fully configured simply because we are using it in a very special-purpose manner. The other element of this approach is the *masquerading*. The patches made to the Linux kernel enable hosts connected by a LAN to use the IP address of the system acting as the router (gateway), in this case 198.139.158.2. Thus, for the Internet, if several people were using Internet resources, it would appear that 198.139.158.2 had an extremely active user, whereas in reality several users would be using that system to reach the Internet. It may also be desirable to add two lines to the routing tables of each of your workstations, explicitly establishing routing links to your Linux machine. At least the Microsoft TCP/IP facility contains a routing command:

```
route add routerIPADDR wkstaIPADDR [e.g., route add 198.139.158.2  198.139.158.3]

route add wkstaIPADDR router IPADDR [e.g., route add 198.139.158.3  198.139.158.2]
```

These statements can be put in a batch file and run in a DOS window, but it must be done *after* Windows is started, not before.

As noted, each workstation must be configured with the Linux machine as its gateway. Ordinarily, when the Linux system forwards a packet to the Internet, the originating workstation's IP address would be replaced by the IP address of the Linux machine. Thus, the workstation would not be able to receive a response from the Internet. The patches to the kernel provide Linux the ability to save the workstation's IP address, so that the workstation remains known throughout the round-trip of any given packet, and have the appropriate IP address restored to an incoming packet. The remote host, out on the Internet, is never aware of these comings and goings. It is necessary to run **ipfw** to configure the masquerading. The method I have used is to have a short script with one entry for each of my workstations, called from */etc/rc.d/rc.local* at boot time. Your file would be similar to mine:

```
#!/bin/sh
/sbin/ipfw a m all from 198.139.158.3/24 to 0.0.0.0/0
/sbin/ipfw a m all from 198.139.158.4/24 to 0.0.0.0/0
/sbin/ipfw a m all from 198.139.158.5/24 to 0.0.0.0/0
/sbin/ipfw a m all from 198.139.158.6/24 to 0.0.0.0/0
```

This approach is at variance from the suggestions made in *INET-2-HOWTO* and in the *ip_masquerade.faq*, but it works. The IP addresses in the foregoing example are those for four of my workstations. Your IP addresses would be different, of course.

The power of this approach is that you should be able to use this technique with any arbitrary ISP regardless of whether they provide SLIP or PPP services. My usual ISP is Global Enterprise Services (GES) of Princeton, NJ, and they offer a SLIP service. When connected, my attached devices look something like the following:

```
Attached Via a SLIP Connection:
# ifconfig -a
lo        Link encap:Local Loopback
```

```
                inet addr:127.0.0.1  Bcast:127.255.255.255  Mask:255.0.0.0
                UP BROADCAST LOOPBACK RUNNING  MTU:2000  Metric:1
                RX packets:0 errors:0 dropped:0 overruns:0
                TX packets:814 errors:0 dropped:0 overruns:0


    sl0         Link encap:Serial Line IP
                inet addr:192.67.236.203  P-t-P:192.67.236.1  Mask:255.255.255.0
                UP POINTOPOINT RUNNING  MTU:1500  Metric:1
                RX packets:352 errors:0 dropped:0 overruns:0
                TX packets:421 errors:0 dropped:0 overruns:0


    eth0        Link encap:10Mbps Ethernet  HWaddr 00:40:95:04:B0:22
                inet addr:198.139.158.2  Bcast:198.139.158.255  Mask:255.255.255.0
                UP BROADCAST RUNNING MULTICAST  MTU:1500  Metric:1
                RX packets:7322 errors:0 dropped:0 overruns:0
                TX packets:7164 errors:0 dropped:0 overruns:0
                Interrupt:5 Base address:0x320
```

I also subscribe to CompuServe and they have a PPP service. I can connect through CompuServe in much the same manner as to GES with the results:

```
    Attached Via a PPP Connection (CompuServe):
    ewcuucp:/etc/dip# ifconfig
    lo          Link encap:Local Loopback
                inet addr:127.0.0.1  Bcast:127.255.255.255  Mask:255.0.0.0
                UP BROADCAST LOOPBACK RUNNING  MTU:2000  Metric:1
                RX packets:0 errors:0 dropped:0 overruns:0
                TX packets:1465 errors:0 dropped:0 overruns:0


    ppp0        Link encap:Point-Point Protocol
                inet addr:199.174.140.156  P-t-P:149.174.210.130  Mask:255.255.255.0
                UP POINTOPOINT RUNNING  MTU:1500  Metric:1
                RX packets:6 errors:0 dropped:0 overruns:0
                TX packets:6 errors:0 dropped:0 overruns:0
```

```
eth0      Link encap:10Mbps Ethernet   HWaddr 00:40:95:04:B0:22
          inet addr:198.139.158.2  Bcast:198.139.158.255  Mask:255.255.255.0
          UP BROADCAST RUNNING MULTICAST  MTU:1500  Metric:1
          RX packets:19868 errors:0 dropped:0 overruns:0
          TX packets:20987 errors:0 dropped:0 overruns:0
          Interrupt:5 Base address:0x320
```

The SLIP service is configured and dialed with **dip** while the PPP service was configured and dialed with **pppd/chat**. Because these programs are described elsewhere in
this chapter, I will not reiterate the discussions here. It may be useful for you to
have my scripts, however. For the SLIP connection I use the following **dip** script:

```
main:
          get $remote 192.67.236.1
          get $mtu 1500
          port cub2
          speed 57600
          reset
          send ATz0\r
          wait OK 2
          if $errlvl != 0 goto error3
          dial 555-1212


Login:
          wait name: 10
          send userid\n
          wait word: 10
          if $errlvl != 0 goto error
          send password\n
          print We are logged in ...
          wait ngo 30
          if $errlvl != 0 goto error
          send slip default\n
          wait address is 30
          if $errlvl !=0 goto error2
```

```
         get $local remote
         if $errlvl != 0 goto error

done:
         print CONNECTED to $remote at $rmtip
         print GATEWAY address $rmtip
         print LOCAL address $local
         default
         proxyarp
         netmask 255.255.255.0
         mode SLIP
         goto exit

error:
         print SLIP to $remote failed
         goto exit

error2:
         print Error 2 - address is not received.
         goto exit

error3:
         print Error 3 - Connection Error

exit:
         print $remote $local $rmtip
```

This version prints the entire process to the screen as well as some additional infor-
mational messages, which will be taken out when I'm convinced it is stable.

The PPP connection requires three files: **ppp-cserve**, an executable shell script that
starts the process; *letc/ppp/options* or the custom options file I have named
letc/ppp/options.cserve, used by **pppd**; and *lusr/lib/ppp/cserve.chat*, the chat script
for doing the dialing. **ppp-cserve** can be placed in a directory, such as *lusr/local/bin*,
where other executables live. It simply calls everything else:

```
#!/bin/sh

#
#        ppp-cserve
#
#        Set up a PPP link with CompuServe
#

LOCKDIR=/var/spool/uucp
DEVICE=cub2

PHONE=555-1212
USER=11111,777
PASSWORD=FIRST.SECOND
OUR_IP_ADDR=0.0.0.0
echo "Variables Initialized"

if [ -f $LOCKDIR/LCK..$DEVICE ]
then
        echo "PPP device is locked"
        exit 1
fi

/usr/lib/ppp/fix-cua $DEVICE
echo $DEVICE "fixed."
echo $USER $PASSWORD $OUR_IP_ADDR
stty 19200 -tostop -parenb cs8 < /dev/$DEVICE > /dev/$DEVICE
echo "stty run."
setserial /dev/$DEVICE spd_hi
echo "setserial run."
chat "" ATZ OK < /dev/$DEVICE > /dev/$DEVICE
echo "Modem Initialized."

(
```

```
if /usr/lib/ppp/pppd file /etc/ppp/options.cserve
then
        #echo "Into the THEN"
        #sleep 5
        echo "You Are Connected."
        exit 0
else
        echo "PPP call failed" 1>&2
        exit 1
fi
) < /dev/$DEVICE > /dev/$DEVICE
```

In this script, several variables are defined at the top that are used only for purposes of display and should probably be taken out. That is a byproduct of the development of the script. **pppd** can use command line options or options placed in a default */etc/ppp/options* file or the custom options file that I have called */etc/ppp/options.cserve*:

My */etc/ppp/options.cserve* file:

```
connect "chat -v -l LCK..cub2 -t 90 -f /usr/lib/ppp/cserve.chat"
-detach
netmask 255.255.255.0
passive
crtscts
modem
defaultroute
proxyarp
/dev/cub2
57600
mru 1500
kdebug 2
```

Finally, of course, we need to dial the ISP. This is actually done with a program called **chat** but called through **pppd**. It also requires a script which I have called */usr/lib/ppp/cserve.chat*:

```
ABORT "NO CARRIER" ABORT BUSY
```

```
''  atdt5551212
CONNECT ''
''  \r\r\r
Name: CIS\r
ID: 11111,777/GO:PPPCONNECT\r
ssword: FIRST.SECOND\r
'address is' ''
```

The CIS network normally functions at a word length of 7 bits and even parity. PPP runs at 8 bits. This can pose a little problem, but by and large both **dip** and **chat** take care of this problem for you. You can write the scripts without reference to this problem. There is a parallel discussion regarding the use of the Windows NT Server 3.5 and when you read that you will see that the Microsoft software must be handled a bit differently.

In any event, the strong point of this approach is that it is inexpensive and it can be set up using almost any service that offers SLIP or PPP. If you happen to have an older PC about, such as a reasonably fast 386 or a 486, by upgrading that machine to 8 or more megabytes of memory, at least a 200 Mb hard disk, and an inexpensive CDROM drive, you can have an adequate system on which to install Linux and configure it as a router/gateway to the Internet. It is relatively easy to get going, although you will have to learn how to patch the kernel and recompile it. The down side is that not all Internet related software will work.

First and foremost, of course, since this is dependent on a dial-access connection, even though you may wish to set up servers for http (World Wide Web), FTP, and others on your own LAN for internal use, such servers are unreachable using this technique. Furthermore, no matter what dial-access technique you use, a dial-access link is not acceptable for offering services to others. This is primarily an issue of availability rather than technology. From your standpoint, however, much of what you would wish to use as a client will work properly. You can use Web browsers such as Netscape or Mosaic, TELNET for logging into remote hosts, and, with limits, FTP for transferring files. If you use an FTP client it must be one that can force the server into PASV mode. One widely used, Windows-based family of FTP clients is called **ws_ftp**. It can be configured for PASV, and when so configured works fine over this kind of link.

The other item that works very well is the use of a POP3 client for accessing a Post-Office Protocol server. There are many POP3 clients available including Eudora and Pegasus Mail. If you have a POP mail service through your ISP, then you can use the link for accessing your email. In fact, if you have a POP mail service somewhere, you can access it from anywhere in the world that you can access the Internet. Thus, if you happen to go in through ISP ABC and your service is on XYZ, you can still log on to your mail server and send and receive mail.

The typical kinds of applications that will not work include *ping*, and various "real-time" chatting programs. The IP_Masquerade software is still undergoing development, however, so by the time you are able to take advantage of this technique, additional services may be available.

Routing with *Route* and *Routed*

Each of the machines on your LAN must also maintain a routing table. The way that the routing table is maintained is the subject of this section. The current status of the routing table may be ascertained by use of the **netstat** command:

```
netstat -r<Enter>
```

Although under Linux you can also display the routing table by issuing the **route** command without any options, this is somewhat nonstandard. The **netstat** command, whether it resides on a Windows machine, a DOS machine, or a *nix machine, works about the same across all platforms. My current routing table, for example, is:

```
Kernel routing table
```

Destination	Gateway	Genmask	Flags	Metric	Ref	Use	Iface
198.67.236.1	*	255.255.255.255	UH	0	0	1	sl0
localnet	*	255.255.255.0	U	0	0	37958	eth0
loopback	*	255.0.0.0	U	0	0	395	lo
default	198.67.236.1	0.0.0.0	UG	0	0	4	sl0

IP address 198.67.236.1 is my ISP's gateway address. Note that the route to the ISP is via SLIP (s10), while the route to the local network is via Ethernet (eth0).

Route manipulates the kernel's IP routing table. Its primary use is to set up static routes to specific hosts or networks via an interface after it has been configured with the **ifconfig** program. In contrast, **routed** is invoked at boot time to manage the network routing tables. The routing daemon uses a variant of the Xerox NS Routing Information Protocol (RIP) in maintaining up-to-date kernel routing table entries. RIP is a generalized protocol capable of use with multiple address types, but is currently used only for Internet routing within a cluster of networks. **Route** is invoked to display, add, or delete routes in one of the following ways:

```
route [ -vn ]


route   [   -v  ] add [ -net | -host ] XXXX [gw GGGG]
        [metric MMMM]     [netmask NNNN] [mss NNNN] [window
        NNNN] [dev DDDD]


route [ -v ] del XXXX
```

You should consult the **route** man page for operational details.

In normal operation **routed** listens for the route service for routing information packets. If the host is an internetwork router, it periodically supplies copies of its routing tables to any directly connected hosts and networks. When **routed** is started, it searches for directly connected interfaces configured into the system and marked "up" (the software loopback interface is ignored). If multiple interfaces are present, it is assumed that the host will forward packets between networks. **routed** then transmits a request packet on each interface (using a broadcast packet if the interface supports it) and enters a loop, listening for request and response packets from other hosts. When a request packet is received, **routed** formulates a reply based on the information maintained in its internal tables. The response packet generated contains a list of known routes, each marked with a *hop count* metric (a count of 16, or greater, is considered infinite). The metric associated with each route returned provides a metric relative to the sender.

ARP and proxyARP

proxyARP allows the assignment of more than one IP address to a single network adapter. This is accomplished by creating an entry in the ARP cache of Linux that associates the additional IP address with the hardware MAC address of the Ethernet controller. This permits the Linux system to respond to an ARP request to translate an IP address to a hardware address. When a remote host connects with some IP address to your system, Linux will add this IP address and the MAC address associated with the eth0 interface (see **ifconfig** above) to the ARP cache. When a request is received to translate that IP address to a MAC address, it will send the entry from its tables to the requester. Assuming that the secondary IP address is associated with a MAC address on your router, then packets directed to that IP address will be sent to the router and the router may then forward them to the remote system. The router on your local network is a proxy for the remote IP address. It can accept packets for the remote IP address and deliver them by responding to the ARP requests providing that the local ARP table has an entry that associates the remote IP address with "real" MAC address on the local network's server. This is frequently the situation when using SLIP/PPP.

Because the Ethernet adapter on the server must be set up as a proxy for a remote IP address that is actually accessible only via a SLIP or PPP adapter, this has led to the view that proxyARP should be used only with extreme caution. If you are configuring a Linux system for use as a SLIP/PPP dial-in server, however, you may have to use proxyARP set up either manually or automatically. Normally, when a host on your Ethernet network wants to talk to you, it knows your IP address but does not know your MAC address. The ARP mechanism is there specifically to provide the mapping function between a network address and MAC (hardware) address. The "pub" argument should be specified. It is this argument that instructs your machine to answer requests for these addresses, even though they are not for your machine. When it answers it will supply the hardware address specified, which is, of course, its own address. If the entry is not found in the cache, a special request is made of all systems attached to the network to resolve the IP address to a MAC address. This is called an ARP request. The response to the ARP request is a reply with the MAC address. The MAC address is then added to the cache so that the translation may be performed subsequently without the aid of ARP.

While proxyARP can be quite useful under many conditions, there are some important situations in which it will not work at all. Unfortunately, these are the conditions you will most frequently confront using a commercial ISP. The principal problem is being confronted with a network address that is foreign to your own. If both your network and the remote network are part of the same network (that is, you are subnetted in some fashion), then proxyARP is a viable routing technique. If that is not the case, then other routing techniques become necessary. If your network address is, for example, 198.139.158.0 and the remote is 198.139.200.0, you are likely to have a problem. This can possibly be handled because they are the same at the next level up (i.e., 198.139.0.0). That would require using a netmask on both ends of the connection of 255.255.0.0, however, and your ISP may not be prepared to handle that situation since that could change the characteristics of other connections they need for proper operation.

There are also some operational conditions that need to be avoided. The primary one is to avoid having more than one system respond to the proxyARP query for a specific IP address. One of the ways this can happen is to try a proxyARP on an IP address already on your local network. In any event, when proxyARP will not work for you, then you will have to move to other routing techniques, such as the use of manual routing, or the use of **gated** or **routed**. ProxyARP is obviously not for everyone, but it is a workable solution in some cases.

Gated—Gateway Routing Daemon

Gated is a routing daemon that handles multiple routing protocols and replaces **routed**, which is routinely distributed with Linux. **Gated** currently handles the RIP, BGP, EGP, HELLO, and OSPF routing protocols. The **gated** process can be configured to perform all routing protocols or any subset of them. **Gated** allows you to configure your *nix (Linux or other) machine as an intelligent IP router for your network. RIP is the most commonly used routing protocol in small networks. If **gated** runs on your gateway, configured for RIP, your Linux machine will periodically broadcast a copy of its routing table to your network. This makes information available to all the hosts on your network concerning the addresses of hosts accessible through your gateway.

Gated is not yet routinely distributed with all of the Linux distributions. The **gated** binaries are available from:

```
sunsite.unc.edu in
        /pub/Linux/system/Network/daemons/gated.linux.bin.tgz
```

As of this writing the man pages and sources were not available from sunsite and the gated project has been moved from Cornell University to the Merit network. The full and latest version can be found at **ftp.gated.merit.edu**. The full source distribution has the latest documentation in html format (which means you will have to use a browser like Mosaic or Netscape to view the documents).

According to the NET-2-HOWTO, the "gated binary distribution comprises three programs and two sample configuration files." The archive I was able to find contained only the executables and there was no indication where anything else might be. The programs are:

Gated—the **gated** daemon

gdc—the operational user interface for *gated*. **gdc** is a tool for managing the *gated* daemon, stopping and starting it, and obtaining its status

ripquery—a diagnostic tool to query the known routes of a gateway using either a rip query or a rip poll.

The **gated** binary distribution will not automatically install the *gated* files in the correct directory. It is, however, relatively easy to do by hand. You might try the following (taken from the NET-2-HOWTO):

```
cd /tmp
gzip -dc .../gated.linux.bin.tgz | tar xvf -
install -m 500 bin/gated /usr/sbin
install -m 444 bin/gated.conf bin/gated.version /etc
install -m 555 bin/ripquery bin/gdc /sbin
rm -rf /tmp/bin
```

The networking daemons are usually found in */usr/sbin*, and that is where this procedure will put **gated**. The sample **gated** configuration file listed below configures **gated** to emulate the old routed daemon. The procedure above assumes that you have untarred the binary distribution in */tmp* and that it creates a */tmp/bin* subdirectory. The version I obtained did not create the */bin* subdirectory and I simply took out the references to *bin* or */bin*.

Gated is normally started in */etc/rc.d/rc.inet2* in place of **routed** or in */etc/rc.d/rc.local* with a relatively simple setup:

```
# Start the gated server.
    if [ -f ${NET}/gated ]; then
            echo -n " gated"
            ${NET}/gated
    fi
```

where "NET" is set in the file to specify the path to the **gated** executable. For example, most of the network daemons are found in:

```
NET=/usr/sbin
```

A configuration file, usually called */etc/gated.conf*, must be written (there are several samples distributed with the full source version from Merit). The simplest one would be something like the following:

```
#
#  This configuration emulates routed.  It runs RIP and only sends
#  updates if there are more than one interfaces up and IP forwarding is
#  enabled in the kernel.
#
#       NOTE that RIP *will not* run if UDP checksums are disabled in
#       the kernel.
#

rip yes ;

static {
        default gateway 198.67.236.1 preference 140 retain ;
} ;
```

The gateway IP address would, of course, have to be changed to your IP gateway.

Gated ensures that there is a route available to each IP interface that is configured and up. Normally this is done by the **ifconfig** command that configures the interface; **gated** does it to ensure consistency. For SLIP/PPP interfaces, **gated** installs some special routes. If the local address on one or more point-to-point interfaces is not shared with a non-point-to-point interface, **gated** installs a route to the local address pointing at the loopback interface with a preference of 110. This ensures that packets originating on this host destined for this local address are handled locally. If the local address of one or more point-to-point interfaces is shared with a non-point-to-point interface, **gated** installs a route to the local with a preference of 0 that will not be installed in the forwarding table. This is to prevent protocols like OSPF from routing packets to this address across a serial interface when this system could be functioning as a host.

When the status of an interface changes, **gated** notifies all the protocols, which take the appropriate action. **Gated** assumes that interfaces that are not marked "up" do not exist. **Gated** also ignores any interfaces that have invalid data for the local, remote or broadcast addresses or the subnet mask. Invalid data includes zeros in any field. **Gated** will also ignore any point-to-point interface that has the same local and remote addresses; it assumes it is in some sort of loopback test mode.

Although **gated** is usually started as described earlier, it comes with an operational user interface called **gdc**. **gdc** provides a user-oriented interface for the operation of the **gated** routing daemon. It provides support for starting and stopping the daemon, for the delivery of signals to manipulate the daemon when it is operating, for the maintenance and syntax checking of configuration files, and for the production and removal of state dumps and core dumps. **gdc** can reliably determine **gated's** running state and produces a reliable exit status when errors occur, making it advantageous for use in shell scripts that manipulate **gated**. Commands executed using **gdc** and, optionally, error messages produced by the execution of those commands, are logged via the same syslogd facility that **gated** itself uses, providing an audit trail of operations performed on the daemon. If installed as a setuid root, program **gdc** will allow nonroot users who are members of a trusted group (by default the gdmaint group) to manipulate the routing daemon while denying access to others. For audit purposes,[14] the name of the user is logged along via syslogd with an indication of each command executed.

named—Internet Domain Name Server

named is the Internet domain name server. See RFC's 1033, 1034, and 1035 for more information on the Internet name-domain system. Without any arguments, **named** will read the default boot file */etc/named.boot*, read any initial data, and listen for queries. In general, for the conditions for which you are reading this book, you should not need to run **named**. The primary situation where you might wish or need to run **named** is to support your own network of networks (several remote offices, for example). In order for you to run a nameserver you must also coordinate with your ISP and it must be registered. Most of the name resolutions (names to IP address) you need can be accomplished with the */etc/hosts* file. Nevertheless, it is important that you understand what **named** can do for you in the event that you should ever need it.

named allows your machine to serve the name lookup requests, not only for itself, but also for other machines on the network. If yours or another machine wants to find the address for "xyz.com," the system would look first in your */etc/hosts* file, then go to your designated Internet nameserver. If you are running **named**, then the name-to-address resolution can take place on your LAN rather than having to access a remote nameserver. The problem with setting up a nameserver is that it can be relatively complicated and it takes resources on the machine on which it is running. Consequently, if it is not needed you are better off without it. When operating a small LAN, using a nameserver can increase your work considerably, but even so, may facilitate the operations of the LAN relative to the Internet.

Network Configuration Files

There are several files that are required to complete your gateway (and that you may need on each of your workstations, as well). The primary files are:

    /etc/hosts
    /etc/networks
    /etc/gateways
    /etc/host.conf
    /etc/resolv.conf
    /etc/HOSTNAME

/etc/hosts

/etc/hosts contains a list of IP addresses and their host names. The translation of human-readable names to IP addresses is called *name-to-address resolution*. A nameserver can provide the same function, but if it is remote from your LAN it will be slower than maintaining your own */etc/hosts* file. Moreover, on your

workstations some of the software you will use requires the presence of a *hosts* file. The minimum */etc/hosts* file is one that contains the line:

```
127.0.0.1        localhost
```

You may also include entries for your gateways and network addresses, as well as for other machines on your LAN. The second line of the */etc/hosts* file will be a reference to the machine on which it is running. A single line will contain the IP address, a fully qualified domain name, and one or more aliases (these can be nicknames for the machines). Thus a typical */etc/hosts* file might look something like this:

```
# /etc/hosts
# List of hostnames and their ip addresses
127.0.0.1          localhost
#Your router if this is the hosts file for the router,
#        or your workstation, if this is the hosts file for your
#        workstation.
200.128.50.1             gate.xyz.com         gate


#Other machines on your LAN:
200.128.50.2             apple.xyz.com        apple
200.128.50.3             pear.xyz.com         pear
200.128.50.4             peach.xyz.com        peach
200.128.50.5             prune.xyz.com        prune


#Your nameserver(s) might be placed here:


#Frequently accessed hosts on the Internet might follow:


# end of hosts
```

If you are working on the machine that has this particular *hosts* file, then you can refer to the other machines by any of the names listed. Each component of each line must be separated by one or more white spaces or tabs.

/etc/networks

The /etc/networks file lists the names and addresses of your own and other networks. It is used by the **route** command, and allows you to specify a network by name. Every network to which you wish to add a route using the **route** command should have an entry in the /etc/networks file, unless you also specify the -net argument in the **route** command line. The format is similar to that of /etc/hosts file above. Such a file might be the following:

```
#

# /etc/networks: list all networks that you wish to add route commands

#                for here

# This file contains network name/network number mappings for

# local networks.  Network numbers are recognized in dotted decimal form.

#

# Format:

#

# <network name>  <network number>     [aliases...]  [#<comment>]

#

# For example:

#

default    0.0.0.0                    #recommended

loopback   127.0.0.0                  #recommended

mynet      198.139.158.0              #change to an appropriate network

yournet    198.139.157.0              #change to an appropriate network

anothernet 128.121.0.0                #change to an appropriate network


# End of /etc/networks
```

/etc/gateways

The man page for **routed** describes /etc/gateways as follows: **routed** supports the notion of *distant* passive and active gateways. When routed is started up, it reads the file /etc/gateways to find gateways that may not be located using only information from the SIOGIFCONF ioctl(2). Gateways specified in this manner should be marked passive if they are not expected to exchange routing information, while gateways marked active should be willing to exchange routing information (i.e., they should have a **routed** process running on the machine). Routes through passive gateways are installed in the kernel's routing tables once on startup. Such routes are not included in any routing information transmitted. Active gateways are treated equally with network interfaces. Routing information is distributed to the gateway and if no routing information is received for a period of time, the associated route is deleted. Gateways marked external are also passive but are not placed in the kernel routing table, nor are they included in routing updates. The function of external entries is to inform **routed** that another routing process will install such a route, and that alternate routes to that destination should not be installed. Such entries are required only when both routers may learn of routes to the same destination.

The */etc/gateways* is comprised of a series of lines, each in the following format:

```
<net | host> name1 gateway name2 metric value <passive | active |external>
```

The net or host keyword indicates if the route is to a network or specific host.

Name1 is the name of the destination network or host. This may be a symbolic name located in */etc/networks* or */etc/hosts* (or, if started after named(8), known to the name server), or an Internet address specified in *dot* notation; see inet(3). *Name2* is the name or address of the gateway to which messages should be forwarded. *Value* is a metric indicating the hop count to the destination host or network.

One of the keywords **passive, active,** or **external** indicates if the gateway should be treated as passive or active (as described above), or whether the gateway is external to the scope of the routed protocol.

A typical *gateways* file might look like the following:

```
# Example of /etc/gateways
#
#net|
#host  name1    gateway  name2         metric value <passive|active|external>


net    0.0.0.0 gateway  198.67.236.1 metric   1       passive
```

/etc/host.conf

The */etc/host.conf* file specifies how your system will look up host names. It functions in conjunction with Resolv+, which is a modified version of the standard Berkeley BIND host resolver library. Enhancements include support for host lookups via the Internet Domain Name System (DNS), the */etc/hosts* file, and Sun's Network Information Service (NIS).

As with the standard resolver library, the file */etc/resolv.conf* must be set up before the resolver can function. In addition, the file */etc/host.conf* contains configuration information specific to Resolv+. It should contain at least the following two lines:

```
order hosts,bind
multi on
```

These two lines tell the resolver libraries to first check the */etc/hosts* file, and then to ask the nameserver (if one is present). *multi* allows the use of multiple IP addresses for a given machine name in */etc/hosts* providing the keyword "on" is used.

/etc/resolv.conf

/etc/resolv.conf actually configures the system name resolver, and contains two types of entries: the addresses of your nameservers (if any), and the name of your domain, if you have one. If you're running your own nameserver (i.e., running **named** on your Linux machine), then the address of your nameserver is 127.0.0.1, the loopback address. Your domain name is your fully qualified hostname (if you're a registered machine on the Internet, for example), with the hostname component removed. That is, if your full hostname is **peach.xyz.com**, then your domain name is **xyz.com**, without the hostname (machine name) peach.

For example, if your machine is **arms.ewc-inc.com**, and it has two nameservers, then your */etc/resolv.conf* file might look like this:

```
domain ewc-inc.com
nameserver 128.121.50.2
nameserver 128.121.50.7
```

You can obviously specify more than one nameserver. Each one must have a nameserver entry in the *resolv.conf* file.

Configuring Your Hostname—/etc/HOSTNAME

The task that remains after everything else is configured is to be sure your own machine has its name properly set. This is required so that application programs like sendmail can accept mail, and so that your machine can identify itself to other machines to which it may be connected. There are two programs that are used to deal with this problem: **hostname** and **domainname**.

Assuming that you are using the **hostname** command that came with net-tools-1.1.38 or later, then you would add a command at the end of your */etc/rc.d/rc.inet1* file like this:

```
/bin/hostname arms.ewc-inc.com
```

Or if you have upgraded from a previous release, you could add:

```
/bin/hostname -F /etc/HOSTNAME
```

and it would behave in the same way as for the earlier version. The **/bin/domainname** command is part of the Berkely Network Information System (NIS) and refers to the NIS domain name, *not* to the DNS domain name. Do not set this unless you are running NIS.

Dialing On-Demand

One of the recurrent themes in this book is the issue of making all these processes relatively automatic for the average user on your local LAN. The average user should be able to execute a program like Mosaic or Netscape, for example, and be automatically attached to the appropriate location (URL). When you are a member of a large organization with a permanent (static) attachment to the Internet, this is exactly how the process works. But what about your smaller organization with a dialup link to the Internet? The process, as we have already noted, is called on-demand dialing. There are various way in which on-demand dialing can be implemented, but one way that it can be done in Linux is through the use of a daemon named **diald** by Eric Schenk (**schenk@cs.toronto.edu**).[15]

diald is a daemon that does on-demand dialing for PPP and SLIP. The purpose of **diald**, according to its author "is to make it transparently appear that you have a permanent connection to a remote site." **diald** works by setting up a "proxy" device which stands in for the physical connection to a remote site. The proxy is continuously monitored, waiting for packets to arrive. When packets do arrive, **diald** will attempt to establish the physical link to the remote site using either SLIP or PPP, and if it succeeds it will forward traffic from the proxy to the physical link. **diald** will also monitor traffic once the physical link is up, and when it has determined that the link is idle, the remote connection is terminated. The connection criteria are configured at run time, and are based upon the type of traffic passing over the link.

The primary problem with using **diald** is that it is not a standard part of the easily available distributions of Linux. As of this writing the most recent release of **diald** was *diald-0.10.tar.gs*, available from ftp://sunsite.unc.edu/pub/Linux/system/Network/serial. You may, however, find it on one or more of the CD distributions of Linux although I have been unable to do so. In addition to being available from sunsite, it can also be found on most sunsite mirrors.

Now that we have a tool for doing on-demand dialing, we can complete our Linux gateway to the Internet. The first thing is to install the software. In order to do this you will have to compile it. When you installed Linux itself you should have installed the C programming language (regardless of whether you know C or not). Perform the following steps:

1. Logon as user *root*.
2. Uncompress (using **gzip**)and untar *diald-0.10.tar.gs* in a convenient location. This will create a subdirectory called *diald-0.10*.
3. Cd into *diald-0.10*.
4. Run "make depend."
5. Run "make."
6. Run "make install." This makes the diald daemon and installs it.
7. Run "make install-configs." This will install the configuration files */etc/diald.defs* and */etc/diald.conf*. After installation you may want to edit */etc/diald.conf* to customize diald to your local site.

8. Read the manual page to find out what */etc/diald.conf* can contain.

There are two documents distributed with **diald** that you are strongly advised to read: Eric Schenk (**schenk@cs.toronot.edu**) and Gordon Soukoreff (**gordon@tradenet.com**), *Linux Diald FAQ*, and Eric Schenk, *diald—demand dialing daemon for SLIP and PPP links*, man page. You will need to read the man page since it offers a detailed explanation of each option for **diald**. Toward the end of the man page are several examples for actually running the program. It is very helpful to review those examples. Rarely, however, are two installations identical. For that reason I am also providing my own setup files and you can compare those to those published in the man page. As with some of the other examples in this book, these illustrate how to connect to an ISP providing a dynamic SLIP connection and one providing a dynamic PPP connection. You should be able to use these general procedures with any randomly selected ISP using either SLIP or PPP.

Earlier in this chapter we discussed the use of **dip** and **chat** for dialing into your ISP. If you elect to use **diald**, you *must* use **chat**. The **chat** program was discussed in the section on using SLIP, above. In fact, you must use **chat** regardless whether you have a PPP or a SLIP connection. We will not redo the discussion of the use of **chat** here. Rather, we will simply provide some appropriate scripts that work in PPP and SLIP environments. First, just a brief comment on */etc/diald.conf*. I have found that the distributed version of the file works "out-of-the-box." If you have some peculiar requirements, you may have to make some minor changes. First, however, get the entire system running, then make changes.

Using SLIP

In order to have a working SLIP connection you might set up the following files:

diald.gojvnc This file can be located anywhere convenient to your system. Possibilities would be */etc/ppp*, */usr/local/bin*, or */usr/sbin*. In this example "jvnc" is a short form of the ISP. The content of *diald.gojvnc* follows. From that file you can see the additional files required:

```
#!/bin/sh
Exec diald /dev/cub2 -m slip local 127.0.0.3 remote 192.67.236.1 \
        defaultroute modem crtscts netmask 255.255.255.0 \
        addroute /etc/ppp/diald.addjvnc \
        delroute /etc/ppp/diald.deljvnc \
```

```
connect "chat -v -f /usr/lib/ppp/jvnc.chat" \
mtu 1500 dynamic dslip-mode local
```

The backslash ("\") is used as a continuation character so that you can have a very long command line physically typed on several "real" lines. This particular ISP provides the IP address for its router (gateway) and you can see it at the end of the first line. All of the entries in this small file are command-line options for **diald**. You must read the man page for an explanation. The remote IP address is the real gateway address, although the "local" IP address is a fictitious stand-in for the address that will be assigned by the ISP.

/etc/ppp/diald.addjvnc and /etc/ppp/diald.deljvnc:

diald does not always add (and delete) appropriate routes to your routing table. Thus, you need to use the options "addroute" and "delroute". I happen to have these files in /etc/ppp, by the way. These are very simple:

Diald.addjvnc:
```
route add 192.67.236.1 gw 255.255.255.255
route add default gw 192.67.236.1
```

Diald.deljvnc:
```
route del default
route del 192.67.236.1
```

You should, of course, name your files appropriately. You *must* also use the gateway address your ISP provides (not 192.67.236.1). If your ISP provides this information dynamically, then you may not need these files. See the man page, entry for "dslip-mode." The alternative may be the need for empty dummy files.

/usr/lib/ppp/jvnc.chat:

When you install PPP one of the directories that is created is */usr/lib/ppp*. The **diald** daemon lives in that directory as well as other files. I have arbitrarily decided to use it to house any of the files that **chat** uses, since **chat** also ends up in that directory. The file to access "jvnc" is:

```
ABORT "NO CARRIER" ABORT BUSY
'' atdt555-1212
CONNECT ''
'' \r
```

```
ame: userid
word: yourpassword
ngo> slip
ostname: default
```

This is a typical **chat** script, as already discussed. The abbreviations used happen to be, in this case, shortforms for "Username:", "Password:", "Ringo>", and "Hostname:". This script logs me onto my ISP, starts SLIP, and provides the SLIP option, "default."

At this point you are all set to try your setup. First, run the command **chmod 677 diald.gojvnc**. That small file is now executable. For an automatic setup place the following line in your */etc/rc.d/rc.local* file:

```
/etc/ppp/diald.gojvnc          (Assuming that this file is in /etc/ppp!)
```

When you boot your machine, the daemon will automatically be executed and be available for the use of anyone on the network. You should be able to use a Web browser or other selected TCP/IP software from any of your connected workstations.

Using PPP

The setup for PPP is analogous to that for SLIP. I use CompuServe as the example to demonstrate that you can use virtually any randomly selected PPP or SLIP service.

```
#!/bin/sh
exec diald /dev/cub2 -m ppp local 127.0.0.3 remote 127.0.0.2 \
        defaultroute modem crtscts \
        addroute /etc/ppp/diald.addcserve \
        delroute /etc/ppp/diald.delcserve \
        connect "chat -f /usr/lib/ppp/cserve.chat" dynamic
```

In this case the local and remote IP numbers that are given are merely fictitious standins. They will ultimately be replaced with the real IP numbers assigned by CompuServe. The routing files are similar to those used in the SLIP example:

/etc/ppp/diald.addcserve:

```
route add cserve gw 255.255.255.255
route add default gw cserve
```

/etc/ppp/diald.delcserve:

```
route del cserve        ("cserve" is my name for CompuServe in my /etc/hosts)
route del 198.139.158.2 (My IP address, not yours)
```

And finally, my **chat** file to log on to CompuServe:

/usr/lib/ppp/chat.cserve:

```
ABORT "NO CARRIER" ABORT BUSY
'' atdt5551212  CONNECT ''
'' \r\r\r
Name: CIS\r
ID: 11111,555/GO:PPPCONNECT\r
ssword: FIRST.SECOND\r
'address is' ''
```

As with the SLIP setup, do a **chmod 677 diald.gocserve** (from the */etc/ppp* directory), and place a line in your */etc/rc.d/rc.local* file something like the following:

```
/etc/ppp/diald.gocserve
```

Or execute the file from your command line.

At this point you should have a working **diald** daemon and the related files.
Assuming that you have followed other instructions in this chapter and in the documents I have suggested you read, you should be able to do on-demand dialing from
any of your LAN-connected Pcs.

Conclusion

This chapter is long and sometimes complicated. What do you actually need to connect your LAN to the Internet with Linux? The simplest, least expensive alternative, once you have installed Linux on a machine attached to your LAN, is to
install *IP_masquerade* and **diald.** Install *IP_masquerade* first, and set up relatively
simple SLIP or PPP connection with your ISP to test out the routing aspects of
IP_masquerade. Then install **diald** and test it out. If you have been able to use a
spare PC on which to install Linux, you should have a solid, working, LAN-based

connection to the Internet that will dial on-demand from any workstation on you LAN. The actual "out-of-pocket" cost will be less than $100 for software, plus your time. What you acquire with your investment of time is an understanding of how all this works. If you cannot or do not wish to contribute the time, then hire a consultant who can follow these instructions.

Now that you have configured your server, you can reboot, dial your ISP, and start surfing the net. Before you can do very much, however, you do need to configure each workstation on the LAN. To get some idea of how to do this, see Chapter 8. For further information on these topics, read the full *NET-2-HOWTO*. You might also wish to consult Olaf Kirch, *Linux Network Administrator's Guide*, and/or Craig Hunt, *TCP/IP Network Administration*. [16]

Notes

1. A helpful source for Linux materials including CDs and printed materials is the ACC Bookstore, 800-546-7274, 203-454-5500, or by email at **info@acc-corp.com**.

2. One relatively inexpensive 8-port board is the Cyclom-8o from Cyclades, Inc., at 510-770-9727 or email at **cyclades@netcom.com**. At this writing the board costs about $300 for the 8-port version.

3. The pertinent HOWTOs are: Serial-HOWTO, Mail-HOWTO, Ethernet-HOWTO, NET-2-HOWTO, and UUCP-HOWTO. The Serial-HOWTO and NET-2-HOWTO should be considered mandatory reading. The latest released version of these documents can be retrieved by anonymous FTP from: **sunsite.unc.edu** in */pub/Linux/docs/HOWTO*. Most software packages also have a man (or manual) page documenting how to use the software. These can be read on-line by typing **man programname**.

4. The remaining field definitions are taken directly from the *gettydefs* man page.

5. The field definitions for */etc/inittab* are taken directly from the *inittab* man page.

6. These are taken directly from the **getty** man page.

7. *Linux NET-2/NET-3 HOWTO*, by Terry Dawson, **terryd@extro.ucc.su.oz.au**, v2.3, 03 Jul 1994.

8. *SUBNET Pro Version 1.0*, Copyright 1995 by Guy Michaud, Halifax, Canada. Email: **gmichaud@cisco.com**.

9. See, particularly, the file *README.linux*, entitled "PPP for Linux, "v1.0.1,based on ppp-2.1.2, June 1994, by Michael Callahan (**callahan@maths.ox.ac.uk**) and Al Longyear (**longyear@netcom.com**).

10. These comments are based on the Slakware distributions.

11. The version I have is published by Specialized Systems Consultants, Inc. (SSC), P.O. Box 55549, Seattle, WA 98155 USA.

12. See also, W. Richard Stevens *TCP/IP Illustrated*, Volume 1 (Reading, MA: Addison-Wesley, 1994), ISBN 0-201-63346-9.

13. For a detailed treatment of the major LAN standards, including 802.3 (Ethernet), see Thomas Wm. Madron, *LANS: Applications of IEEE/ANSI 802 Standards* (New York: Wiley, 1989).

14. Abstracted from the *gated* man page.

15. This subsection is abstracted from Eric Schenk (**schenk@cs.toronot.edu**) and Gordon Soukoreff (**gordon@tradenet.com**), *Linux DialdFAQ*, and Eric Schenk, *diald—demand dialing daemon for SLIP an PPP links*, man page.

16. Olaf Kirch, Linux Network Administrator's Guide (Seattle, WA: Specialized Systems Consultants, 1994); and Craig Hunt, *TCP/IP Network Administration* (Sebastopol, CA: O'Reilly & Associates, 1992).

USING MICROSOFT NT SERVER 3.5 AS A ROUTER

The remaining chapters in this book will not be nearly so long as Chapter 5. The reason is that most of the issues for TCP/IP networking were worked out in the context of networks of Unix machines. The result has been that even when TCP/IP has been implemented on other operating systems it follows, even in language, the way in which it has been accomplished on Unix. In this chapter, therefore, we will cover primarily those elements of the use of NT Server 3.5 that are different from what we have already seen. Before getting started, I must emphasize that if you have decided to use Microsoft NT Server 3.5, you *must* also buy the NT Server Resource Kit. The reason for this is that it contains the documentation for most of the TCP/IP facilities available with the NT Server software.

As with other systems, there are a few things you need to have at hand before you can complete the installation of TCP/IP on your NT Server:

- An Internet Service Provider (ISP).
- From the ISP:

- A determination whether the service is SLIP or PPP. If it is SLIP, you will probably not be able to use the NT Server as a router.

- Whether the IP addresses are statically or dynamically allocated.

- The address of a gateway.

- The addresses of the ISP's domain name servers (DNS).

- A block of IP addresses large enough to cover your current workstations, server, and a few extras for expansion purposes. Your ISP should be able to assist you in acquiring the address block. This can be either a valid Class C network (254+2 addresses), or a block of subnetted addresses.

- A registered domain name, although optional, is helpful as well.

- If your ISP uses the Dynamic Host Configuration Protocol (DHCP) then all the foregoing can be dynamically configured. If not, then it is still likely that your ISP will dynamically provide an IP address although you may have to fill in some blanks with their DNS addresses.

Your Windows NT Server will actually have two IP addresses: one associated with your network interface card (NIC), and one associated with the PPP device that will send the IP datagrams over the phone line.

Our objective in this chapter is to briefly describe one way in which a Windows NT Server 3.5 can be used as a router to access the Internet. As you can see from Figure 6.1 the problem is logically similar to using a Unix server (see Chapter 5). Two major services must be installed in order to make your NT Server function as a router: TCP/IP and RAS (Remote Access Service). Although SLIP is also supplied with Windows NT Server 3.5, it is questionable whether it can be used at all for the link between your LAN and your ISP. You may wish to install it anyway for other purposes, although it is a separate and distinct step. We will follow the Microsoft documentation on this point and assume that PPP will be used for linking your LAN to the Internet. Microsoft also cautions that "Windows NT version 3.5 RAS was not designed to route packets from a local area network over a WAN link."[1] Even though NT Server 3.5 was not designed for this purpose, it can be correctly configured to operate as a router for a *small* LAN. Before going further, however, we need to ensure that the appropriate software is properly installed.

We will not go through a step-by-step description of the software setup process. The Microsoft documents do that well. Suffice it to say that if you did not include RAS and/or TCP/IP when you installed Windows NT Server 3.5, you can add any

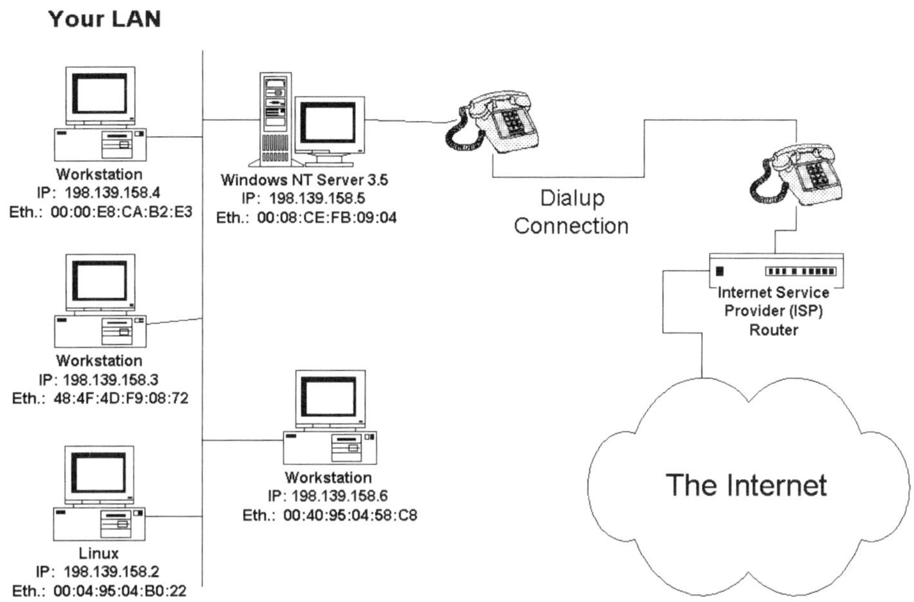

Your LAN

Figure 6.1 A LAN connected to the Internet through an NT Server.

of the additional services at any time. Briefly, you accomplish this by clicking on Main, Control Panel, Network. You end up with the window in Figure 6.2. From Figure 6.2 you can see that there are "Add Software" and "Add Adapters" buttons. With the original CD in your CDROM drive, you can select any of the standard software you did not get the first time around. Once installed, you can configure it by highlighting the service in the Installed Network Software subwindow, then clicking on **Configure**.

Remote Access Service (RAS)

The Remote Access Service allows workstations at remote sites to access network servers transparently, as though they were physically connected to the network. Remote Access connections can be established over public telephone lines, X.25 networks, or ISDN networks. Resources available as a byproduct of RAS also allow servers to dial out to other systems to establish, among other things, links to the Internet. The Remote Access Setup program lets you install the Remote Access drivers, select ports for Remote Access to use, and select how each port will be used

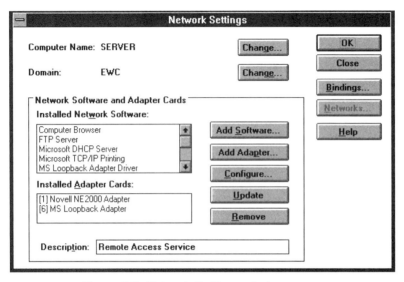

Figure 6.2 Network Settings window.

(for dialing out, receiving calls, or both). If you choose to receive calls, you may choose to give callers access to the entire network or restrict access to the Remote Access server. For our purposes we will concentrate not on the range of RAS capabilities but on the specific issue of dialing out to an ISP using PPP.

In order to have RAS operate properly, you must first select and configure the protocols to use on the LAN. Network protocol configuration applies to all RAS operations for all RAS-enabled ports. The RAS computer may access a LAN as a client or as a server. You must select the LAN protocols RAS will use in each role. A RAS computer's role is determined when you specify how RAS-enabled ports will be used. We are concerned here with the use of RAS in a client mode, since we will be dialing out to an ISP.

The first thing to do is to select the protocols to use when dialing out to a remote access server. If you do not select a protocol in the Dial Out Protocols box, you will be unable to select that protocol later when you configure a phone book entry for dialing out. My own server is configured for the protocols illustrated in Figure 6.3. All I needed were TCP/IP and NETBEUI, since I do not have a Novell server running that requires IPX. NETBEUI, if you don't immediately recall, is the network protocol native to Microsoft networking. If you have not defined any ports for dialout, The Dial Out Protocols box will be dimmed. In this illustrative case, I have defined only a dialout port, as you can see in Figure 6.4.

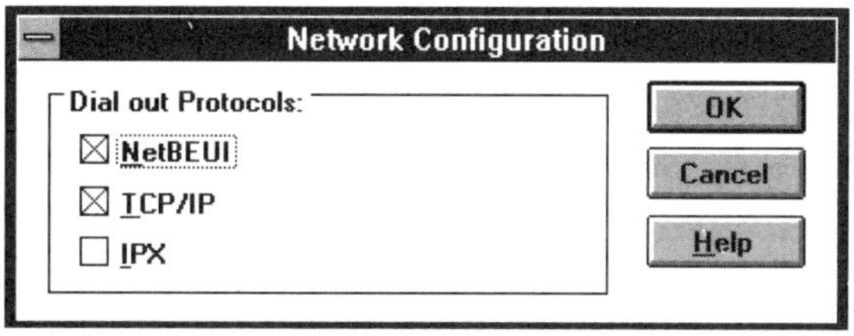

Figure 6.3 Dial-out protocols available.

There are some server settings you may also wish to look at. You can select, for example, the Require Encrypted Authentication check box to require encrypted passwords from all clients. Unless your ISP requires authentication (and most do not), *do not* check this box.

Other protocol parameters may also be configured at this point. The "Help" in each configuration dialog box will provide more detailed information. If no ports are configured to receive calls, the Server Settings box will not appear in the Network Configuration dialog box. If you do decide to allow your RAS server to be used for dial-in as well as dial-out, then there are procedures for providing IP addresses to remote users either statically or dynamically (through DCHP). In particular, if you are allowing others to dial into you, you may wish to enable the authentication capabilities with the appropriate encryption settings.

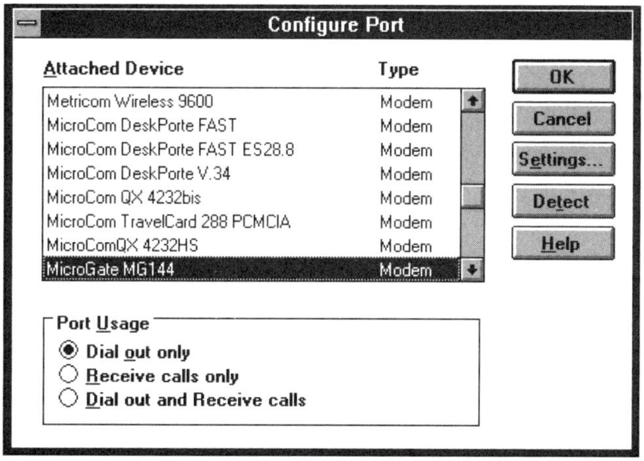

Figure 6.4 Configure Port dialog box.

Configuring TCP/IP

There are two points at which you will have to configure TCP/IP settings. The first, and most general, is in the Network Settings dialog box already illustrated in Figure 6.2. Find the "TCP/IP Protocol" line under "Installed Network Software." Highlight that line, then click on the **Configure** button. Here you are configuring TCP/IP for use primarily within your own LAN (Figure 6.1). When you click on Configure, you will get the dialog box illustrated in Figure 6.5.

General TCP/IP Configuration

Note that at this point you will assign an IP address to your server for the LAN, not for purposes of the Internet. If you had a separate, standalone router (see Chapter 8) attached to the LAN you would also enter the router's IP address as your gateway. Since you do not have such a device (in this scenario), leave the gateway IP address blank at this point. When we configure RAS for dial-out TCP/IP access, we will have an opportunity to fill in an appropriate field at that point. The key here is that you will end up with two IP addresses for your server. The one you assign is shown as in Figure 6.5 (and you cannot use the one illustrated—that is

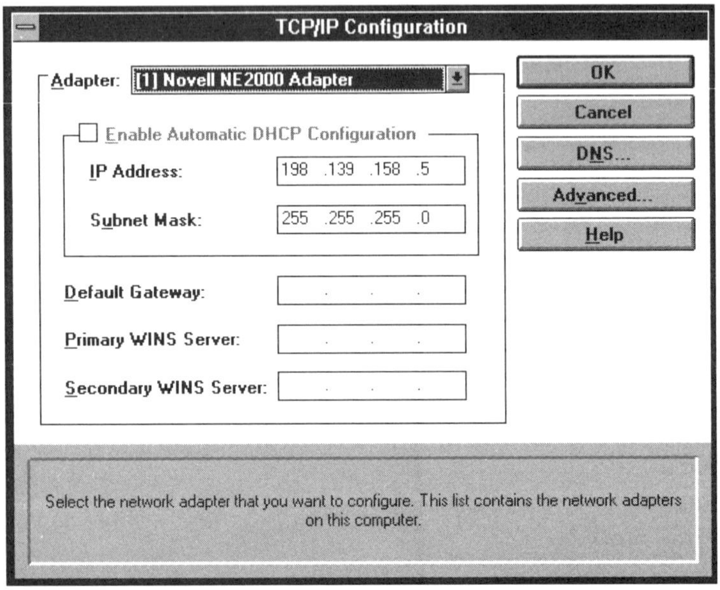

Figure 6.5 TCP/IP configuration.

mine). The subnet mask will most likely be 255.255.255.0, but if your ISP assigns you a block of subnetted addresses for your LAN you may have a subnet mask like 255.255.255.240, or some other number in the fourth subfield. See the discussion of subnetworking in Chapter 5.

Because you will have one IP address assigned to your Ethernet connection and another (from your ISP) assigned to your PPP connection, you can actually use an unregistered block of IP addresses for your LAN from the 192.168.0.0 Class C network. You might, for example, use the block 198.168.100.[0-255], remembering that 198.168.100.0 and 198.168.100.255 will be used for special purposes and should not be used for workstation addresses. Communication to and from the Internet will actually be through the IP address (probably) dynamically allocated by your ISP to your PPP device. This process, as we are describing it, operates similarly to IP_Masquerading discussed in Chapter 5. Now, click on the DNS button.

When you click on the DNS button you will get the dialog box seen in Figure 6.6. Your ISP should provide you with appropriate name server addresses. Those shown happen to be CompuServe's since I will illustrate all this by connecting to the Internet through CompuServe.[2] You will need these DNS addresses again, by the way. The domain suffix

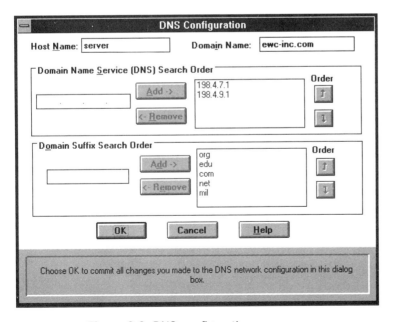

Figure 6.6 DNS configuration.

search order is not critical, but those illustrated are the primary suffixes currently in use. As noted previously, there are a number of others. You will also need to click on **Advanced** and complete some additional information. When this happens you end up with the dialog box found in Figure 6.7. In the Advanced configuration box you have an opportunity to make some additional changes and to add some information.

At the top of Figure 6.7 is a menu bar that will give a list of all the adapters you may have defined. In this illustration you have defined only your NIC, so there is only a single item. You should not have to add or delete any IP addresses at this time. You may or may not want to enable *LMHOSTS*. *LMHOSTS* is the Microsoft equivalent to the *hosts* file we discussed in Chapter 5. In fact, you can set it up exactly as the *hosts* file was described. It is possible to do other things with *LMHOSTS* in addition to the usual *hosts* file information, but you can dispense with that for the moment. I like to use *LMHOSTS* because it means that for any host listed, it will not be necessary to go to a DNS to get an IP address. Moreover, you can define aliases that have short names that you understand but are unrelated to domain and machine names (although you

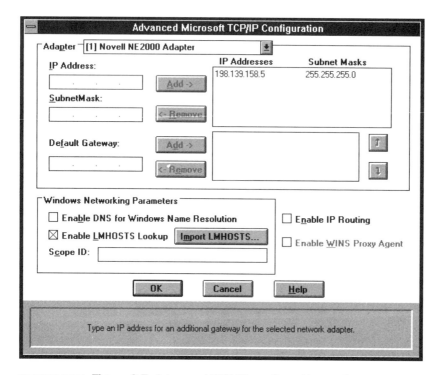

Figure 6.7 Advanced TCP/IP configuration options.

probably should not make them too foreign). At the very least, put an entry for each of your LAN workstations in *LMHOSTS* as well as Internet hosts that you frequently use. Consult the Microsoft documentation for more on the use of *LMHOSTS*.

A couple of final notes for this section are in order. First go to the Ports icon in Control Panel and check the port on which you have your modem. Make certain it is correctly set up. In general, the speed should be at least as fast as the "real" speed of your modem. For a 14.4 Kbps smart modem, set the speed to 38,400 bps or 57,600 bps. It should have been correctly set for your modem when you installed the modem earlier. The other settings should be 8 data bits, no parity, 1 stop bit, and hardware flow control. As you will find when connecting to CompuServe, this causes some minor problems because the CompuServe network typically is set for 7 data bits, even parity, and 1 stop bit. Even if you set this incorrectly, however, RAS, on behalf of PPP, will override. When all of this is finished, shut down NT and reboot your server.

Configuring RAS for TCP/IP

As a result of installing RAS you will have a Remote Access Service program group in Program Manager. One of the icons will be *Remote Access*. Click on **Remote Access** now. The result will be the Remote Access window illustrated in Figure 6.8. I already have some entries for ISPs in mine, but yours will be blank. In fact, you will have to define a service by clicking on **Add**, resulting in the screen in Figure 6.9.

If your "Add Phone Book Entry" box does not look quite like the one shown, don't worry. Rather than the **<<Basic** button you will have an **Advanced>>** button. Just click it and the box will take on the appearance of Figure 6.9. Just type in the name

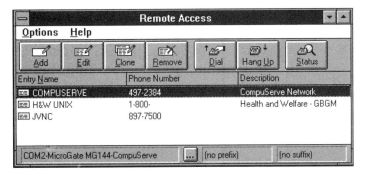

▬▬▬▬ **Figure 6.8** Remote Access window.

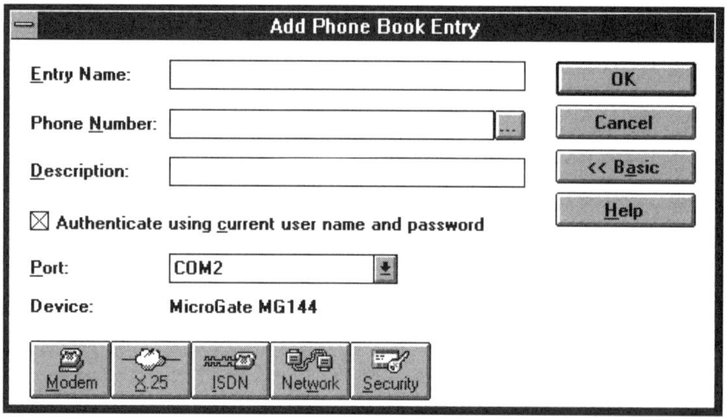

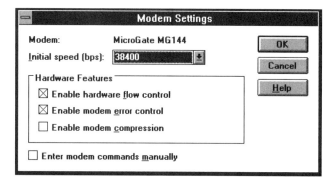

Figure 6.9 Add Phone Book Entry.

of your ISP, a phone number to connect to, and a short description (optional). Check to make sure the port setting is aimed at the correct port. The Authenticate check box defaults to being checked and you can leave it alone. Click on the **Modem** button and check the settings. Make certain they all conform to what you have already done with modems. It should look like Figure 6.10.

Assuming that everything is okay, click on **OK**, get back to the previous screen, and click on Network. The Network box may be seen in Figure 6.11. Here is the second point at which you will deal with TCP/IP. At least TCP/IP should be checked. NETBEUI is not necessary for our purposes, but is shouldn't hurt. When in doubt, turn it off. Then click on the **TCP/IP Settings** button so that you can see Figure 6.12. Yours should look just like the box illustrated, except that you should put

Figure 6.10 Modem Settings.

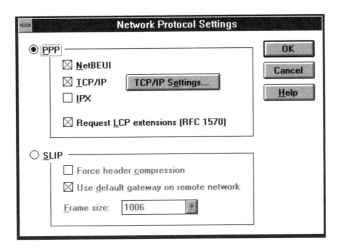

■■■■ **Figure 6.11** Network Protocol Settings.

you own DNS addresses in, unless, of course, you are connecting to CompuServe. You may have to experiment with the "VJ Header Compression," although most ISPs do use header compression. When you connect with your ISP it will assign you an IP address. This IP address will be related to your PPP device, not to your LAN interface card. Thus, while you are connected to the Internet, you will have two IP addresses for your server. The one on the LAN side allows your other workstations

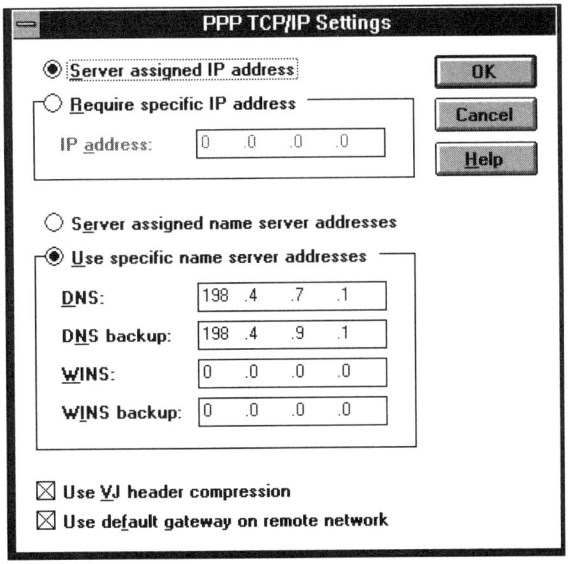

■■■■ **Figure 6.12** PPP TCP/IP Settings.

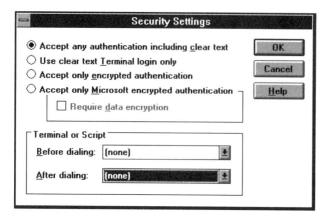

Figure 6.13 Security Settings.

to get into the server, the one on the Internet side lets the server get to the Internet and allows the Internet resources to return information to your server. The server, then, must take care of getting information back out to your LAN.

Click on **OK** until you get back to the Add Phone Book Entry screen. Then click on the **Security** button. This will call up the screen shown in Figure 6.13. What we want to do now is to configure our setup for as automatic an operation as is possible with the NT software in its current state. When dialing out, RAS provides the capability for using either a terminal emulation screen or a script. (In the case of a SLIP connection it ends up being a combination of the two.) The script is in the file *x:\winnt\system32\ras\switch.inf*, where "x:" is the drive letter where you have NT installed. You may also have changed your base directory name from "winnt" (the default), so that should also be changed as necessary.

After we edit the dummy *switch.inf* file that comes with the system, you will be able to click on **After Dialing** under "terminal or script" and get a list of dialing scripts that appear in *switch.inf* (*switch.inf* can contain multiple scripts). The dummy file that is distributed consists only of the first two lines (the copyright notice). We add the rest. My file that accesses CompuServe is the following:

```
; SWITCH.INF for Windows NT Remote Access Service version 3.51
; Copyright 1995 Microsoft Corporation

[CompuServe]
```

```
COMMAND<cr>            ;send a carriage return to wake up the network.


OK=<match>":"          ;look for a colon.
LOOP=<ignore>          ;loop until a colon comes, ignoring all else.



OK=<match>":"          ;find another colon.
LOOP=<ignore>          ;ignore everything except a colon.


COMMAND=11111,222/GO:PPPCONNECT<cr> ;send your userid, then
        ;request PPP services, followed by a CR.


OK=<match>":"        ;wait for another colon.
LOOP=<ignore>        ;ignore everything else.
COMMAND=FIRST.SECOND<cr> ;send your password.


OK=<ignore>          ;expect nothing else and exit script.


; At this point the script successfully ends.  You are ready to
; surf the net.
```

A *switch.inf* file consists of section headers (the "[CompuServe]" in the illustrative file); comment lines (any lines beginning with a semicolon); commands (lines beginning with "COMMAND="); and responses or directives (the "OK=" and "LOOP=" lines). Following each equal sign, depending on whether the line is a command, a response, or a directive, will be a string that you devise, or an instruction or value. For a more detailed treatment of *switch.inf* scripts see the appropriate Microsoft documentation.[3]

In the example given above, the three colons are the colons that follow three prompts. The first is for the service, which in this case is CIS. The second is the end of the prompt "User ID:". And the third is the end of the prompt "Password:". With most ISPs we would use not only the colons, but also part of the longer prompt. Remember, however, that CompuServe expects a 7-bit word length and we have defined the communications condition with an 8-bit word length. If you were doing this by hand and a terminal emulation program you would see that what is being returned is unreadable by humans because of this disparity. Fortunately, colons do not seem to get reprocessed, nor does anything get translated into colons. So we watch for just the colons. This may occasionally result in some degree of unreliability in the process. If so, just redial. Now, go back to the Security screen and highlight **CompuServe** in the option entitled "After Dialing"; click **OK** until you are back to the main RAS screen. At this point you should be able to highlight **CompuServe**, click on the **Dial** button, and connect. But we are not quite finished setting up the server as a router.

Remaking NT Server into a Router

Once all the foregoing has been accomplished, and you have a reliable PPP link with an ISP, it is fairly easy to complete the process. First, you will have to make at least one and possibly two adjustments to the Windows Registry database. You do this with a program called **regedt32.exe**. From Program Manager click on File and Run, then type **x:\winnt\system32\regedt32** and click on **OK**. The registry editor should come up. The first registry path you need to modify or add is:

    \HKEY_LOCAL_MACHINE\System\CurrentControlSet\Services\RasArp\Parameters

Remember that with TCP/IP (and other protocols) we send and receive packets. Those packets have destination and source addresses in their headers. By default, the header of each packet sent by RAS over the PPP link uses the IP address of the RAS computer as the source. Since the packets that come from your LAN workstations are not originating from your server, but from some workstation, we actually want the packet headers to retain the original source address rather than replacing it with the server's address. We accomplish this by setting the value REG_DWORD for the parameter **DisableOtherSrcPacket** to 1. It normally defaults to 0. When in regedt32 you will see buttons that will allow you to add or edit parameters and their values.[4]

The foregoing change is mandatory. The second change also deals with the REG_WORD value, but this time with the registry path:

    \HKEY_LOCAL_MACHINE\System\CurrentControlSet\Services\RasMan\PPP\IPCP

The parameter we will deal with is **PriorityBasedOnSubNetwork**. The issue addressed here goes back to our discussion of subnetworking in Chapter 5. If your LAN has the *same* network address as your ISP, even if the addresses are subnetted, then you can make all packets go across the link by setting the value of REG_WORD for this parameter to 1. Then all packets from your LAN will automatically be sent across the PPP link. You must also have elected to "Use Default Gateway ON Remote Network" in the configurations above. If this addressing condition is not met, however, then you will need to get a gateway address from your ISP and put it in explicitly, and leave the value of this parameter at 0.

Finally, you will have to set the gateways for each of your workstations to the LAN-side IP address of your server. We'll say more on this issue in Chapter 9.

TCP/IP Utilities

There are a number of useful, standard utilities that come with Windows NT Server 3.5. If you have read Chapter 5 carefully, you will already be familiar with many of them, such as **route** and **netstat**. These utilities are documented in the *Windows NT Networking Guide*, in the TCP/IP help file that comes with the operating system, and in "Books Online," which you will find under Program Manager, Main. I will not attempt to replicate those sources here. There are two classes of utilities: diagnostic commands and connectivity commands.

Diagnostic commands:

```
arp, hostname, ipconfig, lpq, nbstat, netstat, ping, route, and tracert.
```

Connectivity commands:

```
finger, ftp, lpr, rcp, rcp, rexec, rsh, telnet, and tftp.
```

The **ftp**, **rexec**, and **telnet** all rely on password authentication by the remote computer. For these utilities, as with their *nix counterparts, passwords are sent clear. If you have a particularly sensitive installation, therefore, it is best that you use different passwords for such services that you use internally on your LAN since all passwords used by Windows networking services are encrypted.

If you want to use one of these utilities, but need help doing so, you can consult the sources mentioned above, or you can simply type **route -?** or whatever command you need help on.

Problems and Opportunities

There are a lot of strong reasons for using Windows NT Server 3.5 as the router for your small LAN into the Internet. The setup is straightforward and (unless you need to use some of the utilities mentioned) completely within a Windows environment. And this may be the very solution for you.

There is one major disadvantage, however. We have discussed several times the issue of on-demand dialing. This means the ability of one of your people at a workstation being able to initiate a dialup connection by requesting an Internet address for some service. This capability does not currently exist, so far as I can find, in the Windows NT Server environment. This means that you (or somebody) must manually go to the server and initiate the call. Depending on your work environment this may or may not be a problem. If on-demand dialing is not critical to you, then Windows NT Server 3.5 may be the best environment for your situation.

Be aware, however, that by the time you read this book software may have become available that solves the problem of on-demand dialing. Check with Microsoft and/or check on shareware at **ftip.cica.indaiana.edu** in */pub/pc/winnt/netutil* or */pub/pc/winnt/misc*, other Internet NT sites, and CompuServe or AOL. Examples of such software that assist with the use of RAS are *Somar(TM) ReDial*, an NT service that maintains a full-time dialup PPP internet or other RAS connection, by redialing whenever the connection is lost. Somar can be contacted at **http://www.somar.com** or **7220,2574@compuserve.com**. Another program, available from the CICA archive, is **startras.exe. startras** is also a program designed to keep the RAS connection to an internet service provider up all day. These programs do not solve the problem of on-demand dialing, but they are examples of emerging software related to this issue. In other words, you should always check out what is currently available in the way of software to assist you in what you wish to accomplish.

Notes

1. *Windows NT Networking Guide* (Redmond, WA: Microsoft Press, 1995), p. 419.

2. In a little paper found on CompuServe, by Nick Radov, entitled "Connecting Windows NT 3.5 RAS to CompuServe PPP," (**nradov@netcom.com**, CompuServe: **74732,3354**), Radov writes: "The Sysop of the Internet Resources forum (GO INETRESOURCE) says that the main DNS address is 149.174.64.41 (mhaak.inhouse.compuserve.com) and the backup is 149.174.64.42 (mhaal.inhouse.compuserve.com). There seems to be something funny about these servers, however; I don't think they are totally reliable and the routers are set up so that they are only accessible from within the compuserve.com domain. The Internic database lists the main name servers for the compuserve.com domain as 198.4.7.1 (arl-img-1.compuserve.com) and 198.4.9.1 (dub-img-1.compuserve.com). If you have problems then you may want to use one of those addresses instead." I would suggest using those illustrated. If you have problems, call CompuServe and ask them for their DNS addresses.

3. *Windows NT Networking Guide*, pp. 141–144.

4. See also *Windows NT Networking Guide,* pp. 419–421.

STANDALONE

ON-DEMAND

DIALUP ROUTERS

We have repeatedly defined "router," but for the sake of completeness, we need to do so one more time. A router is the hardware and software necessary to link two subnetworks together, the hardware and software necessary to link two subnetworks at the network layer of the OSI reference model, and any machine responsible for making decisions about which of several paths network traffic will follow. In the Internet, each IP gateway is a router because it uses IP destination addresses to choose routes. We have seen in the preceding chapters that PCs, equipped with the appropriate operating systems, can be configured to act as routers between your LAN and the Internet.

If, after reading this book, you choose to take the high-end approach to Internet access with a leased telephone line into the nearest node of your Internet Service Provider (ISP), then your ISP will likely deliver a router to you and manage that connection. This solution, which is the most expensive, is also the standard method for large organizations. There is a relatively low-cost alternative for small organizations, however, that provides on-demand access through a router that dials into your ISP whenever a service request is received through your LAN from a workstation. For a one-time cost of about $1,700 to $2,000 you can have a self-contained, dedicated, on-demand dial-access router to service your Internet needs. A typical configuration can be seen in Figure 7.1.

The difference between Figure 7.1 and the similar figures in preceding chapters is that the LAN still has the same number and variety of computers, but now we have included the standalone dial-access router rather than using one of the computers as a router. Note that the router has its own IP and Ethernet addresses on the local LAN. In order to prepare this chapter I was able to obtain on-demand dial-access routers from several manufacturers. This chapter is not designed, however, to provide a comparative analysis or evaluation of the devices now being sold. Rather, I was more concerned about being able to describe the general technology with some degree of accuracy. This issue of connecting your LAN to the Internet is becoming increasingly important for smaller organizations, and new router products for that market are appearing with some frequency. I would like to specifically thank the

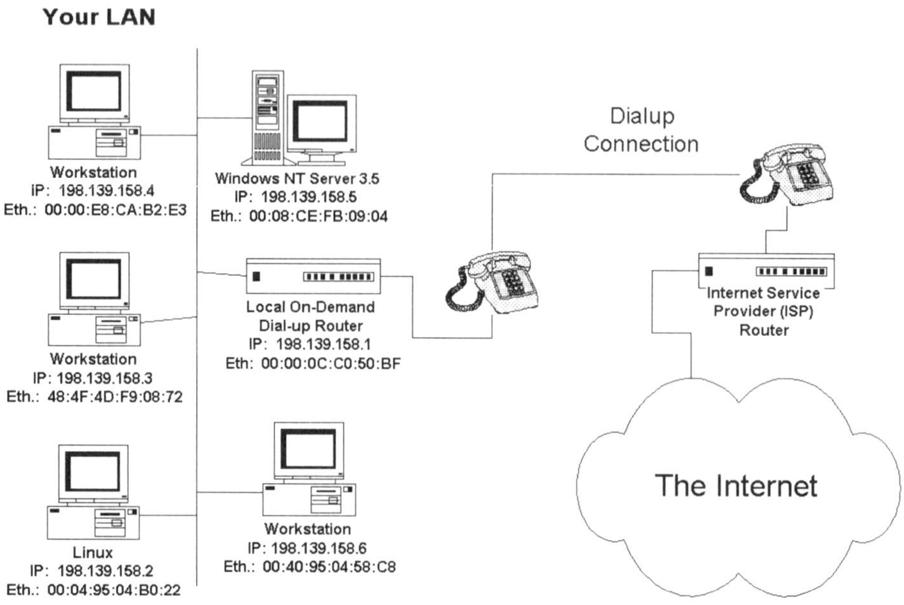

Your LAN

Figure 7.1 Router-to-router dialup connection.

manufacturers that did provide me with routers for review and evaluation: Black Box Corporation (Async Router AR-P); Cisco Systems (Cisco 1020); Network Application Technology, Inc. (LANB/290 Multiprotocol Router, v. 4.00); Rockwell Network Systems (NetHopper); and Shiva Corporation (LanRover/2E Plus). It turns out that the Rockwell NetHopper and the Black Box Async Router are the same device. Rockwell OEM (Original Equipment Manufacturer) manufactures the device from Black Box. The primary difference between the two is not the hardware but the extent and quality of documentation.

What Is an On-Demand Standalone Router?

An on-demand standalone router is a small, dedicated computer that is programmed to provide a single function: routing of packets within the context of specific protocols (usually IP and IPX). Those we are using for purposes of illustration in this chapter can handle outgoing calls to a larger network (such as the Internet) and can accept calls coming in from either an ISP or from a remote workstation. *On-demand* means that the router need not be continuously connected to an ISP, but will automatically dial the ISP when it sees a packet destined for an address outside the local network. In this case *standalone* simply means *dedicated*.

All these devices are relatively easy to program (see below), are relatively small, and work as advertised. The quality of the documentation varies. They all support at least IP and IPX for routing and are able to do this simultaneously. This means that if you want your local LAN to not only access the Internet (or other TCP/IP network using IP) *and* be part of a distributed Novell NetWare network (using IPX), you can accomplish these objectives. All the devices have multiple connectors for communications. The Cisco router requires an external modem while the Black Box/Rockwell and Shiva devices have built-in, high-speed, smart modems. Most have more than one Ethernet interface.

The design objectives of the Cisco and Black Box/Rockwell routers seem to have been similar while the Shiva design is more modular and specialized. The design differences are very important for they dictate what these devices can and cannot do. The Shiva LanRover/2E Plus is called, in its documentation, a "remote access server." It is designed primarily to provide access to your LAN from external systems (either PCs or other LANs). If dial-in access to your LAN is the way in which you want the link configured, then the Shiva approach might be appropriate for your needs. If your ISP is actually the subdivision of a larger organization of which you are also a part, this might be a way that would appeal to the WAN planners. Otherwise, in order to use the LanRover effectively, there would have to be another LanRover on the other end to which it connects. PPP (and SLIP) is, in the general sense, available only on dial-in, not on dial-out. The lack of a scripting capability makes it impossible to dial out with the LanRover to anything but another LanRover. The LanRover is designed primarily to provide access to your LAN.

By the time this book is published, Shiva may have a product that is more directly competitive with the Black Box/Rockwell and Cisco routers, but at the time I started this project, Shiva claimed that the LanRover was its most nearly competitive product. I have included the Shiva in all the comparisons, however, because it may have some specific uses in your environment. It also has some management software that is clearly superior to that of other manufacturers. Specifically, the network administrator can install a *Windows* (there is also a Mac version) program called the Shiva Net Manager that can fully configure the LanRover from a Windows-based workstation. Just as with the others, it is also possible to TELNET into the Shiva and do a command-line configuration, but while documented, it is discouraged.

A device that diverged even more from the intent of this chapter was the Network Application Technology, Inc. *LANB/290 Multiprotocol Router*. The only reason I looked at this product at all was the fact that it supported IP routing over an asynchronous connection such as a dedicated cable or a leased telephone line. With a smart modem (using a stored telephone number in the modem) it might be possible to set up the LANB/290 to function over a dialup connection, but it is unlikely that it would be possible to configure it for on-demand dialing. This particular router also supports other serial connections in addition to RS-232. As a side note, I might also add that the other manufacturers discussed in this chapter also have similar products. An illustration of where such a router might prove useful to a small organization would be in an office complex where the complex supports a high-speed dedicated link into the Internet, and companies that lease office space may have the ability to link their own LANs into that high-speed interface. Under such circumstances a relatively low-cost dedicated router such as the LANB/290 might be the easiest and best way to handle the intracomplex link.

Only the Black Box/Rockwell and Cisco routers do on-demand dialing, however, so most of this chapter should be interpreted to apply to those devices. There are other competitive routers now coming on the market and by the time you read this book you may wish to do more extensive comparison shopping. The logic of how to use such devices, however, will be much the same regardless of the manufacturer.

Advantages/Disadvantages of a Dedicated Router

As with everything, there are both advantages and disadvantages in the use of dedicated routers versus the use of PCs configured for a routing function. You need to be clear on what those advantages and disadvantages are. At the outset, the primary advantage is that the devices work pretty much out-of-the-box. Of the various approaches to handling the problem of routing to the Internet, the use of standalone routers is probably the cleanest and easiest method, and, in general, the advantages outweigh the disadvantages. The principle disadvantage is that the acquisition of a standalone router represents a completely new cost for an organization.

Advantages

- Support for TCP/IP and IPX protocols (and possibly others)
- SLIP/PPP access
- Small footprint
- Management capabilities including SNMP (Simple Network Management Protocol)
- Relative ease of setup
- Support for both outgoing and incoming calls
- Suite of TCP/IP utilities

Disadvantages

The disadvantages of using a standalone router are not technical but economic. The cost for such a router is about the same as it would be for a new, fully configured Intel-based workstation. For many businesses and organizations this is probably not a problem. For others, however, it might represent some difficulties. Disadvantages of a dedicated router include:

- Moderate expense
- The additional LAN cost compared with being able to use an existing machine.

Hardware Attributes

Perhaps the easiest way to gain some scope on dialup routers is to take a comparative look at the hardware. Even with a sample of only three devices it will be easy to understand some of the things you might wish to look for your organization. There is a basic difference between the Shiva router and the others that may be of importance. The Shiva architecture is modular. By adding plug-in circuit boards it is possible to customize the attributes of the device. The other products are not modular: What you see is what you get, although they both come in multiserial-port versions as well as single-port systems. Consider Table 7.1.

With respect to the Ethernet baseband connection there are three options: an AUI (DB15) connector for thick-wire coaxial cable (10BASE5) connections through a transceiver; an RJ45 connector (10BASE-T) for twisted-pair cabling; and a BNC connector (10BASE2) for use with thin-wire RG58 coaxial cable. The Shiva has all three connectors, the Black Box/Rockwell has an AUI and an RJ45 connector, and the Cisco has only an RJ45 connector. To connect the Black Box/Rockwell router to a thin-wire coaxial cable it is necessary to purchase a low-cost transceiver with a DB15 (AUI) connector on one end and a BNC connector on the other end. A *transceiver* is the device that connects the transceiver (AUI) cable to the Ethernet coaxial cable. The transceiver is used to transmit and receive data. For a 10BASE5 802.3 (Ethernet), the transceiver is the specific device that allows connection of a NIC with an AUI interface with a 15-conductor cable to the 802.3 coaxial backbone. If your LAN is wired with twisted-pair copper cable, and your workstations are plugged into a 10BASE-T hub, all using RJ45 connectors, then all these routers can be directly plugged into the hub.

■■■■■■■■ **Table 7.1** Dialup Router Hardware Comparisons

Attribute	Black Box/Rockwell	Cisco	Shiva
AUI (10BASE5)	Yes	No	Yes
RJ45 (10BASE-T)	Yes	Yes	Yes
BNC (10BASE2)	No	No	Yes
Async serial port	Yes	Yes	Yes
Internal modem	Yes	No	No[1]
PCMCI modem slot	No	Yes	No
Int./Ext. power	External	External	Internal
Floppy Disk	Yes	No	No
Memory	1 MB	1 MB	1 MB
Size in inches	9.9Wx8.3Dx2.3H	8.0Wx8.25Dx1.75H	17.0Wx10.0Dx1.72H

[1]May be configured with one or more internal modems.

■■■■■■■■

Initial configuration of all three routers can be a bit cumbersome. Note that they all have an asynchronous serial port. For initial configuration a dumb terminal or a PC with a terminal emulator program can be attached to the serial port and the initial configuration put in place. Once the routers are given an IP address and name, then they can be plugged into your Ethernet and further configuration can take place via TELNET since they all have TELNET servers. The configuration is kept in memory in the Cisco and Shiva routers and on diskette on the Black Box/Rockwell unit. There is one additional advantage of having the diskette drive. The Black Box/Rockwell router comes with a diskette that already has a default configuration. The IP address and machine name can be added with an appropriate program on the floppy inserted into any available PC. This means that it is not necessary to attach a terminal to the unit in order to do initial programming. All three routers can rest on a desk top or be wall mounted. The Shiva can also be rack mounted.

Software Specifications

The basic software that any router needs consists of the ability to configure the protocols, the line, and port that will be handling WAN access, and some selected TCP/IP utilities. Not surprisingly, all three of the routers described here have those capabilities. For the Black Box/Rockwell and Cisco routers configuration is accomplished largely through a configuration program used at the command line of the router itself. The easiest way to do this is through TELNETing into the router. In order to TELNET into the routers, however, they must already have at least an IP address assigned to them. The way that is accomplished on the Cisco 1020 is to hook a terminal or PC directly to its asynchronous port and configure its IP address and network name. The same can also be done with the Black Box/Rockwell router, but an easier way is to take the boot diskette and, using the software provided, install the IP address and network name. The slickest method is used by Shiva: The Shiva Net Manager program, which comes for both Windows and the Apple Macintosh, can directly probe your LAN and discover the device. Once the device has been discovered all the appropriate configuration can take place from the Windows workstation. Table 7.2 illustrates the TCP/IP-related software available on each of these routers once they are configured. (Again, a table of software capabilities is probably the easiest way to provide some idea of the capabilities of these routers.)

All of the devices have additional software features, most notably those having to do with routing of Novell's IPX packets for extended Novell networking. However, that is outside the context of this book. One note about event logging is in order. The Shiva router has its own logging system. The other two routers use syslog, which is a standard log kept on Unix systems through the use of the *syslogd* logging daemon. When a *nix system, with logging turned on, is part of your local LAN, then the syslog option can be invoked to send logging information automatically to the syslog of the *nix machine. Note Table 7.2: Most of the software items are analogous to programs of the same name found on Unix systems.

▅▅▅▅▅ **Table 7.2** Dialup Router Software Feature Comparisons

TCP/IP Utilities[1]	Black Box/Rockwell	Cisco	Shiva
On-demand dialing[2]	Yes	Yes	No
arp	Yes	Yes	Yes
FTP client	No	No	No
FTP server	Yes	No	No
icmp	Yes	Yes	No
ifconfig	Yes	equivalent	equivalent
netstat	Yes	equivalent	equivalent
ping	Yes	Yes	No
ppp	Yes	Yes	Yes
ps	Yes	No	No
rip	Yes	Yes	No
route	Yes	Yes	Yes
snmp	Yes	Yes	No
syslog	Yes	Yes	No
TELNET client	Yes	No	Yes
TELNET server	Yes	Yes	Yes
tftp	No	Yes	Yes
traceroute	Yes	No	No

[1]List includes some features required to effectively use TCP/IP on your LAN.

[2]See text for an explanation of how these three devices differ.

▅▅▅▅▅

Supported Protocols

A protocol, you will remember, is a formal set of conventions governing the format and relative timing of message exchange in a communications network. There are several that are not only helpful, but necessary, in order to do extensive IP routing. The most significant of the TCP/IP-related protocols (some of which we have previously discussed) are listed in Table 7.3.

■■■■■■ **Table 7.3** Protocols Important for Dialup Routers

TCP/IP Protocols	Protocol
ARP	*Address Resolution Protocol (ARP)*. Within TCP/IP, ARP is the protocol that determines whether a packet's source and destination addresses are in the Data Link Control (DLC) or Internet Protocol (IP) format. ARP is necessary for proper packet routing on a TCP/IP network.
CHAP	*Challenge-Handshake Authentication Protocol*. CHAP is used to verify the identity of the peer using a three-way handshake. This is done upon initial link establishment.
FTP	*File Transfer Protocol (FTP)*. FTP is the TCP/IP protocol for file transfer.
ICMP	*Internet Control Message Protocol (ICMP)*. Automatically reports unusual network conditions such as routing errors and network congestion. ICMP is an adjunct to the Internet Protocol and is often used to help diagnose and solve network problems.
IP	*Internet Protocol (IP)*. IP is part of the TCP/IP suite. It is a session-layer protocol that governs packet forwarding.
PAP	*Password Authentication Protocol (PAP)*. Provides a simple method for a peer to establish its identity using a two-way handshake during initial link establishment. PAP is not a robust authentication method. Passwords are sent over the circuit in the clear or in text format and there is no protection from playback.
PPP	*Point-to-Point Protocol (PPP)*. PPP provides router-to-router and host-to-network connections over asynchronous and synchronous connections. It is considered a second-generation Serial Line Interface Protocol (SLIP).
RIP	*Routing Information Protocol (RIP)*. RIP is the routing protocol used by most TCP/IP routers. It is a distance-vector routing protocol, and it measures the shortest distance between the source and destination addresses by the lowest hop count.
SLIP	*Serial Line Internet Protocol (SLIP)*. SLIP is used to run IP over serial lines, such as telephone lines.

▰▰▰▰ **Table 7.3** Continued

TCP/IP Protocols	Protocol
SNMP	*Simple Network Management Protocol (SNMP)*. SNMP is a request-response type protocol that gathers management information from network devices. SNMP is a de facto standard protocol for network management. Two versions exist: SNMP 1 and 2. It provides a means to monitor and set configuration parameters.
TCP/IP	*Transmission Control Protocol/Internet Protocol (TCP/IP)*. TCP/IP is the protocol suite developed by the Advanced Research Projects Agency (ARPA), and is almost exclusively used on the Internet. It is also widely used in corporate internetworks, because of its superior design for WANs. TCP governs how packets are sequenced for transmission on the network. IP provides a connectionless datagram service. The term TCP/IP is often used to generically refer to the entire suite of related protocols.
TELNET	*TELNET*. TELNET is the TCP/IP protocol for terminal emulation.
TFTP	*Trivial File Transfer Protocol (TFTP)*. TFTP is a simplified version of FTP, or the TCP/IP file transfer protocol.
UDP	*User Datagram Protocol*. Provides for user access to low-overhead connectionless datagram communications. UCP is part of the TPC/IP protocol suite.

The issue in evaluating your needs relative to routers then becomes what protocols are supported and to what extent. As can be seen from Table 7.4, the Black Box/Rockwell and Cisco routers are very similar. In fact, the only difference is in the fact that the Black Box/Rockwell router supports an FTP server. The reason for this is that it provides a method for easily transferring updated files (such as configuration files) from a PC-based workstation to the router. That is why it also has no FTP client—there is no need for it. In the case of the Cisco router (and the Shiva, for that matter), there is no disk storage device that retains such files so it makes more sense to directly configure those devices via TELNET or other management software. Cisco supports SLIP and this could be important depending on your ISP.

■■■■ **Table 7.4** Protocols Supported by Selected Dialup Routers

TCP/IP Protocols	Black Box/Rockwell	Cisco	Shiva
ARP	Yes	Yes	Yes
CHAP	Yes	Yes	Yes
FTP	Server	No	No
ICMP	Yes	Yes	No
IP	Yes	Yes	Yes
PAP	Yes	Yes	No
PPP	Yes	Yes	Dial-in only
RIP	Yes	Yes	No
SLIP	No	Yes	Dial-in only
SNMP	Yes	Yes	Yes
TCP/IP	Yes	Yes	Yes
TELNET	Client/Server	Server	Client/Server
UDP	Yes	Yes	Yes

■■■■

All the other protocols are important to the routing process at one time or another. There are some small software and protocol differences between the Black Box offering and the Rockwell router even though the hardware is identical.

Routes and Routing

The documentation for all of these routers provides adequate direction for your setup needs, although see the comments on documentation below. I will not repeat the setup instructions here. Suffice it to say that once properly set up, both the Black Box/Rockwell and Cisco routers can do what we propose they do in the context of this book: They provide on-demand access to the Internet from a small LAN. As we have noted elsewhere, the easiest method for doing this is to have a static IP address for your system, with closely related IP addresses for each of your workstations. In this scenario your ISP would know about, and have listed in the appropriate tables, references to your network IP address. The consequence of this is that IP packets will find you properly and you will be able to send them appropriately. More challenging is the task of routing when your ISP does not know the details of your LAN's IP setup and when it dynamically issues IP addresses. Routing can, of course, still be accomplished, especially for small networks, but it may take a little more effort to set up.

In any event, just to give you some feel for what a completed and working system looks like using a router like the Black Box/Rockwell or Cisco devices, you might take note of the listings that follow. In this instance, my ISP was a remote Unix machine named "hwmin." It is connected to the Internet. My local router is named "arms" and I have workstations named "ewcuucp" (Linux) and "madron" (Windows for Workgroups 3.11). The relevant routes on each of these systems can be seen in their respective routing tables and are shown in **bold** type. The **netstat** command was used on all three systems to print the routing tables. The Unix machine, hwmin, is configured as a local router on the remote LAN, which has a router called "cisco" that is the direct link to the ISP. The arms router has a route to hwmin across a PPP link and each workstation has routes to arms. The appropriate IP addresses were:

arms (router)	198.139.158.1
ewcuucp	198.139.158.2
madron	198.139.158.6
hwmin (remote)	198.139.157.2

I won't go into a detailed explanation of all this here. It is not possible to take such routing tables and simply change machine names and IP addresses and have them work. You will have to work out the routing attributes more carefully than that. The ARP tables can also play a role in making all this work properly. For static IP addresses, however, your ISP would take care of the logical equivalent of hwmin so you would not need to be concerned.

Suffice it to say that on your local LAN your own router and workstations must be able to see one another. Your workstations would normally define your own local router as their gateway, and your router will have to have an appropriate route to the router on the other end of the line. Given these conditions, your LAN should have a connection. When your router is picking up a dynamically assigned IP address it may be necessary for it to have two addresses: one for the Ethernet device and one for the PPP device (which would be the one that is dynamically assigned).

Routing on ewcuucp (Linux machine):

```
ewcuucp:~$ netstat -r
Kernel routing table
Destination   Gateway    Genmask           Flags  Metric  Ref  Use   Iface
arms          *          255.255.255.255   UH     0       0    636   eth0
hwmin         arms       255.255.255.255   UGH    0       0    281   eth0
localnet      *          255.255.255.0     U      0       0    4290  eth0
loopnet       *          255.0.0.0         U      0       0    38    lo
default       arms       0.0.0.0           UG     0       0    58    eth0
ewcuucp:~$
```

Routing on madron (WFW 3.11 with Microsoft TCP/IP [Winsock]):

```
C:\WINDOWS>netstat -r


Route Table
 Network Address          Netmask    Gateway Address       Interface   Metric
   198.139.0.0       255.255.0.0     198.139.158.6     198.139.158.6        1
     224.0.0.0         224.0.0.0     198.139.158.6     198.139.158.6        1
       0.0.0.0           0.0.0.0     198.139.158.1     198.139.158.6        1
       0.0.0.0           0.0.0.0     198.139.157.2     198.139.158.6        1
       0.0.0.0           0.0.0.0     198.139.157.1     198.139.158.6        1
 128.121.50.2   255.255.255.255     198.139.157.2     198.139.158.6
 198.139.158.255 255.255.255.255    198.139.158.6     198.139.158.6        1
 198.139.157.2  255.255.255.255     198.139.158.1     198.139.158.6        1
 198.139.158.6  255.255.255.255         127.0.0.1         127.0.0.1        1
 255.255.255.255 255.255.255.255    198.139.158.6     198.139.158.6        1
   127.0.0.0         255.0.0.0         127.0.0.1         127.0.0.1        1


Active Connections

  Proto   Local Address          Foreign Address         State
```

Routing on hwmin (only the boldface lines concern us here):

```
# netstat -r
Routing tables
Destination            Gateway               Flags   Refs   Use     Interface
moscow                 gbgm-umc.org          UH      0      0       ppp3
hwbbs.gbgm-umc.o       hwbbs.gbgm-umc.org    UGHD    0      3550    pnt0
arms                   hwmin.gbgm-umc.org    UH      0      455     ppp0
localhost.jvnc.n       localhost.jvnc.net    UH      0      0       lo0
ewcuucp                arms                  UGH     0      149     ppp0
198.139.157.50         198.139.157.50        UGHD    0      24      pnt0
gbgm-umc.org           localhost.jvnc.net    UH      4      0       lo0
198.139.157.51         198.139.157.51        UGHD    0      70      pnt0
beta                   arms                  UGH     0      1       ppp0
198.139.157.4          198.139.157.4         UGHD    0      49      pnt0
198.139.157.100        hwmin.gbgm-umc.org    UH      0      6       ppp1
server                 arms                  UGH     0      1       ppp0
madron                 arms                  UGH     1      676     ppp0
198.139.157.7          198.139.157.7         UGHD    0      889     pnt0
errolct                gbgm-umc.org          UH      0      0       ppp2
default                cisco                 UG      2      120274  pnt0
arms1                  arms                  UG      0      0       ppp0
#
```

One thing that you should bear in mind is that you, as your own system manager, will not be the only one to add routes to the routing tables, particularly on your local router. Those routes can come from a number of sources. Typically they will be established in one of several ways:

- By explicit use of the **route** command to establish static routes
- By configuring an interface (Ethernet or PPP)
- By receiving an SNMP setRequest
- Through RIP updates

The source of the routing information will determine the characteristics of the routes established and they are not the same for all methods.

Conclusion

In general, the standalone dedicated, on-demand router is easier to set up and get running than any of the other techniques suggested in this book. You may, in fact, be able to buy one from your ISP and/or you may be able to get your ISP (for a fee) to send someone around to install it for you. I would strongly suggest that you find an ISP that can provide you some guidance whether you elect to use a device such as those discussed in this chapter or opt for the approaches we examined earlier.

8

END-USER SOFTWARE
TO MAKE INTERNET
ACCESS WORK

You are now at a point where it is necessary to give some consideration to setting up your workstations so that each person on your LAN can use the Internet. In Chapter 3 we discussed the need for a TCP/IP protocol stack on each workstation and how you might acquire it. We will not repeat that discussion here, but you may wish to go back and review that section now. The main thing to remember is that you will have to set up a route from each workstation to your router and perhaps from each workstation to the gateway to which your router attaches. Depending on your setup, you may have to set up other routes for your workstations, as well. I would suggest you take one and get it working properly, then configure others. The success or failure of Internet access revolves around two issues: 1. How reliable is the service and 2. How easy is it to make the connection? There is a wide range of software available to answer the second question. That software, what it is, and where it is, is the subject of this chapter.

Basic Software Tools

The individual software items I will briefly discuss are most, although not solely, shareware. They are available from sources on the Internet and from services such as CompuServe and America Online. Many of the programs noted in this chapter are also available in the low-cost Internet access kits available from your local computer store or come as disk inserts in books on the Internet at your favorite bookstore. Consult the software list in Appendix B for a more extended list. The basic categories of software and a few illustrations of such software, are the following:

- Electronic mail (Email)

  In directory: *~ftp/pub/pc/**win3**/winsock*

  On archive: **ftp.cica.indiana.edu** [129.79.26.27]

atisml03.zip	950418	Atismail Winsock mail agent sends/receives email [1.6m]
eudor143.exe	941102	Eudora 1.4.3 WinSockAPI 1.1 POP3/SMTP mail client
		Latest copy may be acquired from **ftp.qualcomm.com**
prontoip.zip	950418	Pronto/IP is an advanced Windows Internet mail client
trp110.zip	950406	Offline news/mail reader, NNTP, SMTP, POP3, fingerd
wsmtpd16.zip	931027	Windows 3.1 and NT SimpleMailTransProtocol daemon

  In directory: *~ftp/pub/pc/**win95**/netutil*

  On archive: **ftp.cica.indiana.edu** [129.79.26.27

  stst07b4.zip   950801 32-Bit SMTP/POP3 daemon for Windows 95

  In directory: *~ftp/pub/pc/**winnt**/netutil*

  On archive: **ftp.cica.indiana.edu** [129.79.26.27]

blat11.zip	941211	Blat is a command-line SMTP mail client for Windows NT
vmail104.zip	930727	VanceMail: SMTP Send mail agent for NT

- FTP programs

  In directory: *~ftp/pub/pc/**win3**/winsock*

  On archive: **ftp.cica.indiana.edu** [129.79.26.27]

cftp14b4.zip	950725	CuteFTP v1.4 Beta 4
ftpsrv11.zip	950312	Serv-U v1.1—FTP server (daemon) for WinSock
wftpd196.zip	950130	Windows FTP daemon 1.96 for Winsock 1.1
ws_ftp.zip	950628	Windows Sockets FTP client Application v94.10.18
ws_ftp32.zip	950628	Windows Sockets FTP client Application v95.04.24

  In directory: *~ftp/pub/pc/**win95**/netutil*

  On archive: **ftp.cica.indiana.edu** [129.79.26.27

  cuteftp32.zip 951001 FTP client

  ws_ftp32.zip 950628 Win95 Sockets FTP client Application for Win 95

  In directory: *~ftp/pub/pc/**winnt**/netutil*

  On archive: **ftp.cica.indiana.edu** [129.79.26.27

wsftp32.zip	950914	FTP client, all NT binaries

- TELNET software

  In directory: *~ftp/pub/pc/**win3**/winsock*

  On archive: **ftp.cica.indiana.edu** [129.79.26.27]

anzl102f.zip	950502	Anzio Lite 10.2f is a Winsock TELNET client
ewan105.zip	941222	EWAN is a free Winsock 1.2 TELNET with VT100
trmptel.zip	940311	Trumpet TELNET (VT100) Terminal for Winsock
wintelb3.zip	931202	NCSA TELNET for MS Windows (unsupported beta 3)
yawtel07.zip	950721	Yet another Windows socket TELNET v0.7 Beta

In directory: *~ftp/pub/pc/win95/netutil*

On archive: **ftp.cica.indiana.edu** [129.79.26.27]

ntcrt10.zip 951003 CRT: A 32-bit Winsock-compliant TELNET client

sptn3209.zip 950912 TELNET/rlogin client including zmodem and kermit

In directory: *~ftp/pub/pc/winnt/netutil*

On archive: **ftp.cica.indiana.edu** [129.79.26.27]

groupsr2.zip   950628   WINNT TCP/IP multiuser chat server, TELNET
                                     clients

- World Wide Web browsers

  Netscape from **http://www.netscape.com** or **ftp.netscape.com**

  Netscape is now available in a commercial version but beta test versions are usually available for evaluation.

N16E11N.EXE	16-bit version of Netscape (the characters following "N16" reflect the current version)
N3212B1.EXE	32-bit version of Netscape

NCSA Mosaic from **ftp.ncsa.uiuc.edu** in /Mosaic/Windows/

mos20fh.exe	Final 2.0 beta (as of this writing for all versions of Windows)

In directory: *~ftp/pub/pc/win3/winsock*

On archive: **ftp.cica.indiana.edu** [129.79.26.27]

cello.zip	940711	Cello WWW browser rel. 1.01a
mmwwwpc1.zip	941008	MultiMedia World Wide Web PC
powwow13.exe	950422	PowWow: Internet chat, file transfer and Web browser
vogon14.zip	950727	Vogon Poetry Web browser
winweb.zip	940810	WinWeb v1.0 A2: Web browser

- WWW Servers for Windows

  Note: Depending on the platforms you have available, Web servers are available for Linux and the Windows NT Server 3.5 Resource Kit comes with an http server. See also the following:

  In directory: *~ftp/pub/pc/**win3**/winsock*

  On archive: **ftp.cica.indiana.edu** [129.79.26.27]

  serweb03.zip   931209   World Wide Web server for Windows 3.1 and NT

  w4serv21.zip   950731   WWW server for your PC v2.1

  In directory: *~ftp/pub/pc/**win95**/netutil*

  On archive: **ftp.cica.indiana.edu** [129.79.26.27]

  w4serv21.zip 950725 W4 server 2.1 is an httpd server

  Even for a system not continuously connected with the Internet, a local http (WWW) server can be useful. It allows you to test pages if you have a Web page elsewhere (say, at your ISP site) and it allows you to maintain internal documents in html formats.

- WinQVT/Net—Multifunction utility.

  WinQVT/Net is a widely used multifunctional utility with a POP3 mail reader, a news reader, an FTP client, and a very good TELNET client. In addition, it has an FTP server built into it.

  In directory: *~ftp/pub/pc/**win3**/winsock*

  On archive: **ftp.cica.indiana.edu** [129.79.26.27]

  qvtw3989.zip   950107   Windows-Sockets-compliant version of TCP/IP

  In directory: *~ftp/pub/pc/**win95**/netutil*

  On archive: **ftp.cica.indiana.edu** [129.79.26.27]

  qvtnt398.zip   950801   TCP/IP for Windows 95 and NT

A basic set of software that would handle your initial needs would be WinQVT/Net and Netscape or Mosaic, although I happen to prefer Qualcomm's Eudora as a mail reader over the one in WinQVT/Net. Let's take a quick look at these three packages.

WinQVT/Net—
Multifunction Utility

WinQVT/Net is relatively easy to install. It is usually just a matter of unzipping the distribution archive in an appropriate directory, usually *c:\qvtnet*, and configuring two files: *qvtnet.ini* and *qvtnet.rc* (see below). Once set up, a screen similar to that found in Figure 8.1 will come up when you first click on the WinQVT/Net icon. You can see from the button bar the client functions available and from the initial screen how a properly configured version of the program should appear. In this case I have started the FTP server as well. That means that others on my LAN, provided they had an appropriate ID and password, could transfer files to and from my PC. The version illustrated here is 3.9. Just as production of this book was being completed, v4.0 was released, which is a Win95 specific implementation organized somewhat differently than v3.9.

In Figure 8.2 is an illustration of the TELNET screen, in this case emulating a VT102 terminal, logged into my own Linux machine. WinQVT/Net also has an *rlogin* (remote login) function that allows access to systems running an rlogin daemon. Such a daemon is available for Windows NT Server 3.5. If you happen to

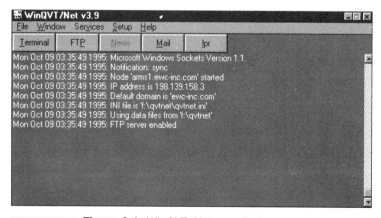

■■■■■■ **Figure 8.1** WinQVT/Net opening screen.

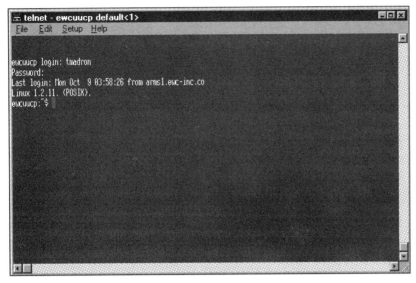

Figure 8.2 WinQVT/Net TELNET screen.

have the rlogin server running (**remote.exe**) then WinQVT/Net could be used to access your NT Server across your LAN.

Setup of all the functions is straightforward. Login scripts can be written for automating selected logins on particular machines. These are all explained in the QVT help file accessible from the main menu. When you click on **help,** screen seen in Figure 8.3 appears. You can see from this screen the basic help available.

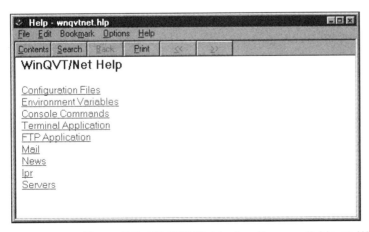

Figure 8.3 WinQVT/Net instructions available as Windows help file.

Configuration Files[1]

WinQVT/Net uses a number of configuration files and database files in the course of normal operations. These files should be located together in the same directory. That will usually be either the directory where the executable files are located, or the directory pointed to by the optional environment variable **QVTNET_DIR**. A possible exception is *qvthost.rc*, which can optionally reside in a separate directory, as specified by the environment variable **QVTHOST_DIR**. If **QVTHOST_DIR** is not found in the environment, WinQVT/Net will look for *qvthost.rc* in the default directory. If you use the Winsock version of QVT, then the *qvthost.rc* file is not used at all.

The files *Qvtnet.ini* and *news.rc* are routinely updated by WinQVT/Net in its normal functioning. In addition, users may wish to create TELNET screen images and logfiles, which requires that the home directory not be read-only. It is, therefore, important that these configuration files *not* be marked as read-only. The two primary configuration files are *qvtnet.ini* and *qvtnet.rc*.

Qvtnet.ini

Qvtnet.ini includes configuration settings for the program as a whole, such as connectivity information, as well as settings for each of the client applications (Terminal, FTP, etc.).

The sections of *qvtnet.ini* are as follows:

[net]	Basic network connectivity information
[tcp]	TCP tuning information
[domain]	Domain nameserver configuration
[localio]	Local I/O ports and devices
[console]	Console window setup and operation
[servers]	FTP and RCP server configuration
[terminal]	Terminal application setup
[ftp]	FTP application setup
[pop]	Mail application setup

[nntp]   News application setup

[lpr]   lpr application setup

Most entries in *qvtnet.ini* are optional, with the exception of the "name=", and "ip=". In non-Winsock versions the "packet_vector" statement was also critical. If you attempt to start WinQVT/Net with one or more of these items missing or invalid, a dialog box will be presented that will allow you to make the entries at that time.

Qvthost.rc

This database file contains a list of the network hosts that you plan to access regularly. It has much the same format as the standard *hosts* file. This file is used only for the packet driver version of QVT. Winsock versions use the standard *hosts* file that is usually found in *c:\windows*. Each line of text in qvthost.rc is of the following format:

```
<IP address> <host name>
```

For example,

```
28.1.5.39 myhost
```

There are some features available when using *qvthost.rc* that are unavailable in the use of *hosts*. For example, if you plan to use a domain nameserver to acquire the IP address for a host, you should use all zeros for that machine's *qvthost.rc* entry (i.e., 0.0.0.0). In *qvthost.rc*, the comment character is the #. Comment characters can appear either at the beginning of the line, or in-line. Everything to the right of # will be ignored.

Qvtnet.rc

Alternate configurations for the Terminal application (the default configuration is stored in *qvtnet.ini*) are stored in *qvtnet.rc*. Each configuration consists of a series of text lines. The first line will always be a line of the form:

```
name=<configuration name>
```

If the name includes embedded blanks, it must be enclosed in double quotes. The remainder of the configuration consists of a series of lines of the form:

```
<item>=<value>
```

where <item> is a configurable item, and <value> is the value being assigned to that item.

Available configurable items are those found in the [terminal] section of *qvtnet.ini*. One important item that is available only in *qvtnet.rc* is the "host=" directive, which allows you to specify a default host to associate with a configuration. The argument to this directive should be the name of a host as found in *qvthost.rc*.

Browsing with Netscape

Netscape is currently the hottest browser on the Internet. It has a graphical interface, and it works fairly rapidly over a dialup line. The opening screen can be seen in Figure 8.4. In my case I have the opening URL pointed at a local file since I have http servers running on both the Linux machine and the NT Server machine. I have a number of other services running on Linux and on my NT Server.

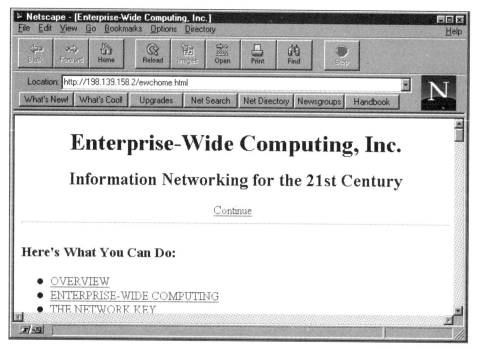

■■■■■■■ **Figure 8.4** Netscape opening screen.

Netscape is downloaded as a self-extracting archive file. It is expanded in a temporary directory, then **setup.exe** is executed from that temporary file. Setup expands and copies relevant information to a permanent directory of your own choosing.

There are several Netscape products. The one most commonly available, and the one already referenced, is *Netscape Navigator Personal Edition*. The version that is sold in computer stores provides its own Winsock (which can be very annoying because it will conflict with an already-installed Winsock). Another Netscape product, *Netscape Navigator LAN Edition*, is actually more appropriate for use in your LAN environment. The LAN version is designed for users who already have an Internet connection or the know-how to gain access. You may wish to find out more about the LAN version by sending email to **info@netscape.com**.

Eudora and POP Mail

The Eudora for Windows email software was developed by QUALCOMM Incorporated in San Diego, California. The program was written by Jeff Beckley, Mark Erikson, and Jeff Gehlhaar. The program is copyright ©1992–1994 by QUALCOMM Incorporated and further information may be obtained by writing to **info@qualcomm.com**. The inbox screen of Eudora may be seen in Figure 8.5.

Eudora is a POP3 mail client. POP3 is one variation of the Post Office Protocol, which is designed to allow single-user hosts to read mail from a server. There are three versions: POP, POP2, and POP3. Later versions are *not* compatible with earlier versions. Neither Eudora nor other POP mail clients are actually designed for direct use within a LAN, particularly when the POP mail server is somewhere outside the LAN. In Chapter 4 we examine one way around this issue.

The basic approach you should take on a LAN that is not continuously connected to an ISP is to bring all the mail for any user on your LAN to a server on your local LAN at periodic intervals. Chapter 4 presents a method for redistributing such mail through MS Mail. Another approach would be to bring the mail down with some sort of a POP mail client and redistribute it through a local POP mail server. This approach can probably be most easily set up on a Linux machine where a POP mail client is available that will bring mail down, then redistribute it to existing user ID's

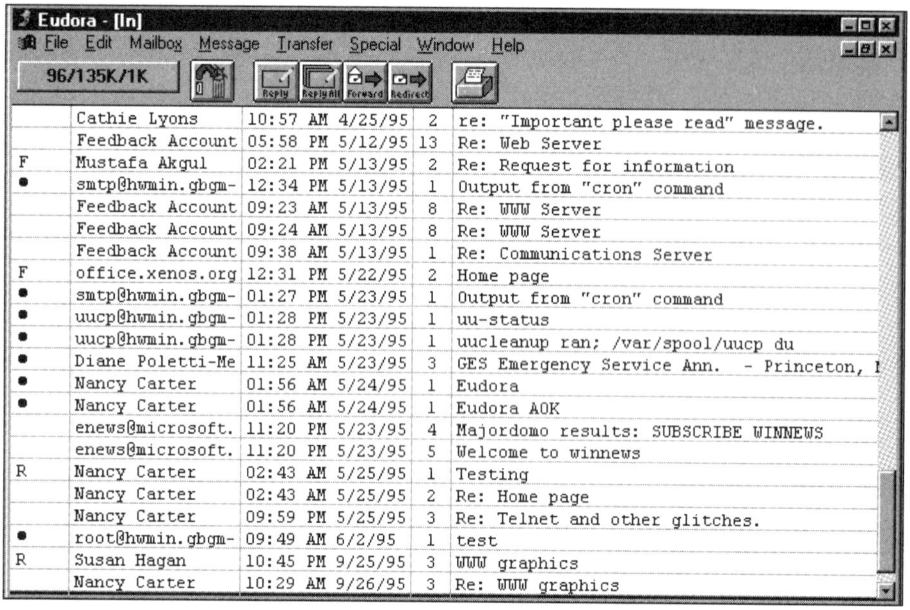

```
Eudora - [In]                                                    _ □ ×
  File  Edit  Mailbox  Message  Transfer  Special  Window  Help   _ 回 ×
  96/135K/1K

         Cathie Lyons    10:57 AM 4/25/95  2   re: "Important please read" message.
         Feedback Account 05:58 PM 5/12/95  13  Re: Web Server
  F      Mustafa Akgul   02:21 PM 5/13/95   2   Re: Request for information
  •      smtp@hwmin.gbgm- 12:34 PM 5/13/95   1   Output from "cron" command
         Feedback Account 09:23 AM 5/13/95   8   Re: WWW Server
         Feedback Account 09:24 AM 5/13/95   8   Re: WWW Server
         Feedback Account 09:38 AM 5/13/95   1   Re: Communications Server
  F      office.xenos.org 12:31 PM 5/22/95   2   Home page
  •      smtp@hwmin.gbgm- 01:27 PM 5/23/95   1   Output from "cron" command
  •      uucp@hwmin.gbgm- 01:28 PM 5/23/95   1   uu-status
  •      uucp@hwmin.gbgm- 01:28 PM 5/23/95   1   uucleanup ran; /var/spool/uucp du
  •      Diane Poletti-Me 11:25 AM 5/23/95   3   GES Emergency Service Ann.  - Princeton, I
  •      Nancy Carter     01:56 AM 5/24/95   1   Eudora
  •      Nancy Carter     01:56 AM 5/24/95   1   Eudora AOK
         enews@microsoft. 11:20 PM 5/23/95   4   Majordomo results: SUBSCRIBE WINNEWS
         enews@microsoft. 11:20 PM 5/23/95   5   Welcome to winnews
  R      Nancy Carter     02:43 AM 5/25/95   1   Testing
         Nancy Carter     02:43 AM 5/25/95   2   Re: Home page
         Nancy Carter     09:59 AM 5/25/95   3   Re: Telnet and other glitches.
  •      root@hwmin.gbgm-  09:49 AM 6/2/95    1   test
  R      Susan Hagan      10:45 PM 9/25/95   3   WWW graphics
         Nancy Carter     10:29 AM 9/26/95   3   Re: WWW graphics
```

Figure 8.5 Eudora input mail screen.

on the Linux system, which are then accessible by other POP mail clients from other machines. My ISP acquired a domain name for me and my company (**ewc-inc.com**). Email destined for **anybody@ewc-inc.com** is forwarded to my "real" POP mail account. I can, therefore, easily pick up all the mail for everyone on my LAN through a single POP mail account. The task on my LAN, then, is to automatically redistribute the mail either by the method described in Chapter 4 or through the Linux machine.

Briefly, through the Linux machine and the use of *popclient* I can set up an automatic login to my ISP, run *popclient*, and the mail it retrieves it simply sends into the local *nix mail system; if a username is consistent with someone with an account on my Linux system, the mail will be automatically directed to that person. Note the following fragment of the *popclient* man page:

```
NAME

        popclient - retrieve mail from a mailserver using Post
        Office Protocol.

SYNOPSIS
```

```
        popclient [-2 | -3] [-Vksv] [-u server-userid] [-p
        server-password]
        [-f remote-folder] [-c | -o local-folder] host
DESCRIPTION
        popclient is a Post Office Protocol compliant mail
        retrieval client which supports both POP2 (as specified in
        RFC 937) and POP3 (RFC 1225).


        Typically, popclient will be used to download mail in
        batch from the remote mailserver specified by host to a
        mail folder on the local disk. The retrieved mail will
        then be manipulated using a local mail reader, such as mail or elm.
```

I have a POP3 mail server running on the Linux system, so others on my LAN can retrieve their mail using Eudora or some other POP mail client on their own machines.

Executing Remote Commands

One final comment in the nature of a final caveat: Throughout this book I have made much of the concept of on-demand dialing. On-demand dialing, while very useful under the circumstances I have described, is not a technology without flaws. Sometimes it will be necessary for you to more directly manipulate your connection—either by bringing it up or cutting it off. One way to do that, if you have set up a Linux or Unix server, is to TELNET into your server and execute shell scripts that will bring up or take down the connection. You can, in a similar manner, log onto a router and do the same thing. For a Windows NT Server you may have to walk over to that machine and enter commands on its console. A semi-automated method for handling these situations is to use remote execution techniques whereby a program is run on a local workstation that will invoke an appropriate command or script on the server. A relatively standard part of Unix and Unix-like systems is the ability to enable remote execution for selected programs by trusted users. With Unix, remote execution usually runs as a daemon to provide the server side of the mechanism. On the workstation end there must also be a some client that initiates the procedure.

There is software available for Windows that provides the client-side of the remote execution system. One such program is *WinRSH*, described by the author [William Cheung (**wcheung@ee.ubc.ca**)] as a remote shell for Windows. The price for *WinRSH|WinRSH32* is right, since it is free software. If remote execution is enabled on your Linux machine, then you can configure **winrsh.exe** or **winrsh32-exe** to execute your shell scripts that manipulate your connection with your ISP from a workstation and you can give that ability to others on your LAN as necessary. *WinRSH* is available from most of the sources I have already cited for the acquisition of inexpensive or free software.

If you have opted for a Windows NT Server, all is not lost. You will still have to run a program on the Server that is the equivalent of the daemon run on Unix. One alternative is *WinsockRSH/NT*. This small system is the Windows NT version of the Unix Remote Shell Daemon. It accepts requests from remote hosts (Unix or other PCs) via the standard **rsh** and **rexec** commands and executes them on the PC running Winsock RSHD/NT. It runs as a Windows NT service. This particular piece of software is useful because it has a special SendKeys extension that allows some remote control of Windows programs even from Unix. This is important in the Windows environment where you are often asked to "press a button" or some similar approach. *Winsock RSHDINT* is also available from places like CICA and CompuServe. By installing *Winsock RSHDINT* on your NT Server, you can have a functionality similar to that on a Unix host.

These programs are not literally necessary for the operation of your LAN connection to the Internet. They are, however, illustrations of software that can make your operations much smoother. You will likely find it desirable at some time to invest some time in looking into these software packages as well as others.

Conclusion

We have seen in this chapter that you will need some basic user applications for the effective use of the Internet in your office. The precise distribution of software both functionally and in terms of products will be a byproduct of what you want to accomplish with your Internet connection. As with other elements of this book, it is unlikely that you will configure your LAN in exactly the same way I do. The other point you should keep in mind as you are preparing a budget for this project is the fact that there are costs involved in providing end-user software as well as in setting up the system itself. If you accept the approach outlined in this chapter you will need to register sufficient copies of WinQVT/Net for each of your users, purchase a copy of the LAN-based version of Netscape, and purchase sufficient copies of Eudora for each of your workstations.

Note

1. This section draws heavily on the WinQVT/Net help file distributed with the system.

GO FOR IT

There is one lesson that you should now have learned above all others: There are many ways to connect your LAN to the Internet. We have attempted to describe a range of approaches in this book but not all have been covered. Since starting the book I have found other interesting approaches but as a practical matter have not been able to cover them. Even among the various solutions I have described, if you carefully analyze your situation you will find that you might benefit by using some combination of the techniques contained here.

The guiding principle of this book has been the assumption that for smaller businesses and organizations—those with limited resources—solutions are needed that minimize cost and minimize the ongoing commitment of personnel time. At the same time you will want to maximize ease and extent of access. Even with smaller organizations, however, there are two critical business decisions that must be made: What is the potential intensity of use of the Internet and how mission-critical is your use of the Internet to the success of your organization? If your answers to these questions are "high" and "very," then you may not wish to go the least expensive route.

Prices on software, hardware, and services are also changing rapidly so what may not have been feasible for you six months ago may be acceptable today.

Some Topics We Have Missed

There are several issues that we could have included in this book, but have not. For LAN server-based Internet connections we focused, for example, in Windows NT Server 3.5. For many people Novell NetWare 4.x would be a better choice. NetWare, however, proved to be much more complicated to deal with in this book that had been anticipated. Moreover, there was already at least one book that specifically dealt with this topic.[1] Most of the tools discussed in this book are available under NetWare. The total cost of a NetWare solution, even for a small installation, will likely be greater than any of the solutions offered here. NetWare is normally a solution applied in larger organizations rather in smaller companies.

A second issue that we have alluded to rather than discussing is the question of security. Network security is a complex subject and not easily handled in a single chapter. Security is, however, an issue with which you should probably become familiar. It is probably somewhat less problematic in a dialup environment than one in which you are permanently attached to your Internet service provider. There are, however, many books on network security. A good introduction is my own *Network Security in the '90s*.[2] Coming to the market are Internet-specific security books, as well. If you feel the need for a firewall, for example, you might consult William R. Cheswick and Steven M. Bellovin, *Firewalls and Internet Security: Repelling the Wiley Hacker*.[3]

Combining Ideas

I noted above that you might find that some other combination of the techniques I have described may provide the solution you need. For example, although I described a specific method for dealing with Internet email in Chapter 4, you could implement an email-only solution using a Windows NT Server (Chapter 6) or a Linux server (Chapter 5). You could then grow into other uses of the Internet. Several of the solutions also lend themselves to incremental upgrading.

Incremental Upgrading

You may, for example, wish to start out with a Linux Internet server as described in Chapter 5, using a technique such as *IP_Masquerading* with on-demand dialing implemented with *diald*. For such a solution you do not need registered IP addresses on your LAN and any randomly selected SLIP or PPP service can provide you access. As your needs increase, however, you may find that the upgrade path to following could be the following:

1. Start with *IP_Masquerading* and on-demand dialing with *diald* using a Linux server.

2. Increment your service with your Internet Service Provider (ISP) so that you pay a flat monthly fee and keep your dialup link going the entire work day so that you do not have to wait for the dialing action.

3. Increment your service to upgrade from voice-grade dialup service to ISDN for faster access.

4. Have your ISP help you get a block of official IP addresses and a domain name for your LAN and move from the use of *IP_Masquerading* to one of the other routing techniques discussed in Chapter 5. This will allow you to establish services on your LAN that others can access, at least while your dialup link is up. These services might include World Wide Web server software, an FTP server, or other services.

5. Replace your dialup link with a 56 Kbps leased line (from your telephone company) to your ISP, thus requiring a more elaborate router on your LAN.

6. Increase the speed of your leased line to T1 (1.44 Mbps) line.

By the time you get to item 6, above, you will have very fast Internet access and will be able to provide a full set of services to the Internet as well as make use of the services of others.

Using WWW and Other Internet Tools Effectively

Even if you are using access techniques that prevent you from offering Internet services to people outside your own LAN, there may be reasons for you to set up some "Internet" services for internal use. An example might be a World Wide Web (WWW) server. If you set up your access so that you can obtain information from the WWW, it might assist your employees or members to access the resources you need by setting up your own local home page. This could be very simple and have only a menu of specific links to Web sites that affect your business.

With this scenario you would still not be offering information to the Web, but you would be using Web tools to assist your own people to work more effectively. Web server software is currently available for Unix (Linux), Windows NT, Win95, and WFW 3.11, among other platforms. Because you have a LAN you would not typically need to have an internal FTP server, although if you are running Linux as your Internet server, it would be convenient to run the FTP daemon on Linux so that you could easily pass files from your Windows workstations to the Linux system.

On my own small office LAN I actually operate two WWW servers, one on my Windows NT Server and one on my Linux machine. Part of the reason for this is to distribute resources across the disk storage available. I, of course, as a writer of networking books, need a test-bed for software that you will probably not find desirable. On my Linux machine, however, I have set up a home page that provides a set of menus for accessing WWW resources outside my own office. I am currently running *ip_masquerading* and *diald* so I cannot provide WWW services to others. One of my menus is found in Figure 9.1.

Similar comments can be made regarding the use of an FTP server. If you have files that people outside your own office need to acquire, even with a dial-access connection you could schedule availability so that such files could be available through the File Transfer Protocol. That would require a little finesse, but it could be implemented, even when using *IP_Masquerading*, on your Linux machine. Another method for making files available might be through email using a list server. In other words, there are many emendations you might make to the basic set of tools described earlier in this book.

Conclusion

If you wish to have your organization enter the Internet arena, the ideas provided in this book will allow you to do so in a cost-effective manner. As your use of the Internet increases, or as your requirements increase, you may have to move beyond what we have presented here. Even in that event, however, you will find that many

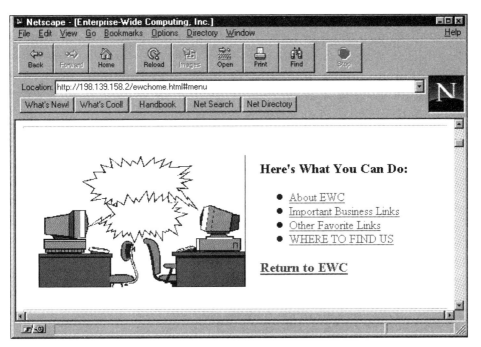

▬▬▬▬ **Figure 9.1** Local menu.

of the ideas presented here will carry over as you move from dialup access to the Internet to a permanent connection.

Notes

1. See Paul Singh, Rick Fairweath, and Dan Ladermann, Connecting *NetWare to the Internet* (Indianapolis, IN: New Riders Publishing, 1995).

2. Thomas Wm. Madron, *Network Security in the '90s: Issues and Solutions for Managers* (New York: John Wiley & Sons, 1992).

3. William R. Cheswick and Steven M. Bellovin, *Firewalls and Internet Security: Repelling the Wiley Hacker* (Reading, MA: Addison-Wesley Publishing Co., 1994).

APPENDIX

A

PROVIDERS OF

COMMERCIAL

INTERNET ACCESS

This document is reprinted with the permission of the author and of the Celestin Company, Inc.

```
Providers of Commercial Internet Access

The TEXT version of the POCIA Directory

=======================================


 *** AUGUST 1995 VERSION ***


Copyright 1994-1995 by Celestin Company, Inc. All rights reserved worldwide.

The information in this directory is provided as-is and without any expressed

or implied warranties, including, without limitation, the implied warranties

of merchantability and fitness for a particular purpose. You may use the

information in this directory for non-commercial purposes only. Contact us

if you wish to use the directory for a commercial purpose. For example, if

you would like to post this file on a public BBS, you may do so. However, if
```

you would like to reproduce this file (in whole or in part) in a newsletter, book,article, or other commercial media, please contact me.

All of the information in this directory was supplied to Celestin Company directly by the service providers and is subject to change without notice. Celestin Company does not endorse any of the providers in this directory. If you do not see a provider listed for your area, please do not ask us about it, as we only know about providers in this directory. This directory is brought to you as a public service. Celestin Company does not receive any compensation from the providers listed here. Since Internet service providers come and go, and frequently change their offers, we strongly urge you to contact them for additional information and/or restrictions.

The latest version of this document is available at the following location:

  ftp://ftp.celestin.com/biz/celestin/pocia/pocia.txt

You may also retrieve the latest copy (as well as additional information on Celestin Company and its products) using email. For information on how this works, send a blank message to:

  info@celestin.com

If you have web access, try http://www.celestin.com/pocia/ for the hypertext version of this list, which includes addresses, telephone numbers, fax numbers, email addresses, and pricing.

Items designated by an asterisk (*) are new this month.

DOMESTIC

========

A listing of Internet service providers in the U.S. and Canada, sorted by area code. Fields are area code, service provider name, voice phone number, and email address for more information.

Coffee Shops and Service Bureaus

The following companies and organizations provide walk-in access to the
Internet. Usually, you can sit at a terminal and have coffee and pastries.
Charges can be hourly, monthly, or a combination of both.

```
 206   Speakeasy Cafe                     206 782 9770   cafe@speakeasy.org
```

Free Service Providers

For the cost of a long distance phone call, you can dial any of these Internet
providers and give the Internet a try.

```
        Cyberspace (shell,slip,ppp)      modem -> 515 945 7000   info@cyberspace.com
        Free.org (shell,slip,ppp)        modem -> 715 743 1600   info@free.org
        Free.I.Net (must dial via AT&T)  modem -> 801 471 2266   info@free.i.net
        SLIPNET (shell,slip,ppp)         modem -> 217 792 2777   info@slip.net
```

Nationwide Service Providers

The following access providers provide service to more than just one part of
the United States/Canada. Many of them provide service regardless of your
geographic location, but may charge a higher price than local service providers.

```
        AGIS (Apex Global Information Services)   313 730 1130   info@agis.net
        ANS                                       703 758 7700   info@ans.net
        Concentric Research Corporation           800 745 2747   info@cris.com
   *    CRL Network Services                       415 837 5300   sales@crl.com
        Delphi Internet Services Corporation      800 695 4005   info@delphi.com
        Global Connect, Inc.                      804 229 4484   info@gc.net
        Information Access Technologies (Holonet)  510 704 0160   info@holonet.net
```

```
*       Institute for Global Communications     415 442 0220   igc-info@igc.apc.org
        MIDnet                                   800 682 5550   info@mid.net
        Moran Communications                     716 639 1254   info@moran.com
        NETCOM On-Line Communications Services   408 554 8649   info@netcom.com
        Netrex, Inc                              800 3 NETREX   info@netrex.com
        Network 99, Inc.                         800 NET 99IP   net99@cluster.mcs.net
        Performance Systems International        800 827 7482   all-info@psi.com
        Portal Information Network               408 973 9111   info@portal.com
        SprintLink - Nationwide 56K - 45M access 800 817 7755   info@sprint.net
*       The ThoughtPort Authority Inc.           800 ISP 6870   info@thoughtport.com
*       WareNet                                  714 348 3295   info@ware.net
        Zocalo Engineering                       510 540 8000   info@zocalo.net
```

Toll-Free Service Providers

These access providers allow you to dial a toll-free 800 number to connect to
the Internet. Most of them charge for this privilege, but it may save you money
over long distance charges if you do not have local Internet access.

```
        Allied Access Inc.                       618 684 2255   sales@intrnet.net
        American Information Systems, Inc.       708 413 8400   info@ais.net
        Association for Computing Machinery      817 776 6876   account-info@acm.org
        CICNet, Inc.                             313 998 6103   info@cic.net
*       Cogent Software, Inc.                    818 585 2788   info@cogsoft.com
*       Cyberius Online Inc.                     613 233 1215   info@cyberus.ca
        Colorado SuperNet, Inc.                  303 296 8202   info@csn.org
        DataBank, Inc.                           913 842 6699   info@databank.com
        EarthLink Network, Inc.                  213 644 9500   sales@earthlink.net
        Global Connect, Inc.                     804 229 4484   info@gc.net
        Internet Express                         719 592 1240   info@usa.net
        Mnematics, Incorporated                  914 359 4546   service@mne.com
        Msen, Inc.                               313 998 4562   info@msen.com
        NeoSoft, Inc.                            713 684 5969   info@neosoft.com
```

```
New Mexico Technet, Inc.              505 345 6555   granoff@technet.nm.org
Pacific Rim Network, Inc.             360 650 0442   info@pacificrim.net
Rocky Mountain Internet               800 900 7644   info@rmii.com
Synergy Communications, Inc.          800 345 9669   info@synergy.net
WLN                                   800 342 5956   info@wln.com
```

Regional Service Providers

These access providers specialize in particular regions, some as small as a
town of a thousand people, others as large as the San Francisco Bay Area.

```
201  Carroll-Net                              201 488 1332   info@carroll.com
201  Digital Express Group                    301 847 5000   info@digex.net
201  Eclipse Internet Access                  800 483 1223   info@eclipse.net
201  Galaxy Networks                          201 825 2310   info@galaxy.net
201  GBN InternetAccess                       201 343 6427   gbninfo@gbn.net
201  INTAC Access Corporation                 800 504 6822   info@intac.com
*201 Interactive Networks, Inc.               201 881 1878   info@interactive.net
201  InterCom Online                          212 714 7183   info@intercom.com
201  The Internet Connection Corp.            201 435 4414   info@cnct.com
201  Internet Online Services       x226 ->   201 928 1000   help@ios.com
201  Mordor International BBS                  201 433 4222   ritz@mordor.com
201  NETCOM On-Line Communications Services   408 554 8649   info@netcom.com
201  New York Net                             718 776 6811   sales@new-york.net
201  NIC - Neighborhood Internet Connection   201 934 1445   info@nic.com

*202 American Information Network              410 855 2353   info@ai.net
202  CAPCON Library Network                   202 331 5771   info@capcon.net
202  Charm.Net                                410 558 3900   info@charm.net
202  Digital Express Group                    301 847 5000   info@digex.net
202  Genuine Computing Resources              703 878 4680   info@gcr.com
202  I-Link Ltd                               800 ILINK 99   info@i-link.net
202  Internet Online, Inc.                    301 652 4468   info@intr.net
```

202	Interpath	800 849 6305	info@interpath.net
202	LaserNet	703 591 4232	info@laser.net
202	Quantum Networking Solutions, Inc.	805 538 2028	info@qnet.com
202	RadixNet Internet Services	301 567 9831	info@radix.net
202	US Net, Incorporated	301 572 5926	info@us.net
*202	World Web Limited	703 838 2000	info@worldweb.net
203	Computerized Horizons	203 335 7431	sysop@fcc.com
203	Connix: Connecticut Internet Exchange	203 349 7059	info@connix.com
203	Futuris Networks, Inc.	203 359 8868	info@futuris.net
203	I-2000, Inc.	516 867 6379	info@i-2000.com
203	NETPLEX	203 233 1111	info@ntplx.net
203	North American Internet Company	800 952 INET	info@nai.net
203	Paradigm Communications, Inc.	203 250 7397	info@pcnet.com
*204	Cycor Communications Incorporated	902 892 7354	signup@cycor.ca
*205	AIRnet Internet Services, Inc.	800 247 6388	efelton@AIRnet.net
205	Community Internet Connect, Inc.	205 722 0199	info@cici.com
205	HiWAAY Information Services	205 533 3131	info@HiWAAY.net
205	interQuest, Inc.	205 464 8280	info@iquest.com
205	MindSpring Enterprises, Inc.	800 719 4332	info@mindspring.com
205	Scott Network Services, Inc.	205 987 5889	info@scott.net
*206	Blarg! Online Services	206 782 6578	info@blarg.com
206	Eskimo North	206 367 7457	nanook@eskimo.com
206	I-Link Ltd	800 ILINK 99	info@i-link.net
206	InEx Net	206 670 1131	info@inex.com
206	Interconnected Associates Inc. (IXA)	206 622 7337	mike@ixa.com
206	Internet Express	719 592 1240	info@usa.net
206	ISOMEDIA.COM	206 881 8769	info@isomedia.com
206	Olympic Computing Solutions	206 989 6698	ocs@oz.net
206	NETCOM On-Line Communications Services	408 554 8649	info@netcom.com
206	Northwest Nexus, Inc.	206 455 3505	info@nwnexus.wa.com

206	Pacific Rim Network, Inc.	360 650 0442	info@pacificrim.net
206	Seanet Online Services	206 343 7828	info@seanet.com
206	SenseMedia	408 335 9400	sm@picosof.com
206	Structured Network Systems, Inc.	503 656 3530	info@structured.net
206	Teleport, Inc.	503 223 4245	info@teleport.com
206	Transport Logic	503 243 1940	sales@transport.com
206	WLN	800 342 5956	info@wln.com
207	Agate Internet Services	207 947 8248	ais@agate.net
207	MV Communications, Inc.	603 429 2223	info@mv.mv.com
208	Micron Internet Services	208 368 5400	sales@micron.net
208	Minnesota Regional Network	612 342 2570	info@mr.net
208	NICOH Net	208 233 5802	info@nicoh.com
208	Primenet	602 870 1010	info@primenet.com
208	Transport Logic	503 243 1940	sales@transport.com
209	Cybergate Information Services	209 486 4283	cis@cybergate.com
209	InterNex Tiara	408 496 5466	info@internex.net
*209	Primenet	602 870 1010	info@primenet.com
209	ValleyNet Communications	209 486 8638	info@valleynet.com
209	West Coast Online	707 586 3060	info@calon.com
*210	The Eden Matrix	512 478 9900	info@eden.com
210	I-Link Ltd	800 ILINK 99	info@i-link.net
212	Alternet (UUNET Technologies, Inc.)	703 204 8000	info@alter.net
212	Blythe Systems	212 226 7171	infodesk@blythe.org
212	BrainLINK	718 805 6559	info@beast.brainlink.com
212	Calyx Internet Access	212 475 5051	info@calyx.net
212	Creative Data Consultants (SILLY.COM)	718 229 0489	info@silly.com
212	Digital Express Group	301 847 5000	info@digex.net
212	Echo Communications Group	212 255 3839	info@echonyc.com
212	escape.com - Kazan Corp	212 888 8780	info@escape.com

212	I-2000, Inc.	516 867 6379	info@i-2000.com
212	I-Link Ltd	800 ILINK 99	info@i-link.net
212	Ingress Communications Inc.	212 679 2838	info@ingress.com
212	INTAC Access Corporation	800 504 6822	info@intac.com
*212	Interactive Networks, Inc.	201 881 1878	info@interactive.net
212	InterCom Online	212 714 7183	info@intercom.com
212	The Internet Connection Corp.	201 435 4414	info@cnct.com
212	Internet Online Services x226 ->	201 928 1000	help@ios.com
212	Interport Communications Corp.	212 989 1128	info@interport.net
212	Mordor International BBS	201 433 4222	ritz@mordor.com
212	Mnematics, Incorporated	914 359 4546	service@mne.com
212	NETCOM On-Line Communications Services	408 554 8649	info@netcom.com
212	New York Net	718 776 6811	sales@new-york.net
212	NY WEBB, Inc.	800 458 4660	wayne@webb.com
212	Panix (Public Access uNIX)	212 741 4545	info@panix.com
212	Phantom Access Technologies, Inc.	212 989 2418	bruce@phantom.com
212	Pipeline New York	212 267 3636	info@pipeline.com
*212	The ThoughtPort Authority Inc.	800 ISP 6870	info@thoughtport.com
*212	ThoughtPort of New York City	212 645 7970	info@precipice.com
213	Abode Computer Service	818 287 5115	eric@abode.ttank.com
*213	Cogent Software, Inc.	818 585 2788	info@cogsoft.com
213	Delta Internet Services	714 778 0370	info@deltanet.com
213	DigiLink Network Services	310 542 7421	info@digilink.net
213	DirectNet	213 383 3144	info@directnet.com
213	EarthLink Network, Inc.	213 644 9500	sales@earthlink.net
213	Electriciti	619 338 9000	info@powergrid.electriciti.com
213	Exodus Communications, Inc.	408 522 8450	info@exodus.net
213	I-Link Ltd	800 ILINK 99	info@i-link.net
213	The Loop Internet Switch Co.	213 465 1311	info@loop.com
213	KAIWAN Internet	714 638 2139	info@kaiwan.com
213	Leonardo Internet	310 395 5500	jimp@leonardo.net
213	Liberty Information Network	800 218 5157	info@liberty.com

213	Network Intensive	714 450 8400	info@ni.net
213	Primenet	602 870 1010	info@primenet.com
213	ViaNet Communications	415 903 2242	info@via.net
214	Alternet (UUNET Technologies, Inc.)	703 204 8000	info@alter.net
*214	CompuTek	214 994 0190	info@computek.net
214	DFW Internet Services, Inc.	817 332 5116	info@dfw.net
214	I-Link Ltd	800 ILINK 99	info@i-link.net
214	NETCOM On-Line Communications Services	408 554 8649	info@netcom.com
214	OnRamp Technologies, Inc.	214 746 4710	info@onramp.net
214	Texas Metronet, Inc.	214 705 2900	info@metronet.com
215	Digital Express Group	301 847 5000	info@digex.net
215	FishNet	610 337 9994	info@pond.com
215	GlobalQUEST, Inc.		
215	Microserve Information Systems	717 779 4430	info@microserve.com
215	Net Access	215 576 8669	support@netaxs.com
215	Network Analysis Group	800 624 9240	nag@good.freedom.net
215	Oasis Telecommunications, Inc.	610 439 8560	staff@oasis.ot.com
215	You Tools Corporation / FASTNET	610 954 5910	info@fast.net
216	APK Public Access UNI* Site	216 481 9436	info@wariat.org
216	Branch Information Services	313 741 4442	branch-info@branch.com
216	ExchangeNet	216 261 4593	info@en.com
216	OARnet (corporate clients only)	614 728 8100	info@oar.net
*216	Multiverse, Inc.	216 344 3080	multiverse.com
216	New Age Consulting Service	216 524 3162	damin@nacs.net
217	Allied Access Inc.	618 684 2255	sales@intrnet.net
217	Sol Tec, Inc.	317 920 1SOL	info@soltec.com
218	Red River Net	701 232 2227	info@rrnet.com
218	Protocol Communications, Inc.	612 541 9900	info@protocom.com
*301	American Information Network	410 855 2353	info@ai.net

301	Charm.Net	410 558 3900	info@charm.net
301	Clark Internet Services, Inc. ClarkNet	410 995 0691	info@clark.net
301	Digital Express Group	301 847 5000	info@digex.net
301	FredNet	301 631 5300	info@fred.net
301	Genuine Computing Resources	703 878 4680	info@gcr.com
301	Internet Online, Inc.	301 652 4468	info@intr.net
301	LaserNet	703 591 4232	info@laser.net
301	Quantum Networking Solutions, Inc.	805 538 2028	info@qnet.com
301	RadixNet Internet Services	301 567 9831	info@radix.net
301	SURAnet	301 982 4600	marketing@sura.net
301	US Net, Incorporated	301 572 5926	info@us.net
*301	World Web Limited	703 838 2000	info@worldweb.net
302	Delaware Common Access Network	302 654 1019	info@dca.net
302	The Magnetic Page (tmp) O N L I N E	302 651 9753	info@magpage.com
302	SSNet, Inc.	302 378 1386	info@ssnet.com
303	ABWAM, Inc.	303 730 6050	info@entertain.com
303	Colorado SuperNet, Inc.	303 296 8202	info@csn.org
303	CSDC, Inc.	303 665 8053	support@ares.csd.net
303	The Denver Exchange, Inc.	303 455 4252	info@tde.com
303	ENVISIONET, Inc.	303 770 2408	info@envisionet.net
303	EZLink Internet Access	970 482 0807	ezadmin@ezlink.com
303	I-Link Ltd	800 ILINK 99	info@i-link.net
303	Indra's Net, Inc.	303 546 9151	info@indra.com
303	Internet Express	719 592 1240	info@usa.net
303	NETCOM On-Line Communications Services	408 554 8649	info@netcom.com
303	NetWay 2001, Inc.	303 794 1000	info@netway.net
303	New Mexico Technet, Inc.	505 345 6555	granoff@technet.nm.org
303	Rocky Mountain Internet	800 900 7644	info@rmii.com
303	Shaman Exchange, Inc.	303 674 9784	info@dash.com
303	Stonehenge Internet Communications	800 RUN INET	info@henge.com

304	RAM Technologies Inc.	800 950 1726	info@ramlink.net
305	Acquired Knowledge Systems, Inc.	305 525 2574	info@aksi.net
305	CyberGate, Inc.	305 428 4283	sales@gate.net
305	InteleCom Data Systems, Inc.	401 885 6855	info@ids.net
305	Internet Providers of Florida, Inc	305 273 7978	office@ipof.fla.net
305	NetMiami Internet Corporation	305 554 4463	picard@netmiami.com
*305	Netpoint Communications, Inc.	305 891 1955	info@netpoint.net
305	NetRunner Inc	305 255 5800	info@netrunner.net
305	PSS InterNet Services	800 463 8499	support@america.com
305	SatelNET Communications, Inc.	305 434 8738	admin@satelnet.org
*306	Cycor Communications Incorporated	902 892 7354	signup@cycor.ca
307	wyoming.com	307 332 3030	info@wyoming.com
308	Synergy Communications, Inc.	800 345 9669	info@synergy.net
310	Abode Computer Service	818 287 5115	eric@abode.ttank.com
310	Cloverleaf Communications	714 895 3075	sales@cloverleaf.com
*310	Cogent Software, Inc.	818 585 2788	info@cogsoft.com
310	Delta Internet Services	714 778 0370	info@deltanet.com
310	DigiLink Network Services	310 542 7421	info@digilink.net
310	EarthLink Network, Inc.	213 644 9500	sales@earthlink.net
310	Exodus Communications, Inc.	408 522 8450	info@exodus.net
310	The Loop Internet Switch Co.	213 465 1311	info@loop.com
310	KAIWAN Internet	714 638 2139	info@kaiwan.com
310	Leonardo Internet	310 395 5500	jimp@leonardo.net
310	Liberty Information Network	800 218 5157	info@liberty.com
310	Lightside, Inc.	818 858 9261	Lightside@Lightside.Com
310	NETCOM On-Line Communications Services	408 554 8649	info@netcom.com
310	Network Intensive	714 450 8400	info@ni.net
310	SoftAware	310 305 0275	info@softaware.com
310	ViaNet Communications	415 903 2242	info@via.net
312	American Information Systems, Inc.	708 413 8400	info@ais.net
312	CICNet, Inc.	313 998 6103	info@cic.net

312	InterAccess Co.	800 967 1580	info@interaccess.com
312	Interactive Network Systems, Inc.	312 881 3039	info@insnet.com
312	MCSNet	312 248 8649	info@mcs.net
312	NETCOM On-Line Communications Services	408 554 8649	info@netcom.com
312	Open Business Systems, Inc.	708 250 0260	info@obs.net
312	Ripco Communications, Inc.	312 477 6210	info@ripco.com
312	Tezcatlipoca, Inc.	312 850 0181	info@tezcat.com
*312	The ThoughtPort Authority Inc.	800 ISP 6870	info@thoughtport.com
312	WorldWide Access	708 367 1870	info@wwa.com
313	Branch Information Services	313 741 4442	branch-info@branch.com
313	CICNet, Inc.	313 998 6103	info@cic.net
313	ICNET / Innovative Concepts	313 998 0090	info@ic.net
313	Isthmus Corporation	313 973 2100	info@izzy.net
313	Michigan Internet Cooperative Association	810 355 1438	info@coop.mica.net
313	Msen, Inc.	313 998 4562	info@msen.com
313	RustNet, Inc.	810 650 6812	info@rust.net
314	Allied Access Inc.	618 684 2255	sales@intrnet.net
314	Inlink	314 432 0935	support@inlink.com
314	NeoSoft, Inc.	713 684 5969	info@neosoft.com
*314	Online Information Access Network	618 692 9813	info@oia.net
314	P-Net, Inc.	314 731 2252	info@MO.NET
*314	The ThoughtPort Authority Inc.	800 ISP 6870	info@thoughtport.com
315	ServiceTech, Inc.	716 263 3360	info@servtech.com
315	Spectra.net	607 798 7300	info@spectra.net
*315	Syracuse Internet	315 233 1948	info@vcomm.net
*316	Elysian Fields, Inc.	316 267 2636	info@elysian.net
316	SouthWind Internet Access, Inc.	316 263 7963	info@southwind.net
317	Branch Information Services	313 741 4442	branch-info@branch.com
317	HolliCom Internet Services	317 883 4500	cale@holli.com
317	IQuest Network Services	317 259 5050	info@iquest.net

317	Metropolitan Data Networks Limited	317 449 0539	info@mdn.com
317	Net Direct	317 251 5252	kat@inetdirect.net
317	Sol Tec, Inc.	317 920 1SOL	info@soltec.com
318	Linknet Internet Services	318 442 5465	rdalton@linknet.net
319	Gryffin Information Services	319 399 3690	Info@gryffin.com
334	OnLine Montgomery	334 271 9576	rverble@bbs.olm.com
334	MindSpring Enterprises, Inc.	800 719 4332	info@mindspring.com
334	Scott Network Services, Inc.	205 987 5889	info@scott.net
334	WSNetwork Communications Services, Inc.	334 263 5505	custserv@wsnet.com
360	Interconnected Associates Inc. (IXA)	206 622 7337	mike@ixa.com
360	NorthWest CommLink	360 336 0103	info@nwcl.net
360	Pacifier Computers	360 693 2116	info@pacifier.com
360	Pacific Rim Network, Inc.	360 650 0442	info@pacificrim.net
360	Premier1 Internet Services	360 793 3658	info@premier1.net
360	Skagit On-Line Services	360 755 0190	info@sos.net
360	Townsend Communications, Inc.	360 385 0464	info@olympus.net
360	Transport Logic	503 243 1940	sales@transport.com
360	Whidbey Connections, Inc.	360 678 1070	info@whidbey.net
360	WLN	800 342 5956	info@wln.com
*401	brainiac services inc.	401 539 9050	info@brainiac.com
401	InteleCom Data Systems, Inc.	401 885 6855	info@ids.net
401	The Internet Connection, Inc.	508 261 0383	info@ici.net
401	Plymouth Commercial Internet Exchange	617 741 5900	info@pcix.com
402	Internet Nebraska	402 434 8680	info@inetnebr.com
402	Synergy Communications, Inc.	800 345 9669	info@synergy.net
*403	Alberta SuperNet Inc.	403 441 3663	info@supernet.ab.ca
403	CCI Networks	403 450 6787	info@ccinet.ab.ca
*403	Cycor Communications Incorporated	902 892 7354	signup@cycor.ca

403	Debug Computer Services	403 248 5798	root@debug.cuc.ab.ca
403	UUNET Canada, Inc.	416 368 6621	info@uunet.ca
404	CyberNet Communications Corporation	404 518 5711	sfeingold@atlwin.com
404	I-Link Ltd	800 ILINK 99	info@i-link.net
404	Internet Atlanta	404 410 9000	info@atlanta.com
404	MindSpring Enterprises, Inc.	800 719 4332	info@mindspring.com
404	NETCOM On-Line Communications Services	408 554 8649	info@netcom.com
404	Random Access, Inc.	404 804 1190	sales@randomc.com
405	Internet Oklahoma	405 721 1580	info@ionet.net
405	Questar Network Services	405 848 3228	info@qns.net
406	CyberPort Montana	406 863 3221	skippy@cyberport.net
406	Internet Montana	406 255 9699	support@comp-unltd.com
406	Montana Online	406 721 4952	info@montana.com
407	Acquired Knowledge Systems, Inc.	305 525 2574	info@aksi.net
407	CyberGate, Inc.	305 428 4283	sales@gate.net
407	The EmiNet Domain	407 731 0222	info@emi.net
407	Florida Online	407 635 8888	info@digital.net
407	I-Link Ltd	800 ILINK 99	info@i-link.net
407	InteleCom Data Systems, Inc.	401 885 6855	info@ids.net
407	Internet Providers of Florida, Inc	305 273 7978	office@ipof.fla.net
407	InternetU	407 952 8487	info@iu.net
407	MagicNet, Inc.	407 657 2202	info@magicnet.net
407	MetroLink Internet Services	407 726 6707	jtaylor@metrolink.net
407	PSS InterNet Services	800 463 8499	support@america.com
408	Aimnet Information Services	408 257 0900	info@aimnet.com
408	Alternet (UUNET Technologies, Inc.)	703 204 8000	info@alter.net
408	Brainstorm's Internet Power Connection	415 473-6411	info@brainstorm.net
408	BTR Communications Company	415 966 1429	support@btr.com
408	Direct Net Access Incorporated	510 649 6110	support@dnai.com

408	The Duck Pond Public Unix modem ->	408 249 9630	postmaster@kfu.com
408	Electriciti	619 338 9000	info@powergrid.electriciti.com
408	Exodus Communications, Inc.	408 522 8450	info@exodus.net
408	Infoserv Connections	408 335 5600	root@infoserv.com
408	InterNex Tiara	408 496 5466	info@internex.net
408	ISP Networks	408 653 0100	info@isp.net
408	Liberty Information Network	800 218 5157	info@liberty.com
408	MediaCity World	415 321 6800	info@MediaCity.com
408	NETCOM On-Line Communications Services	408 554 8649	info@netcom.com
408	NetGate Communications	408 565 9601	sales@netgate.net
408	Scruz-Net	408 457 5050	info@scruz.net
408	SenseMedia	408 335 9400	sm@picosof.com
408	South Valley Internet	408 683 4533	info@garlic.com
408	West Coast Online	707 586 3060	info@calon.com
408	zNET	619 755 7772	info@znet.com
408	Zocalo Engineering	510 540 8000	info@zocalo.net
409	Brazos Information Highway Services	409 693 9336	info@bihs.net
*409	Cybercom Corporation	409 268 0771	www@cy-net.net
409	Internet Connect Services, Inc.	512 572 9987	info@icsi.net
*410	American Information Network	410 855 2353	info@ai.net
410	CAPCON Library Network	202 331 5771	info@capcon.net
410	Charm.Net	410 558 3900	info@charm.net
410	Clark Internet Services, Inc. ClarkNet	410 995 0691	info@clark.net
410	Digital Express Group	301 847 5000	info@digex.net
410	jaguNET Access Services	410 931 3157	info@jagunet.com
410	Softaid Internet Services Inc.	410 290 7763	sales@softaid.net
410	US Net, Incorporated	301 572 5926	info@us.net
*412	CityNet, Inc.	412 481 5406	info@city-net.com
412	FYI Networks	412 898 2323	info@fyi.net
*412	Pittsburgh OnLine Inc.	412 681 6130	sales@pgh.net
*412	Stargate Industries, Inc.	412 942 4218	info@sgi.net

412	Telerama Public Access Internet	412 481 3505	info@telerama.lm.com
*412	The ThoughtPort Authority Inc.	800 ISP 6870	info@thoughtport.com
413	Mallard Electronics, Inc.	413 732 0214	gheacock@map.com
413	MediaCity World	415 321 6800	info@MediaCity.com
413	ShaysNet.COM	413 772 3774	staff@shaysnet.com
413	the spa!, inc.	413 539 9818	info@the-spa.com
414	Excel.Net, Inc.	414 452 0455	manager@excel.net
414	Exec-PC, Inc.	414 789 4200	info@execpc.com
414	FullFeed Communications	608 246 4239	info@fullfeed.com
414	MIX Communications	414 351 1868	info@mixcom.com
414	NetNet, Inc.	414 499 1339	info@netnet.net
415	Aimnet Information Services	408 257 0900	info@aimnet.com
415	Alternet (UUNET Technologies, Inc.)	703 204 8000	info@alter.net
415	Brainstorm's Internet Power Connection	415 473-6411	info@brainstorm.net
415	BTR Communications Company	415 966 1429	support@btr.com
415	Community ConneXion - NEXUS-Berkeley	510 549 1383	info@c2.org
415	Datatamers ISP	415 367 7919	info@datatamers.com
415	Direct Net Access Incorporated	510 649 6110	support@dnai.com
415	Exodus Communications, Inc.	408 522 8450	info@exodus.net
415	I-Link Ltd	800 ILINK 99	info@i-link.net
415	Idiom Consulting	510 644 0441	info@idiom.com
415	InterNex Tiara	408 496 5466	info@internex.net
415	LanMinds, Inc.	510 843 6389	info@lanminds.com
415	Liberty Information Network	800 218 5157	info@liberty.com
415	LineX Communications	415 455 1650	info@linex.com
415	MediaCity World	415 321 6800	info@MediaCity.com
415	NETCOM On-Line Communications Services	408 554 8649	info@netcom.com
415	NetGate Communications	408 565 9601	sales@netgate.net
415	QuakeNet	415 655 6607	info@quake.net
415	Sirius	415 284 4700	info@sirius.com
415	SLIPNET	415 281 3132	info@slip.net

```
415   ViaNet Communications                415 903 2242   info@via.net

415   The WELL                             415 332 4335   info@well.com

415   West Coast Online                    707 586 3060   info@calon.com

415   zNET                                 619 755 7772   info@znet.com

415   Zocalo Engineering                   510 540 8000   info@zocalo.net


*416  Cycor Communications Incorporated    902 892 7354   signup@cycor.ca

416   HookUp Communications                905 847 8000   info@hookup.net

416   Internex Online, Inc.                416 363 8676   support@io.org

416   InterLog Internet Services           416 975 2655   internet@interlog.com

*416  Internet Light and Power             416 502 1512   staff@ilap.com

416   UUNET Canada, Inc.                   416 368 6621   info@uunet.ca


417   Woodtech Information Systems, Inc.   417 886 0234   info@woodtech.com


418   UUNET Canada, Inc.                   416 368 6621   info@uunet.ca


419   Branch Information Services          313 741 4442   branch-info@branch.com

419   OARnet (corporate clients only)      614 728 8100   info@oar.net

*419  Primenet                             602 870 1010   info@primenet.com


501   Cloverleaf Technologies              903 832 1367   helpdesk@clover.cleaf.com

501   IntelliNet ISP                       501 376 7676   info@intellinet.com


502   IgLou Internet Services              800 436 4456   info@iglou.com

502   Mikrotec Internet Services, Inc.     606 225 1488   info@mis.net


503   Alternet (UUNET Technologies, Inc.)  703 204 8000   info@alter.net

503   aracnet.com                          503 626 8696   info@aracnet.com

503   Cenornet                             503 557 9047   info@cenornet.com

503   Colossus Inc.            x19 ->      312 528 1000   colossus@romney.mtjeff.com

503   Data Research Group, Inc.            503 465 3282   info@ordata.com

503   DTR Communications Services          503 252 5059   info@dtr.com

*503  Gorge Networks                       503 386 8300   postmaster@gorge.net
```

503	Europa	503 222 9508	info@europa.com
503	Hevanet Communications	503 228 3520	info@hevanet.com
503	I-Link Ltd	800 ILINK 99	info@i-link.net
503	Interconnected Associates Inc. (IXA)	206 622 7337	mike@ixa.com
503	NETCOM On-Line Communications Services	408 554 8649	info@netcom.com
503	Open Door Networks, Inc.	503 488 4127	info@opendoor.com
503	Pacifier Computers	360 693 2116	info@pacifier.com
503	RainDrop Laboratories/Agora	503 293 1772	info@agora.rdrop.com
503	Structured Network Systems, Inc.	503 656 3530	info@structured.net
503	Teleport, Inc.	503 223 4245	info@teleport.com
503	Transport Logic	503 243 1940	sales@transport.com
503	WLN	800 342 5956	info@wln.com
504	AccessCom Internet Services	504 887 0022	info@accesscom.net
504	Communique Inc.	504 527 6200	info@communique.net
504	I-Link Ltd	800 ILINK 99	info@i-link.net
504	NeoSoft, Inc.	713 684 5969	info@neosoft.com
505	Computer Systems Consulting	505 984 0085	info@spy.org
505	Internet Direct, Inc.	800 879 3624	info@direct.net
505	Internet Express	719 592 1240	info@usa.net
505	Network Intensive	714 450 8400	info@ni.net
505	New Mexico Technet, Inc.	505 345 6555	granoff@technet.nm.org
505	Southwest Cyberport	505 271 0009	info@swcp.com
505	WhiteHorse Communications ,Inc.	915 584 6630	whc.net.html
505	ZyNet SouthWest	505 343 8846	zycor@zynet.com
506	Agate Internet Services	207 947 8248	ais@agate.net
*506	Cycor Communications Incorporated	902 892 7354	signup@cycor.ca
507	Desktop Media	507 373 2155	isp@dm.deskmedia.com
507	Internet Connections, Inc.	507 625 7320	info@ic.mankato.mn.us
507	Millennium Communications, Inc.	612 338 5509	info@millcomm.com
507	Minnesota Regional Network	612 342 2570	info@mr.net
507	Protocol Communications, Inc.	612 541 9900	info@protocom.com

*508	Argo Communications	508 261 6121	info@argo.net
508	Channel 1	617 864 0100	support@channel1.com
508	The Destek Group, Inc.	603 635 3857	inquire@destek.net
508	Empire.Net, Inc.	603 889 1220	info@empire.net
508	FOURnet Information Network	508 291 2900	info@four.net
508	The Internet Access Company (TIAC)	617 276 7200	info@tiac.net
508	The Internet Connection, Inc.	508 261 0383	info@ici.net
508	intuitive information, inc.	508 342 1100	info@iii.net
508	MV Communications, Inc.	603 429 2223	info@mv.mv.com
508	North Shore Access	617 593 3110	info@shore.net
508	Pioneer Global Telecommunications, Inc.	617 375 0200	info@pn.com
508	Plymouth Commercial Internet Exchange	617 741 5900	info@pcix.com
508	StarNet	508 922 8238	info@venus.star.net
508	TerraNet, Inc.	617 450 9000	info@terra.net
508	UltraNet Communications, Inc.	508 229 8400	info@ultra.net.com
508	The World	617 739 0202	info@world.std.com
508	Wrentham Internet Services	508 384 1404	info@riva.com
508	Wilder Systems, Inc.	617 933 8810	info@id.wing.net
*509	Cascade Connections, Inc.	509 663 4259	carrie@cascade.net
509	Interconnected Associates Inc. (IXA)	206 622 7337	mike@ixa.com
509	Internet On-Ramp, Inc.	509 624 RAMP	info@on-ramp.ior.com
509	Transport Logic	503 243 1940	sales@transport.com
509	WLN	800 342 5956	info@wln.com
510	Aimnet Information Services	408 257 0900	info@aimnet.com
510	Alternet (UUNET Technologies, Inc.)	703 204 8000	info@alter.net
510	BTR Communications Company	415 966 1429	support@btr.com
510	Community ConneXion - NEXUS-Berkeley	510 549 1383	info@c2.org
510	Direct Net Access Incorporated	510 649 6110	support@dnai.com
510	Exodus Communications, Inc.	408 522 8450	info@exodus.net
510	Idiom Consulting	510 644 0441	info@idiom.com
510	InterNex Tiara	408 496 5466	info@internex.net

510	LanMinds, Inc.	510 843 6389	info@lanminds.com
510	Liberty Information Network	800 218 5157	info@liberty.com
510	LineX Communications	415 455 1650	info@linex.com
510	MediaCity World	415 321 6800	info@MediaCity.com
510	NETCOM On-Line Communications Services	408 554 8649	info@netcom.com
510	Sirius	415 284 4700	info@sirius.com
510	SLIPNET	415 281 3132	info@slip.net
510	West Coast Online	707 586 3060	info@calon.com
510	Zocalo Engineering	510 540 8000	info@zocalo.net
512	@sig.net	512 306 0700	sales@aus.sig.net
*512	The Eden Matrix	512 478 9900	info@eden.com
512	I-Link Ltd	800 ILINK 99	info@i-link.net
512	Illuminati Online	512 462 0999	info@io.com
512	Internet Connect Services, Inc.	512 572 9987	info@icsi.net
512	NETCOM On-Line Communications Services	408 554 8649	info@netcom.com
512	OuterNet Connection Strategies	512 345 3573	question@outer.net
512	Real/Time Communications	512 451 0046	info@realtime.net
512	Turning Point Information Services, Inc.	512 499 8400	info@tpoint.net
512	Zilker Internet Park, Inc.	512 206 3850	info@zilker.net
513	The Dayton Network Access Company	513 237 6868	info@dnaco.net
513	IgLou Internet Services	800 436 4456	info@iglou.com
513	Internet Access Cincinnati	513 887 8877	info@iac.net
513	Local Internet Gateway Co.	510 503 9227	sdw@lig.net
513	OARnet (corporate clients only)	614 728 8100	info@oar.net
513	Premier Internet Cincinnati, Inc.	513 561 6245	pic@cinti.net
*514	Accent Internet	514 737 6077	admin@accent.net
514	CiteNet Telecom Inc.	514 721 1351	info@citenet.net
514	Communication Accessibles Montreal	514 288 2581	info@cam.org
514	Communications Inter-Acces	514 367 0002	info@interax.net
*514	Cycor Communications Incorporated	902 892 7354	signup@cycor.ca

514	Odyssee Internet	514 861 3432	info@odyssee.net
514	UUNET Canada, Inc.	416 368 6621	info@uunet.ca
515	JTM MultiMedia, Inc.	515 277 1990	jtm@ecity.net
515	Synergy Communications, Inc.	800 345 9669	info@synergy.net
516	ASB Internet Services	516 981 1953	info@asb.com
516	Creative Data Consultants (SILLY.COM)	718 229 0489	info@silly.com
516	Echo Communications Group	212 255 3839	info@echonyc.com
516	I-2000, Inc.	516 867 6379	info@i-2000.com
516	INTAC Access Corporation	800 504 6822	info@intac.com
516	LI Net, Inc.	516 476 1168	info@li.net
516	Long Island Information, Inc.	516 294 0124	info@liii.com
516	Network Internet Services	516 543 0234	info@netusa.net
516	Panix (Public Access uNIX)	212 741 4545	info@panix.com
516	Pipeline New York	212 267 3636	info@pipeline.com
517	Msen, Inc.	313 998 4562	info@msen.com
517	Branch Information Services	313 741 4442	branch-info@branch.com
518	Wizvax Communications	518 273 4325	info@wizvax.com
519	HookUp Communications	905 847 8000	info@hookup.net
*519	Inter*Com Information Services	519 679 1620	info@icis.on.ca
519	MGL Systems Computer Technologies Inc.	519 651 2713	info@mgl.ca
519	UUNET Canada, Inc.	416 368 6621	info@uunet.ca
*519	Windsor Infromation Network Company	519 945 9462	kim@wincom.net
520	Internet Direct, Inc.	800 879 3624	info@direct.net
520	Opus One	602 324 0494	sales@opus1.com
*520	Primenet	602 870 1010	info@primenet.com
520	RTD Systems & Networking, Inc.	602 318 0696	info@rtd.com
520	Sedona Internet Services, Inc.	520 204 2247	info@sedona.net

601	Datasync Internet Services	601 872 0001	info@datasync.com
602	Crossroads Communications	602 813 9040	crossroads@xroads.com
602	I-Link Ltd	800 ILINK 99	info@i-link.net
602	Internet Direct, Inc.	800 879 3624	info@direct.net
602	Internet Express	719 592 1240	info@usa.net
602	NETCOM On-Line Communications Services	408 554 8649	info@netcom.com
602	New Mexico Technet, Inc.	505 345 6555	granoff@technet.nm.org
602	Opus One	602 324 0494	sales@opus1.com
602	Primenet	602 870 1010	info@primenet.com
602	RTD Systems & Networking, Inc.	602 318 0696	info@rtd.com
602	Systems Solutions Inc.	602 955 5566	support@syspac.com
603	Agate Internet Services	207 947 8248	ais@agate.net
603	Empire.Net, Inc.	603 889 1220	info@empire.net
603	The Destek Group, Inc.	603 635 3857	inquire@destek.net
603	MV Communications, Inc.	603 429 2223	info@mv.mv.com
603	NETIS Public Access Internet	603 437 1811	epoole@leotech.mv.com
603	StarNet	508 922 8238	info@venus.star.net
604	AMT Solutions Group, Inc. Island Net	604 727 6030	info@islandnet.com
*604	Cycor Communications Incorporated	902 892 7354	signup@cycor.ca
*604	The InterNet Shop Inc.	604 376 3710	info@netshop.net
604	Mind Link!	604 534 5663	info@mindlink.bc.ca
604	Okanagan Internet Junction	604 549 1036	info@junction.net
604	Sunshine Net, Inc.	604 886 4120	admin@sunshine.net
604	UUNET Canada, Inc.	416 368 6621	info@uunet.ca
606	IgLou Internet Services	800 436 4456	info@iglou.com
606	Internet Access Cincinnati	513 887 8877	info@iac.net
606	Mikrotec Internet Services, Inc.	606 225 1488	info@mis.net
606	RAM Technologies Inc.	800 950 1726	info@ramlink.net
607	ServiceTech, Inc.	716 263 3360	info@servtech.com
607	Spectra.net	607 798 7300	info@spectra.net

608	FullFeed Communications	608 246 4239	info@fullfeed.com
609	Digital Express Group	301 847 5000	info@digex.net
609	Eclipse Internet Access	800 483 1223	info@eclipse.net
609	K2NE Software	609 893 0673	vince-q@k2nesoft.com
609	Net Access	215 576 8669	support@netaxs.com
609	New Jersey Computer Connection	609 896 2799	info@pluto.njcc.com
609	Texel International	908 297 0290	info@texel.com
610	Digital Express Group	301 847 5000	info@digex.net
610	FishNet	610 337 9994	info@pond.com
610	GlobalQUEST, Inc.		
610	Microserve Information Systems	717 779 4430	info@microserve.com
610	Net Access	215 576 8669	support@netaxs.com
610	Network Analysis Group	800 624 9240	nag@good.freedom.net
610	SSNet, Inc.	302 378 1386	info@ssnet.com
610	Oasis Telecommunications, Inc.	610 439 8560	staff@oasis.ot.com
610	You Tools Corporation / FASTNET	610 954 5910	info@fast.net
612	DCC Inc.	612 378 4000	kgastony@dcc.com
612	GlobalCom	612 920 9920	info@globalc.com
612	James River Group Inc	612 339 2521	jriver@jriver.jriver.COM
612	Millennium Communications, Inc.	612 338 5509	info@millcomm.com
612	Minnesota Regional Network	612 342 2570	info@mr.net
*612	Orbis Internet Services, Inc.	612 645 9663	info@orbis.net
612	pclink.com	612 541 5656	infomatic@pclink.com
*612	Primenet	602 870 1010	info@primenet.com
612	Protocol Communications, Inc.	612 541 9900	info@protocom.com
612	StarNet Communications, Inc.	612 941 9177	info@winternet.com
612	Synergy Communications, Inc.	800 345 9669	info@synergy.net
*613	Cyberius Online Inc.	613 233 1215	info@cyberus.ca
*613	Cycor Communications Incorporated	902 892 7354	signup@cycor.ca
613	Information Gateway Services (Ottawa)	613 592 5619	info@igs.net

*613	Interactive Telecom Inc.	613 727 5258	info@intertel.net
613	HookUp Communications	905 847 8000	info@hookup.net
613	o://info.web	613 225 3354	kevin@magi.com
613	UUNET Canada, Inc.	416 368 6621	info@uunet.ca
*614	ASCInet (Columbus)	614 798 5321	info@ascinet.com
614	Branch Information Services	313 741 4442	branch-info@branch.com
614	Internet Access Cincinnati	513 887 8877	info@iac.net
614	OARnet (corporate clients only)	614 728 8100	info@oar.net
614	RAM Technologies Inc.	800 950 1726	info@ramlink.net
615	ERC, Inc. / The Edge	615 455 9915	staff@edge.ercnet.com
615	GoldSword Systems	615 691 6498	info@goldsword.com
615	ISDN-Net Inc	615 377 7672	jdunlap@rex.isdn.net
615	The Telalink Corporation	615 321 9100	sales@telalink.net
615	The Tri-Cities Connection	615 378 5355	info@tricon.net
*615	U.S. Internet	615 522 6788	info@usit.net
616	Branch Information Services	313 741 4442	branch-info@branch.com
616	Msen, Inc.	313 998 4562	info@msen.com
616	Traverse Communication Company	616 935 1705	info@traverse.com
617	Alternet (UUNET Technologies, Inc.)	703 204 8000	info@alter.net
*617	Argo Communications	508 261 6121	info@argo.net
617	Channel 1	617 864 0100	support@channel1.com
617	COWZ Technologies	617 497 0058	system@cow.net
617	Cyber Access Internet Communications, Inc	617 396 0491	info@cybercom.net
617	FOURnet Information Network	508 291 2900	info@four.net
617	The Internet Access Company (TIAC)	617 276 7200	info@tiac.net
617	intuitive information, inc.	508 342 1100	info@iii.net
617	NETCOM On-Line Communications Services	408 554 8649	info@netcom.com
617	North Shore Access	617 593 3110	info@shore.net
617	Pioneer Global Telecommunications, Inc.	617 375 0200	info@pn.com
617	Plymouth Commercial Internet Exchange	617 741 5900	info@pcix.com

617	TerraNet, Inc.	617 450 9000	info@terra.net
617	UltraNet Communications, Inc.	508 229 8400	info@ultra.net.com
617	The World	617 739 0202	info@world.std.com
617	Wilder Systems, Inc.	617 933 8810	info@id.wing.net
618	Allied Access Inc.	618 684 2255	sales@intrnet.net
*618	Online Information Access Network	618 692 9813	info@oia.net
618	P-Net, Inc.	314 731 2252	info@MO.NET
619	CONNECTnet Internet Network Services	619 450 0254	info@connectnet.com
619	CTS Network Services	619 637 3637	info@cts.com
619	The Cyberspace Station	619 634 2894	info@cyber.net
619	Electriciti	619 338 9000	info@powergrid.electriciti.com
619	I-Link Ltd	800 ILINK 99	info@i-link.net
619	Liberty Information Network	800 218 5157	info@liberty.com
619	NETCOM On-Line Communications Services	408 554 8649	info@netcom.com
*619	Primenet	602 870 1010	info@primenet.com
619	RidgeNET	619 371 3501	saic@owens.ridgecrest.ca.us
619	Sierra-Net	702 831 3353	giles@sierra.net
701	Red River Net	701 232 2227	info@rrnet.com
702	@wizard.com	702 871 4461	info@wizard.com
*702	Connectus, Inc.	702 323 2008	info@connectus.com
702	Great Basin Internet Services	702 829 2244	info@greatbasin.com
702	InterMind	702 878 6111	support@terminus.intermind.net
702	NETCOM On-Line Communications Services	408 554 8649	info@netcom.com
702	Sierra-Net	702 831 3353	giles@sierra.net
703	Alternet (UUNET Technologies, Inc.)	703 204 8000	info@alter.net
703	CAPCON Library Network	202 331 5771	info@capcon.net
703	Charm.Net	410 558 3900	info@charm.net
703	Clark Internet Services, Inc. ClarkNet	410 995 0691	info@clark.net
703	DataBank, Inc.	913 842 6699	info@databank.com

703	Digital Express Group	301 847 5000	info@digex.net
703	Genuine Computing Resources	703 878 4680	info@gcr.com
703	Internet Online, Inc.	301 652 4468	info@intr.net
703	Interpath	800 849 6305	info@interpath.net
703	LaserNet	703 591 4232	info@laser.net
703	NETCOM On-Line Communications Services	408 554 8649	info@netcom.com
703	Quantum Networking Solutions, Inc.	805 538 2028	info@qnet.com
703	RadixNet Internet Services	301 567 9831	info@radix.net
703	US Net, Incorporated	301 572 5926	info@us.net
*703	World Web Limited	703 838 2000	info@worldweb.net
704	Interpath	800 849 6305	info@interpath.net
704	SunBelt.Net	803 328 1500	info@sunbelt.net
704	Vnet Internet Access	704 334 3282	info@vnet.net
705	Barrie Connex Inc.	705 725 0819	info@bconnex.net
705	Mindemoya Computing	705 523 0243	info@mcd.on.ca
*705	SooNet Corporation	705 253 4700	service@soonet.ca
706	InteliNet	803 279 9775	administrator@intelinet.net
706	Internet Atlanta	404 410 9000	info@atlanta.com
706	MindSpring Enterprises, Inc.	800 719 4332	info@mindspring.com
707	Liberty Information Network	800 218 5157	info@liberty.com
707	West Coast Online	707 586 3060	info@calon.com
707	Zocalo Engineering	510 540 8000	info@zocalo.net
708	American Information Systems, Inc.	708 413 8400	info@ais.net
708	CICNet, Inc.	313 998 6103	info@cic.net
*708	I Connection, Inc.	708 662 0877	info@iconnect.net
708	InterAccess Co.	800 967 1580	info@interaccess.com
708	Interactive Network Systems, Inc.	312 881 3039	info@insnet.com
708	MCSNet	312 248 8649	info@mcs.net
708	Open Business Systems, Inc.	708 250 0260	info@obs.net

708	Ripco Communications, Inc.	312 477 6210	info@ripco.com
708	Tezcatlipoca, Inc.	312 850 0181	info@tezcat.com
708	WorldWide Access	708 367 1870	info@wwa.com
*709	InterActions Limited	709 745 4638	connect@nfld.com
712	Synergy Communications, Inc.	800 345 9669	info@synergy.net
713	Alternet (UUNET Technologies, Inc.)	703 204 8000	info@alter.net
713	The Black Box	713 480 2684	info@blkbox.com
713	ELECTROTEX, Inc.	713 526 3456	info@electrotex.com
713	I-Link Ltd	800 ILINK 99	info@i-link.net
713	Internet Connect Services, Inc.	512 572 9987	info@icsi.net
713	NeoSoft, Inc.	713 684 5969	info@neosoft.com
713	OnRamp Technologies, Inc.	214 746 4710	info@onramp.net
713	USiS	713 682 1666	admin@usis.com
714	Cloverleaf Communications	714 895 3075	sales@cloverleaf.com
*714	Cogent Software, Inc.	818 585 2788	info@cogsoft.com
714	Dana Point Communications	714 443 4172	connect@beach.net
714	Delta Internet Services	714 778 0370	info@deltanet.com
714	DigiLink Network Services	310 542 7421	info@digilink.net
714	EarthLink Network, Inc.	213 644 9500	sales@earthlink.net
714	Electriciti	619 338 9000	info@powergrid.electriciti.com
714	Exodus Communications, Inc.	408 522 8450	info@exodus.net
714	InterNex Tiara	408 496 5466	info@internex.net
714	KAIWAN Internet	714 638 2139	info@kaiwan.com
714	Liberty Information Network	800 218 5157	info@liberty.com
714	Lightside, Inc.	818 858 9261	Lightside@Lightside.Com
714	NETCOM On-Line Communications Services	408 554 8649	info@netcom.com
714	Network Intensive	714 450 8400	info@ni.net
714	Primenet	602 870 1010	info@primenet.com
715	FullFeed Communications	608 246 4239	info@fullfeed.com

*716	BuffNET	800 463 6499	info@buffnet.net
716	E-Znet, Inc.	716 262 2485	
716	ServiceTech, Inc.	716 263 3360	info@servtech.com
*717	The Internet Cafe	717 344 1969	info@lydian.scranton.com
717	Keystone Information Access Systems	717 741 2626	office@yrkpa.kias.com
717	Microserve Information Systems	717 779 4430	info@microserve.com
717	Oasis Telecommunications, Inc.	610 439 8560	staff@oasis.ot.com
717	PenNet	717 368 1577	safrye@pennet.net
717	Spectra.net	607 798 7300	info@spectra.net
717	You Tools Corporation / FASTNET	610 954 5910	info@fast.net
718	Blythe Systems	212 226 7171	infodesk@blythe.org
718	BrainLINK	718 805 6559	info@beast.brainlink.com
718	Creative Data Consultants (SILLY.COM)	718 229 0489	info@silly.com
718	escape.com - Kazan Corp	212 888 8780	info@escape.com
718	I-2000, Inc.	516 867 6379	info@i-2000.com
718	Ingress Communications Inc.	212 679 2838	info@ingress.com
718	INTAC Access Corporation	800 504 6822	info@intac.com
718	InterCom Online	212 714 7183	info@intercom.com
718	Interport Communications Corp.	212 989 1128	info@interport.net
718	Long Island Information, Inc.	516 294 0124	info@liii.com
718	Mnematics, Incorporated	914 359 4546	service@mne.com
718	Mordor International BBS	201 433 4222	ritz@mordor.com
718	Panix (Public Access uNIX)	212 741 4545	info@panix.com
718	Phantom Access Technologies, Inc.	212 989 2418	bruce@phantom.com
718	Pipeline New York	212 267 3636	info@pipeline.com
*718	ThoughtPort of New York City	212 645 7970	info@precipice.com
719	Colorado SuperNet, Inc.	303 296 8202	info@csn.org
719	Internet Express	719 592 1240	info@usa.net
719	Old Colorado City Communications	719 528 5849	thefox@oldcolo.com
719	Rocky Mountain Internet	800 900 7644	info@rmii.com

801	DataBank, Inc.	913 842 6699	info@databank.com
801	I-Link Ltd	800 ILINK 99	info@i-link.net
801	Infonaut Communication Services	801 370 3068	info@infonaut.com
801	Internet Technology Systems (I.T.S.)	801 375 0538	admin@itsnet.com
*801	The ThoughtPort Authority Inc.	800 ISP 6870	info@thoughtport.com
801	XMission	801 539 0852	support@xmission.com
803	A World of Difference, Inc.	803 769 4488	info@awod.com
803	Global Vision Inc.	803 241 0901	info@globalvision.net
*803	Hargray Telephone Company	803 686 5000	info@hargray.com
803	InteliNet	803 279 9775	administrator@intelinet.net
803	Interpath	800 849 6305	info@interpath.net
803	SIMS, Inc.	803 762 4956	info@sims.net
803	SunBelt.Net	803 328 1500	info@sunbelt.net
804	Widomaker Communication Service	804 253 7621	bloyall@widowmaker.com
805	The Catalina BBS InterNet Services	fax->805 687 1185	help@catalina.org
805	The Central Connection	818 735 3000	info@centcon.com
*805	Cogent Software, Inc.	818 585 2788	info@cogsoft.com
805	EarthLink Network, Inc.	213 644 9500	sales@earthlink.net
805	Internet Access of Ventura County	805 383 3500	info@vcnet.com
805	KAIWAN Internet	714 638 2139	info@kaiwan.com
*805	Lancaster Internet (California)	805 943 2112	dennis@gargamel.ptw.com
805	Liberty Information Network	800 218 5157	info@liberty.com
*805	Netport Internet Access	805 538 2860	info@netport.com
805	Network Intensive	714 450 8400	info@ni.net
805	Quantum Networking Solutions, Inc.	805 538 2028	info@qnet.com
805	Regional Alliance for Info Networking	805 967 7246	info@rain.org
805	ValleyNet Communications	209 486 8638	info@valleynet.com
805	WestNet Communications, Inc.	805 892 2133	info@west.net
806	OnRamp Technologies, Inc.	214 746 4710	info@onramp.net

808	FlexNet Inc.	808 732 8849	info@aloha.com
808	Hawaii OnLine	808 533 6981	support@aloha.net
808	Inter-Pacific Network Services	808 935 5550	sales@interpac.net
808	LavaNet, Inc.	808 545 5282	info@lava.net
808	Pacific Information Exchange, Inc.	808 596 7494	info@pixi.com
810	Branch Information Services	313 741 4442	branch-info@branch.com
810	ICNET / Innovative Concepts	313 998 0090	info@ic.net
810	Local Internet Service Provider	810 687 4221	hostmaster@lisp.com
810	Michigan Internet Cooperative Association	810 355 1438	info@coop.mica.net
810	Msen, Inc.	313 998 4562	info@msen.com
810	RustNet, Inc.	810 650 6812	info@rust.net
812	HolliCom Internet Services	317 883 4500	cale@holli.com
812	IgLou Internet Services	800 436 4456	info@iglou.com
812	World Connection Services	812 479 1700	info@evansville.net
813	CFTnet	813 980 1317	sales@cftnet.com
813	CocoNet Corporation	813 945 0055	info@coconet.com
813	CyberGate, Inc.	305 428 4283	sales@gate.net
813	Florida Online	407 635 8888	info@digital.net
813	Intelligence Network Online, Inc. x22 ->	813 442 0114	info@intnet.net
813	PacketWorks, Inc.	813 446 8826	info@packet.net
*813	The ThoughtPort Authority Inc.	800 ISP 6870	info@thoughtport.com
814	PenNet	717 368 1577	safrye@pennet.net
815	American Information Systems, Inc.	708 413 8400	info@ais.net
815	InterAccess Co.	800 967 1580	info@interaccess.com
815	T.B.C. Online Data-Net	815 758 5040	info@tbcnet.com
816	Interstate Networking Corporation	816 472 4949	staff@interstate.net
816	Primenet	602 870 1010	info@primenet.com

817	Association for Computing Machinery	817 776 6876	account-info@acm.org
*817	CompuTek	214 994 0190	info@computek.net
817	DFW Internet Services, Inc.	817 332 5116	info@dfw.net
817	OnRamp Technologies, Inc.	214 746 4710	info@onramp.net
817	Texas Metronet, Inc.	214 705 2900	info@metronet.com
818	The Central Connection	818 735 3000	info@centcon.com
*818	Cogent Software, Inc.	818 585 2788	info@cogsoft.com
818	Delta Internet Services	714 778 0370	info@deltanet.com
818	DigiLink Network Services	310 542 7421	info@digilink.net
818	EarthLink Network, Inc.	213 644 9500	sales@earthlink.net
818	Exodus Communications, Inc.	408 522 8450	info@exodus.net
818	InterNex Tiara	408 496 5466	info@internex.net
818	KAIWAN Internet	714 638 2139	info@kaiwan.com
818	Leonardo Internet	310 395 5500	jimp@leonardo.net
818	Liberty Information Network	800 218 5157	info@liberty.com
818	Lightside, Inc.	818 858 9261	Lightside@Lightside.Com
818	The Loop Internet Switch Co.	213 465 1311	info@loop.com
818	NETCOM On-Line Communications Services	408 554 8649	info@netcom.com
818	Network Intensive	714 450 8400	info@ni.net
		602 870 1010	info@primenet.com
818	Regional Alliance for Info Networking	805 967 7246	info@rain.org
818	ViaNet Communications	415 903 2242	info@via.net
819	Information Gateway Services (Ottawa)	613 592 5619	info@igs.net
*819	Interactive Telecom Inc.	613 727 5258	info@intertel.net
819	o://info.web	613 225 3354	kevin@magi.com
901	ISDN-Net Inc	615 377 7672	jdunlap@rex.isdn.net
901	Magibox Incorporated	901 757 7835	info@magibox.net
*902	Cycor Communications Incorporated	902 892 7354	signup@cycor.ca
903	Cloverleaf Technologies	903 832 1367	helpdesk@clover.cleaf.com

904	CyberGate, Inc.	305 428 4283	sales@gate.net
904	Florida Online	407 635 8888	info@digital.net
904	Internet Connect Company	904 375 2912	info@atlantic.net
*904	Jax Gateway to the World	904 730 7692	sales@gttw.com
904	MagicNet, Inc.	407 657 2202	info@magicnet.net
904	Polaris Network, Inc.	904 878 9745	staff@polaris.net
904	PSS InterNet Services	800 463 8499	support@america.com
904	SymNet	904 385 1061	info@symnet.net
*905	Cycor Communications Incorporated	902 892 7354	signup@cycor.ca
905	HookUp Communications	905 847 8000	info@hookup.net
*905	iCOM Internet Services	905 522 1220	sales@icom.ca
905	InterLog Internet Services	416 975 2655	internet@interlog.com
905	Internet Connect Niagara Inc	905 988 9909	info@niagara.com
905	Internex Online, Inc.	416 363 8676	support@io.org
*905	Times.net	905 775 4471	rfonger@times.net
905	Vaxxine Computer Systems Inc.	905 562 3500	admin@vaxxine.com
906	Branch Information Services	313 741 4442	branch-info@branch.com
906	Msen, Inc.	313 998 4562	info@msen.com
906	The Portage at Micro + Computers	906 487 9832	admin@mail.portup.com
908	Castle Network, Inc.	908 548 8881	request@castle.net
908	Digital Express Group	301 847 5000	info@digex.net
908	Eclipse Internet Access	800 483 1223	info@eclipse.net
908	I-2000, Inc.	516 867 6379	info@i-2000.com
908	INTAC Access Corporation	800 504 6822	info@intac.com
908	Internet For 'U'	800 NET WAY1	info@ifu.net
908	Internet Online Services x226 ->	201 928 1000	help@ios.com
908	Texel International	908 297 0290	info@texel.com
908	You Tools Corporation / FASTNET	610 954 5910	info@fast.net
*909	Cogent Software, Inc.	818 585 2788	info@cogsoft.com
909	CONNECTnet Internet Network Services	619 450 0254	info@connectnet.com

909	Dana Point Communications	714 443 4172	connect@beach.net
909	Delta Internet Services	714 778 0370	info@deltanet.com
*909	EmpireNet	909 787 4969	support@empirenet.com
909	KAIWAN Internet	714 638 2139	info@kaiwan.com
909	Liberty Information Network	800 218 5157	info@liberty.com
909	Lightside, Inc.	818 858 9261	Lightside@Lightside.Com
909	Network Intensive	714 450 8400	info@ni.net
*909	Primenet	602 870 1010	info@primenet.com
910	Interpath	800 849 6305	info@interpath.net
910	Red Barn Data Center	910 750 9809	tom@rbdc.rbdc.com
910	Vnet Internet Access	704 334 3282	info@vnet.net
*912	Hargray Telephone Company	803 686 5000	info@hargray.com
912	Internet Atlanta	404 410 9000	info@atlanta.com
912	MindSpring Enterprises, Inc.	800 719 4332	info@mindspring.com
913	DataBank, Inc.	913 842 6699	info@databank.com
913	Interstate Networking Corporation	816 472 4949	staff@interstate.net
914	Cloud 9 Internet	914 682 0626	info@cloud9.net
914	Computer Solutions by Hawkinson	914 229 9853	info@mhv.net
914	Creative Data Consultants (SILLY.COM)	718 229 0489	info@silly.com
914	DataBank, Inc.	913 842 6699	info@databank.com
914	GBN InternetAccess	201 343 6427	gbninfo@gbn.net
914	ICU On-Line	914 627 3800	info@icu.com
914	INTAC Access Corporation	800 504 6822	info@intac.com
914	I-2000, Inc.	516 867 6379	info@i-2000.com
914	InteleCom Data Systems, Inc.	401 885 6855	info@ids.net
914	Mnematics, Incorporated	914 359 4546	service@mne.com
914	Panix (Public Access uNIX)	212 741 4545	info@panix.com
914	Pipeline New York	212 267 3636	info@pipeline.com
914	TZ-Link Internet	914 353 5443	info@j51.com
914	WestNet Internet Services	914 967 7816	info@westnet.com

915	New Mexico Technet, Inc.	505 345 6555	granoff@technet.nm.org
*915	Primenet	602 870 1010	info@primenet.com
915	WhiteHorse Communications ,Inc.	915 584 6630	whc.net.html
*916	Connectus, Inc.	702 323 2008	info@connectus.com
916	Great Basin Internet Services	702 829 2244	info@greatbasin.com
916	mother.com	916 757 8070	info@mail.mother.com
*916	InterStar Network Services	916 224 6866	gfrank@shasta.com
916	NETCOM On-Line Communications Services	408 554 8649	info@netcom.com
916	Psyberware Internet Access	916 645 9451	info@psyber.com
916	Sacramento Network Access	916 565 4500	info@sna.com
916	Sierra-Net	702 831 3353	giles@sierra.net
916	VFR, Inc.	916 652 7237	vfr@vfr.net
916	West Coast Online	707 586 3060	info@calon.com
916	Zocalo Engineering	510 540 8000	info@zocalo.net
918	Galaxy Star Systems	918 835 3655	info@galstar.com
918	Internet Oklahoma	918 583 1161	info@ionet.net
919	Interpath	800 849 6305	info@interpath.net
919	NETCOM On-Line Communications Services	408 554 8649	info@netcom.com
919	Vnet Internet Access	704 334 3282	info@vnet.net
941	Net Sarasota	941 371 1966	info@netsrq.com
941	PacketWorks, Inc.	813 446 8826	info@packet.net
970	EZLink Internet Access	970 482 0807	ezadmin@ezlink.com
970	Frontier Internet, Inc.	970 385 4177	info@frontier.net

FOREIGN

=======

A listing of Internet service providers in countries other than the U.S.
and Canada, sorted by country. Fields are country, service provider name,
voice phone number, and email address for more information.

Australia	APANA	+61 42 965015	wollongong@apana.org.au
Australia	arrakis.apana.org.au	+61 8 296 6200	greg@arrakis.apana.org.au
Australia	AusNet Services Pty Ltd	+61 2 241 5888	sales@world.net
Australia	Byron Public Access	+61 18 823 541	admin@byron.apana.org.au
Australia	DIALix Services	+61 2 948 6995	justin@sydney.dialix.oz.au
Australia	Highway 1	+61 9 370 4584	info@highway1.com.au
Australia	Hunter Network Association	+61 49 621783	mbrown@hna.com.au
Australia	iiNet Technologies	+61 9 3071183	iinet@iinet.com.au
Australia	Kralizec Dialup Unix System	+61 2 837 1397	nick@kralizec.zeta.org.au
Australia	Informed Technology	+61 9 245 2279	info@it.com.au
Australia	The Message eXchange Pty Ltd	+61 2 550 5014	info@tmx.com.au
Australia	Microplex Pty. Ltd.	+61 2 888 3685	info@mpx.com.au
Australia	Pegasus Networks Pty Ltd	+61 7 257 1111	fwhitmee@peg.apc.org
Australia	PPIT Pty. Ltd. (059 051 320)	+61 3 747 9823	info@ppit.com.au
Australia	Stour System Services	+61 9 571 1949	stour@stour.net.au
Australia	Winthrop Technology	+61 9 380 3564	wthelp@yarrow.wt.uwa.edu.au
Australia	Zip Australia Pty. Ltd.	+61 2 482 7015	info@zip.com.au
Austria	ARGE DATEN	+43 1 4897893	info@email.ad.or.at
Austria	EUnet EDV	+43 1 3174969	info@austria.eu.net
Austria	Hochschuelerschaft	+43 1 586 1868	sysop@link-atu.comlink.apc.org
Austria	Net4You	+43 4242 257367	office@net4you.co.at
*Austria	netwing	+43 5337 65315	info@netwing.at
Austria	PING EDV	+43 1 3194336	info@ping.at
Austria	Vianet Austria Ltd.	+43 1 5892920	info@via.at
Bashkiria	UD JV 'DiasPro'	+7 3472 387454	iskander@diaspro.bashkiria.su
Belarus	Open Contact, Ltd.	+7 017 2206134	admin@brc.minsk.by
Belgium	EUnet Belgium NV	+32 16 236099	info@belgium.eu.net
Belgium	Infoboard Telematics SA	+32 2 475 25 31	ocaeymaex@infoboard.be
Belgium	INnet NV/SA	+32 14 319937	info@inbe.net
Belgium	KnoopPunt VZW	+32 9 2333 686	support@knooppunt.be

Bulgaria	EUnet Bulgaria	+359 52 259135	info@bulgaria.eu.net
Denmark	DKnet / EUnet Denmark	+45 3917 9900	info@dknet.dk
Finland	Clinet Ltd	+358 0 437 5209	clinet@clinet.fi
Finland	EUnet Finland Ltd.	+358 0 400 2060	helpdesk@eunet.fi
France	French Data Network	+33 1 4797 5873	info@fdn.org
France	Internet Way	+33 1 4143 2110	info@iway.fr
France	OLEANE	+33 1 4328 3232	info-internet@oleane.net
France	REMCOMP SARL	+33 1 4479 0642	info@liber.net
France	STI	+33 1 3463 1919	fb101@calvacom.fr
Georgia	Mimosi Hard	+7 8832 232857	kisho@sanet.ge
Germany	bbTT Electronic Networks	+49 30 817 42 06	willem@b-2.de.contrib.net
Germany	EUnet Germany GmbH	+49 231 972 2222	info@germany.eu.net
Germany	Individual Network e.V.	+49 441 980 8556	in-info@individual.net
Germany	INS Inter Networking Systems	+49 2305 356505	info@ins.net
Germany	Internet PoP Frankfurt	+49 69 94439192	joerg@pop-frankfurt.com
Germany	MUC.DE e.V.	+49 89 324 683 0	postmaster@muc.de
Germany	Onlineservice Nuernberg	+49 911 9933882	info@osn.de
Germany	PFM News & Mail Xlink POP	+49 171 331 0862	info@pfm.pfm-mainz.de
Germany	Point of Presence GmbH	+49 40 2519 2025	info@pop.de
Germany	POP Contrib.Net Netzdienste	+49 521 9683011	info@teuto.de
Germany	SpaceNet GmbH	+49 89 324 683 0	info@space.net
Germany	TouchNET GmbH	+49 89 5447 1111	info@touch.net
Germany	Westend GbR	+49 241 911879	info@westend.com
Ghana	Chonia Informatica	+233 21 66 94 20	info@ghana.net
Greece	Ariadne	+30 1 651 3392	dialup@leon.nrcps.ariadne-t.gr
Greece	Foundation of Research	+30 81 221171	forthnet-pr@forthnet.gr
*Hong Kong	Asia On-Line Limited	+852 2866 6018	info@asiaonline.net

Hong Kong	Hong Kong SuperNet	+852 358 7924	trouble@hk.super.net
Iceland	SURIS / ISnet	+354 1 694747	isnet-info@isnet.is
Ireland	Cork Internet Services	+353 21 277124	info@cis.ie
Ireland	Ieunet Limited	+353 1 679 0832	info@ieunet.ie
Ireland	Ireland On-Line	+353 91 592727	info@iol.ie
Israel	Elronet	+972 313534	info@elron.net
Israel	NetVision LTD.	+972 550330	info@netvision.net.il
*Italy	Abacom s.a.s.	+39 434 660911	info@system.abacom.it
Italy	ITnet S.p.A.	+39 10 6563324	info@it.net
Japan	Asahi Net	+81 3 3666 2811	info@asahi-net.or.jp
Japan	Global OnLine	+81 3 5330 9380	info@gol.org
Japan	Internet Initiative Japan	+81 3 3580 3781	info@iij.ad.jp
Japan	M.R.T., Inc.	+81 3 3255 8880	sysop@janis-tok.com
Japan	TWICS	+81 3 3351 5977	info@twics.com
Japan	Typhoon Inc.	+81 3 3757 2118	info@typhoon.co.jp
Kazakhstan	Bogas Soft Laboratory Co.	+7 322 262 4990	pasha@sl.semsk.su
Kuwait	Gulfnet Kuwait	+965 242 6728	info@kw.us.com
Latvia	LvNet-Teleport	+371 2 551133	vit@riga.lv
Latvia	Versia Ltd.	+371 2 417000	postmaster@vernet.lv
Lisboa	Esoterica	716 2395	info@esoterica.com
Luxemburg	EUnet Luxemburg	+352 47 02 61 361	info@luxemburg.eu.net
Mexico	Datanet S.A. de C.V.	+52 5 1075400	info@data.net.mx
*Mexico	Internet de Mexico S.A.	+52 5 3602931	info@mail.internet.com.mx

Netherlands	The Delft Connection	+31 15560079	info@void.tdcnet.nl
Netherlands	Hobbynet	+31 365361683	henk@hgatenl.hobby.nl
Netherlands	Internet Access Foundation	+31 5982 2720	mail-server@iafnl.iaf.nl
Netherlands	NEST	+31 206265566	info@nest.nl
Netherlands	NetLand	+31 206943664	info@netland.nl
Netherlands	NLnet (EUnet)	+31 206639366	info@nl.net
Netherlands	Psyline	+31 80445801	postmaster@psyline.nl
Netherlands	Simplex Networking	+31 206932433	skelmir@simplex.nl
Netherlands	Stichting XS4ALL	+31 206225222	helpdesk@xs4all.nl
New Zealand	Actrix Networks Limited	+64 4 389 6356	john@actrix.gen.nz
New Zealand	Efficient Software Limited	+64 3 4738274	bart@dunedin.es.co.nz
Norway	Oslonett A/S	+47 22 46 10 99	oslonett@oslonett.no
Poland	PDi Ltd. - Public Internet	+48 42 30 21 94	info@pdi.lodz.pl
Romania	EUnet Romania SRL	+40 1 312 6886	info@romania.eu.net
Russia	ELCOM	+7 092 223 2208	root@centre.elcom.ru
Russia	GlasNet	+7 95 262 7079	support@glas.apc.org
Russia	InterCommunications Ltd.	+7 8632 620562	postmaster@icomm.rnd.su
Russia	NEVAlink Ltd.	+7 812 592 3737	serg@arcom.spb.su
Russia	Relcom CO	+7 95 194 25 40	postmaster@ussr.eu.net
Russia	SvjazInform	+7 351 265 3600	pol@rich.chel.su
Singapore	Singapore Telecom Limited	+65 7308079	admin@singnet.com.sg
Slovakia	EUnet Slovakia	+42 7 725 306	info@slovakia.eu.net
Slovenia	NIL, System Integration	+386 61 1405 183	info@slovenia.eu.net
South Africa	Aztec	+27 21 419 2690	info@aztec.co.za
South Africa	Internet Africa	+27 0800 020003	info@iaccess.za
South Africa	The Internet Solution	+27 11 447 5566	info@is.co.za

Spain	OFFCAMPUS SL	+34 1 577 3026	infonet@offcampus.es
Sweden	NetGuide	+46 31 28 03 73	info@netg.se
Switzerland	EUnet AG, Zurich	+41 1 291 45 80	info@eunet.ch
Switzerland	EUnet SA, Geneva	+41 22 348 80 45	deffer@eunet.ch
Switzerland	SWITCH	+41 1 268 1515	postmaster@switch.ch
Switzerland	XGP Switzerland	+41 61 8115635	service@xgp.spn.com
Tataretan	KAMAZ Incorporated	+7 8439 53 03 34	postmaster@kamaz.kazan.su
Ukraine	ConCom, Ltd.	+7 0572 27 69 13	igor@ktts.kharkov.ua
Ukraine	Crimea Communication Centre	+380 0652 257214	sem@snail.crimea.ua
Ukraine	Electronni Visti	+7 44 2713457	info%elvisti.kiev.ua@kiae.su
Ukraine	PACO Links Int'l Ltd.	+7 48 2200057	info@vista.odessa.ua
Ukraine	UkrCom-Kherson Ltd	+7 5522 64098	postmaster@ukrcom.kherson.ua
United Kingdom	Compulink (CIX Ltd)	+44 181 390 8446	cixadmin@cix.compulink.co.uk
United Kingdom	CONNECT - PC User Group	+44 181 863 1191	info@ibmpcug.co.uk
United Kingdom	Demon Internet Limited	+44 181 371 1000	internet@demon.net
United Kingdom	The Direct Connection	+44 81 313 0100	helpdesk@dircon.co.uk
United Kingdom	EUnet GB	+44 1227 266466	sales@britain.eu.net
United Kingdom	ExNet Systems Ltd.	+44 81 244 0077	info@exnet.com
United Kingdom	Frontier Internet Services	+44 171 242 3383	info@ftech.net
United Kingdom	GreenNet	+44 71 713 1941	support@gn.apc.org
United Kingdom	Lunatech Research	+44 1734 791900	info@luna.co.uk
United Kingdom	Pavilion Internet plc	+44 1273 606072	info@pavilion.co.uk
United Kingdom	Sound & Visions BBS	+44 1932 253131	info@span.com
United Kingdom	Specialix	+44 932 3522251	keith@specialix.co.uk
United Kingdom	WinNET (UK)	+44 181 863 1191	info@win-uk.ne
Venezuela	Internet Comunicaciones c.a.	+58 9599550	admin@ccs.internet.ve

*** END OF LIST ***

INTERNET TOOLS

SUMMARY

This document is reprinted with the permission of John December.

```
Internet Tools Summary
================================================================================
AUTHOR:     John December (decemj@rpi.edu)


DATE:       02 Dec 94; Release 1.77


COPYRIGHT:  1994 by John December (decemj@rpi.edu). You may use this
document for any personal or educational purpose. For-profit
distribution requires permission.


DISCLAIMER: Provided "as is" without expressed or implied warranty.
```

PURPOSE: to list tools available on the Internet that are used for
network information retrieval (NIR) and Computer-Mediated Communication
(CMC). This is not meant to be a strict categorization or an exhaustive
list, rather a reference catalog. I welcome c omments and suggestions.

AUDIENCE: those getting started in understanding what you can do on the
Internet in NIR and CMC; for experienced users, it collects and
summarizes sources of information.

ASSUMPTION: You have access to and know how to use finger, ftp,
gopher, http, telnet, email, World Wide Web, or Usenet newsgroups.

REFERENCES: The references which are listed at the end of this
document provide very useful guides to these tools.

ACTION: The Action notation that I had described in earlier versions
of this document is in the internet-tools.tax file.

NOTES:

1. Respect your access privileges to these tools.

2. This information changes;additions/comments welcome.

3. For demo purposes, I have used Unix commands; certainly Unix
is not the only operating system required for these tools and
forums. Apologies to those who don't have Unix.

4. On the classification (NIR v. CMC): some tools could be used
for either, such as telnet and email. I've placed them in what
I feel are "principle use" categories, e.g., telnet is used mostly
for NIR, and email is commonly used for CMC (although both have
applications in the other category).

5. Many of these tools have applicability off the Internet.
Usenet, for example, is not confined to the Internet, and
Internet email (and thus LISTSERV files) can be exchanged with
communication systems off the Internet (BITNET, fidonet, commercial
service s.) So this list is not Internet (only) tools, but tools that
can be used on the Internet.

6. A $ sign indicates a non-public domain tool or interface.

7. The easiest way to use this list is to access the hypertext
version at URL http://www.rpi.edu/Internet/Guides/decemj/itools/top.html

Information about updates of this document:
>John December: contact for comments, corrections, updates
(mailto:decemj@rpi.edu).
----
* Section -1- ABOUT THIS INFORMATION
==
o Notes
~~~~~~
These are some explanatory files for using this information and
describing this project. >Segmented: describes how to use the
segmented hypertext format of this information
(http://www.rpi.edu/Internet/Guides/decemj/itools/top.html).
>README: describes Internet tools project and other formats of the
information
(ftp://ftp.rpi.edu/pub/communications/internet-tools.readme).
>Using: some tips and instructions on using the access methods
mentioned in this file
(ftp://ftp.rpi.edu/pub/communications/internet-tools.use).
>Taxonomy: some notes toward a taxonomy of Internet tools
(ftp://ftp.rpi.edu/pub/communications/internet-tools.tax).
o Formats
~~~~~~

These are the other formats for this information. Note that the files
at the ftp site (ftp.rpi.edu) will not be as current as those on the
web server. >Database: the raw database in my own, simple markup
language from which I generate all versions of this information
(warning--this is a large file)
(ftp://ftp.rpi.edu/pub/communications/internet-tools.dat).
>DVI: the device-independent file (generated from LaTeX source file)
(ftp://ftp.rpi.edu/pub/communications/internet-tools.dvi).
>HTML 1 big page: HTML version of this information on one big page
(http://www.rpi.edu/Internet/Guides/decemj/itools/internet-tools.html).
>HTML segmented: HTML version of this information in a web of pages
divided by section, sub-section, and sub-sub-section
(http://www.rpi.edu/Internet/Guides/decemj/itools/top.html).
>LaTeX: source for the LaTeX version of this information
(ftp://ftp.rpi.edu/pub/communications/internet-tools.tex).
>Postscript: postscript version of this information
(ftp://ftp.rpi.edu/pub/communications/internet-tools.ps.Z).
>Text Wide: text version of this information >80 columns wide
(ftp://ftp.rpi.edu/pub/communications/internet-tools).
>Text 80: text version of this information, 80 columns wide
(ftp://ftp.rpi.edu/pub/communications/internet-tools.txt).
----
* Section -2- NIR = NETWORK INFORMATION RETRIEVAL
==
o Utilities
~~~~~~
- Finger
....
Definition: Finger retrieves information about a user registered on a
host computer. >Finger description: Unix manual page for finger
(unix:man finger).
>Finger Protocol: The Finger User Information Protocol, by D.
Zimmerman (ftp://nic.merit.edu/documents/rfc/rfc1288.txt).
>Finger via email: (mailto:dlangley@netcom.com Subject: "#finger
USER@HOST.DOMAIN").

>Finger via gopher: gopher to HOST, port 79, path 0USER-ID
(gopher://rpi.edu:79/0decemj).

>Finger via telnet: access finger via telnet HOST=host on which USER
is located, then type USER (telnet://rpi.edu:79).

>FingerInfo: a script to get information via finger, by Scott Yanoff
(ftp://csd4.csd.uwm.edu/pub/fingerinfo).

>FingerInfo via WWW: a hypertext version of Scott Yanoff's FingerInfo
script, by A. Daviel (http://sundae.triumf.ca/fingerinfo.html).

>Logfinger: A Program to Log a Fingerer
(gopher://twinbrook.cis.uab.edu:79/0logfinger).

- Netfind
....

Definition: Netfind provides a simple Internet 'white pages' user
directory. >Netfind description: a way to find someone on the
Internet, by Michael F. Schwartz
(ftp://ftp.cs.colorado.edu/pub/cs/distribs/netfind/README).

>Netfind info/EARN: an overview and introduction to Netfind, from
European Academic Research Network Association (EARN)
(http://www.earn.net/gnrt/netfind.html).

>Netfind source: (ftp://ftp.cs.colorado.edu/cs/distribs/netfind/).

>Netfind via Web: (http://alpha.acast.nova.edu/netfind.html).

>Netfind via telnet: using telnet to find someone on the Internet
(telnet://netfind@ds.internic.net).

>Netfind via email: use email to find someone on the Internet
(mailto:listserv@brownvm.brown.edu Body: get netfind help).

- Nslookup
....

Definition: Nslookup is an interactive program to query Internet domain
name servers (gives IP address). >Nslookup man page: Unix man page
(unix:man nslookup).

>Nslookup command: command to find out about command-name
(unix:nslookup domain-name).

- Ping
....

Definition: Ping requests echo from network host; see if remote host is up. >Ping source: source code and a description of Ping and its use (README) (ftp://vixen.cso.uiuc.edu/utils/ping/).

>Ping demo: check to see if host uwm.edu is up and roundtrip time (unix:/usr/etc/ping -s uwm.edu).

>WWWPing: simple internet pinging, and for HTTP pinging, with server identification, by Jonathon Fletcher (http://www.stir.ac.uk/jsbin/wwping).

- Shepherd

....

Definition: Shepherd monitors information servers (gopher, WAIS, WWW, jughead) to make sure they are responding. >Shepherd: monitoring tool for gopher, WAIS, WWW, jughead (ftp://inform.umd.edu/software/Gopher/).

- TIA = The Internet Adapter (tm)

....

Definition: The Internet Adapter (tm) $, allows you to use TCP/IP applications using a UNIX shell account. This is classified as an "Internet access utility." >TIA: The Internet Adapter (tm), $ (http://marketplace.com/0/tia/tiahome.html).

- WHOIS

....

Definition: WHOIS provides information on registered computer network users, domains, and organizations. >Whois info/EARN: overview and introductory information about WHOIS, from European Academic Research Network Association (EARN) (http://www.earn.net/gnrt/whois.html).

>Whois specs: NICNAME/WHOIS, by Harrenstien, Stahl, Feinler (October 1985) (ftp://nic.merit.edu/documents/rfc/rfc0954.txt).

>Whois Servers List: List of Internet whois servers, by Matt Power (ftp://sipb.mit.edu/pub/whois/whois-servers.list).

>Whois via email: (mailto:service@nic.ddn.mil Subject: whois HOST.DOMAIN).

>Whois via gopher: enter HOST.DOMAIN to query
(gopher://phantom.bsu.edu:4320/7whois%20rs.internic.net).

>Whois via telnet: at the prompt, enter whois host-name
(telnet://rs.internic.net).

>Whois via Unix: the Unix command for whois, where 'string' is the
organization/person name or Internet domain name (unix:whois
"string").

- X.500
....
Definition: X.500 (OSI Directory Service) provides globally distributed
directory service. >X.500 Definition: Executive Introduction to
Directory Services Using the X.500 Protocol
(ftp://nic.merit.edu/documents/fyi/fyi_13.txt).

>X.500 info/EARN: overview and introduction to X.500, from European
Academic Research Network Association (EARN)
(http://www.earn.net/gnrt/x500.html).

>X.500 Implement: A Revised Catalog of Available X.500 Implementations
(ftp://nic.merit.edu/documents/fyi/fyi_11.txt).

>X.500 Technical: Technical Overview of Directory Services Using the
X.500 Protocol (ftp://nic.merit.edu/documents/fyi/fyi_14.txt).

>X.500 via telnet: at the prompt, enter X500whois host-name
(telnet://rs.internic.net).

>X.500 via gopher: (gopher://judgmentday.rs.itd.umich.edu:7777).

>X.500 via WWW: from the X.500 Group at Brunel University
(http://http1.brunel.ac.uk:8080/wlu.html).

o Tools
~~~~~~
- Alibi = Adaptive Location of Internetworked Bases of Information
....
Definition: Alibi provides a query interface to retrieve information by
keywords >Alibi info: source code for Alibi, by Dave Flater
(ftp://speckle.ncsl.nist.gov/flater/sources/).

>Dave Flater: developer of Alibi (mailto:dave@case50.ncsl.nist.gov).

- Archie
....

Definition: Archie locates files at anonymous FTP sites by filename (or string expression) search. >Archie description: archie - An Electronic Directory Service for the Internet, by Deutsch, Emtage, and Heelan (ftp://archie.ans.net/pub/archie/doc/whatis.archie).

>Archie info/EARN: overview and information about Archie, from European Academic Research Network Association (EARN) (http://www.earn.net/gnrt/archie.html).

>Archie manual page: reference manual page for archie (ftp://archie.ans.net/pub/archie/doc/archie.man.txt).

>Archie via telnet: a telnet demo of archie (telnet://archie@archie.ans.net).

>Archie via gopher: a collection of information and links about archie, from Texas A and M University (gopher://gopher.tamu.edu/11/.dir/archie.dir).

>Archie via WWW: List of Hypertext Archie Servers (ArchiePlex), by Martijn Koster (http://web.nexor.co.uk/archie.html).

>Archie via Unix: Unix command line for hosts with installed archie client, search for STRING (unix:archie -s STRING).

>Archie via email: use archie via email (mailto:archie@archie.unl.edu Body: help).

>Anarchie: a Mac client that integrates archie searches and ftp requests, by Peter Lewis (ftp://amug.org/pub/ftp1/peterlewis/).

- Astra
....
Definition: Astra retrieve documents from databases. >Astra Help: the help file for Astra (mailto:astradb@icnucevm.bitnet Body: help).

>Astra documentation: Astra User Guide (mailto:astradb@icnucevm.bitnet Body: GET META DOCUMENT).

- Bitftp
....
Definition: Bitftp allows the user to use electronic mail to obtain files at an ftp site via email. >Bitftp info/EARN: from European Academic Research Network Association (EARN)

(http://www.earn.net/gnrt/notice.html).

- Essence

....

Definition: Essence is a resource discovery system using indexes.

>Essence description: The distribution includes the following files
and directories
(ftp://ftp.cs.colorado.edu/pub/cs/distribs/essence/README).

>Essence document: Essence -- A Resource Discovery System Based on
Semantic File Indexing
(ftp://ftp.cs.colorado.edu/pub/cs/distribs/essence/Essence.txt.Z).

- FSP = File Service Protocol

....

Definition: FSP is a conectionless protocol for transferring files.

>FSP INFO: an overview and description of FSP
(ftp://ftp.germany.eu.net/pub/network/inet/fsp/INFO).

>FSP FAQ: Frequently Asked Questions about FSP
(ftp://ftp.germany.eu.net/pub/network/inet/fsp/FAQ).

>FSP Sites: (mailto:charro@ee.ualberta.ca Subject: fsp list Body:
help).

>FSP software: (ftp://ftp.germany.eu.net/pub/network/inet/fsp/).

>FSP Discussion: an unmoderated Usenet discussion group about FSP
(news:alt.comp.fsp).

- FTP = File Transfer Protocol

....

Definition: FTP retrieves or puts copies of files at remote FTP sites.

>FTP how to: A guide to using ftp
(ftp://ftp.sura.net/pub/nic/network.service.guides/how.to.ftp.guide).

>FTP: File Transfer Protocol
(ftp://nic.merit.edu/documents/rfc/rfc0959.txt).

>FTP FAQ: Anonymous FTP Frequently Asked Questions (FAQ) List
(ftp://rtfm.mit.edu/pub/usenet-by-group/news.answers/ftp-list/faq).

>FTP Interface: look at ftp site lists
(http://hoohoo.ncsa.uiuc.edu/ftp-interface.html).

>FTP via Unix: Unix command for ftp, once in, type help (unix:ftp).

>FTP via email: get files at anonymous ftp sites via email.

(mailto:ftpmail@decwrl.dec.com Body: help).

>FTP via telnet: site at Univ of IA (telnet://grind.isca.uiowa.edu).

>File Compression: File compression, archiving, and text<->binary

formats, by David Lemson

(ftp://ftp.cso.uiuc.edu/doc/pcnet/compression).

>FTP setup: (ftp://cert.org/pub/tech_tips/anonymous_ftp).

- Jughead

....

Definition: Jughead gets menu information from gopher servers.

>Jughead description: description of Jonzy's Universal Gopher

Hierarchy Excavation And Display (JUGHEAD) current status, by Rhett

'Jonzy' Jones

(ftp://boombox.micro.umn.edu/pub/gopher/Unix/GopherTools/jughead/jughead.ReadMe).

>Jughead Search: (gopher://liberty.uc.wlu.edu:3002/7).

- Knowbot

....

Definition: Knowbot provides a uniform interface to heterogeneous

remote directory services. >Knowbot via telnet: use a knowbot service

via telnet; at the prompt, type 'help'

(telnet://info.cnri.reston.va.us:185).

- Maltshop

....

Definition: Maltshop builds a veronica-access menu on your local gopher

server. >Maltshop script:

(ftp://veronica.scs.unr.edu/veronica-code/).

- Netserv

....

Definition: Netserv is a server for access to data files and programs

of general interest. >Netserv: a server for access to data files and

programs of general interest (mailto:netserv@frmop11.bitnet Body: get

netserv helpfile).

>Netserv info/EARN: from European Academic Research Network

Association (EARN) (http://www.earn.net/gnrt/netserv.html).

- Soft-Pages

....

Definition: Soft Pages aids in retrieval of documents, software, and other resources from servers. >Soft Pages documentation: (ftp://ftp.tohoku.ac.jp/pub/spp).

>Project description: Soft Pages Project, by Johannsen and Mansfield (ftp://cs.ucl.ac.uk/osi-ds/osi-ds-39-00.txt).

- Spiders

....

Definition: Spiders are a class of software programs that traverse network hosts gathering information from and about resources. >Web Spiders: World Wide Web Robots, Wanderers, and Spiders, by Martijn Koster (http://web.nexor.co.uk/mak/doc/robots/robots.html).

>Yahoo List: Reference--Searching the Web--Robots, Spiders, etc., from Yahoo (http://akebono.stanford.edu/yahoo/Reference/Searching_the_Web/Robots__Spiders__etc_/). A selected list of Web spiders: >Web Ants: a project for cooperating, distributed Web spiders (http://thule.mt.cs.cmu.edu:8001/jrrl-space/webants.html).

>Harvest Brokers: (http://rd.cs.colorado.edu/brokers/).

>Crawler: gathers indexes of the total contents of documents, as well as URLSs and titles, by Brian Pinkerton (http://www.biotech.washington.edu/WebQuery.html).

>JumpStation: indexes the titles and headers of documents on the Web, by Jonathon Fletcher (http://www.stir.ac.uk/jsbin/js/).

>Lycos: uses information metrics to record the 100 most important words in a document, along with the first 20 lines, so that users can often determine the value of a WWW document without retrieving it (http://fuzine.mt.cs.cmu.edu/mlm/lycos-home.html).

>MOMspider: a spider that you can install on your system (Unix/Perl) (http://www.ics.uci.edu/WebSoft/MOMspider/).

>NIKOS: allows a topic-oriented search of a spider database (http://www.rns.com/cgi-bin/nikos).

>RBSE URL: a database of URL references, with full WAIS indexing of
the contents of the documents, by David Eichmann
(http://rbse.jsc.nasa.gov/eichmann/urlsearch.html).
>SG-Scout: a robot for finding Web servers
(http://www-swiss.ai.mit.edu/~ptbb/SG-Scout.html).
>Wandex: index from the World Wide Web Wanderer, by Matthew Gray
(http://www.mit.edu:8001/cgi/wandex/index).
>Worm: gathers information about titles and URLs from Web servers, by
Oliver McBryan (http://www.cs.colorado.edu/home/mcbryan/WWWW.html).
- Telnet
....
Definition: Telnet allows a user to login to a remote computer to use
applications. >Telnet how: a guide to using telnet
(ftp://ftp.sura.net/pub/nic/network.service.guides/how.to.telnet.guide).
>Telnet tips:
(http://kufacts.cc.ukans.edu/hytelnet_html/TELNET.html).
>TELNET: Telnet Protocol
(ftp://nic.merit.edu/documents/rfc/rfc0818.txt).
>Telnet demo: check the weather
(telnet://downwind.sprl.umich.edu:3000).
>Telnet search: find telnet connections based on keyword search
(gopher://liberty.uc.wlu.edu:3004/7).
- Trickle
....
Definition: Trickle is an electronic mail-based alternative to
obtaining files at FTP sites. >Trickle: an email-based alternative to
FTP, information
(gopher://gopher.earn.net/11/doc/gnrt-by-chapters/TRICKLE).
>Trickle info/EARN: from European Academic Research Network
Association (EARN) (http://www.earn.net/gnrt/trickle.html).
>Trickle guide: (mailto:listserv@earncc.bitnet Body: get trickle
memo).
- Veronica
....

Definition: Veronica locates titles of Gopher items by keyword search.

>Veronica info: information about veronica

(ftp://veronica.scs.unr.edu/pub/veronica/).

>Veronica Queries:

(ftp://veronica.scs.unr.edu/veronica-docs/how-to-query-veronica).

>Gopher/Veronica documentation:

(ftp://ftp.cso.uiuc.edu/doc/net/uiucnet/vol6no1.txt).

>Veronica via gopher: Search ALL of Gopherspace using veronica

(gopher://veronica.scs.unr.edu/11/veronica).

o Systems

~~~~~~

- Alex

....

Definition: Alex provides transparent read of remote files at anonymous

FTP sites. >Alex description: NIR (Networked Information Retrieval)

description of Alex (ftp://alex.sp.cs.cmu.edu/usr0/anon/doc/NIR.Tool).

>Alex Web Page: Alex FTP Filesystem

(ftp://alex.sp.cs.cmu.edu/usr0/anon/www/alex.html).

>Alex document: (ftp://alex.sp.cs.cmu.edu/usr0/anon/doc/intro.ps).

- GN

....

Definition: GN is a multi-protocol (gopher0, http/1.0) server. >GN

Description: (ftp://ftp.acns.nwu.edu/pub/gn/README).

>GN Source: (ftp://ftp.acns.nwu.edu/pub/gn/).

- Gopher

....

Definition: Gopher provides access to resources using a graph of

menus. >Gopher guide: Internet Gopher User's Guide, ed. Paul Linder

(ftp://boombox.micro.umn.edu/pub/gopher/docs/).

>Gopher info/EARN: gopher overview and introduction, from European

Academic Research Network Association (EARN)

(http://www.earn.net/gnrt/gopher.html).

>Gopher sources/info: gopher client/server source code, as well as

general information (e.g. gopher conference, gopherMoo, etc.)

(ftp://boombox.micro.umn.edu/pub/gopher/).

>Gopher demo: a session demonstrating gopher at Univ of Minnesota
(gopher://gopher.micro.umn.edu).

>Gopher via telnet: (telnet://gopher@consultant.micro.umn.edu).

>Gopher via email/Japan: use a gopher via email
(mailto:gophermail@ncc.go.jp Body: help).

>Gopher via email/USA: use a gopher via email
(mailto:gophermail@calvin.edu Body: help).

>Gopher FAQ: Common Questions and Answers about the Internet Gopher, a
client/server protocol for making a world wide information service,
with many implementations
(ftp://rtfm.mit.edu/pub/usenet/news.answers/gopher-faq).

>Gopher-Web: Gopher in the World-Wide Web, gopher-Web interactions
(gopher://gopher.ocf.berkeley.edu/00/gopher/gopher-www).

>Gopher/Veronica article: Exploring the Power of the Internet Gopher,
by Lynn Ward; an article from the University of Illinois publication
UIUCnet, Dec. 1992 - Jan. 1993, Vol. 6, No. 1, a newsletter covering
campus networking issues
(ftp://ftp.cso.uiuc.edu/doc/net/uiucnet/vol6no1.txt).

>Discussion: unmoderated Usenet newsgroup devoted to gopher
(news:comp.infosystems.gopher).

- Prospero
....
Definition: Prospero provides user-centered view of remote files.

>Prospero document: Prospero user's manual, by Neuman and Augart
(ftp://prospero.isi.edu/pub/prospero/doc/prospero-user-manual.tex.Z).

>Prospero info/EARN: from European Academic Research Network
Association (EARN) (http://www.earn.net/gnrt/prospero.html).

>Prospero documentation: description of prospero documentation
available
(ftp://prospero.isi.edu/pub/prospero/doc/README-prospero-documents).

- WAIS = Wide Area Information Server
....

Definition: WAIS(tm) responds to natural language queries by searching
indexes of databases and retrieving resources. >WAIS overview:
Overview of Wide Area Information Servers, by Brewster Kahle (April
1991) (ftp://quake.think.com/wais/doc/overview.txt).
>WAIS: A Sketch of An Overview, by Jeff Kallem
(ftp://sunsite.unc.edu/pub/docs/about-the-net/libsoft/wais.txt).
>WAIS info/EARN: WAIS overview and introduction, from European
Academic Research Network Association (EARN)
(http://www.earn.net/gnrt/wais.html).
>WAIS documentation: information on WAIS, Inc. and products
(ftp://quake.think.com/pub/wais-inc-doc/).
>WAIS, Inc. web: interactive on-line publishing systems and services
to organizations (http://server.wais.com).
>WAIS clients: client to WAIS in different interfaces (X)
(ftp://sunsite.unc.edu/pub/wais/clients/).
>freeWAIS: a UNIX based, freely available information server.
(ftp://ftp.cnidr.org/pub/NIDR.tools/freewais/).
>WAIS via telnet: (telnet://wais@quake.think.com).
>WAISGATE: WAIS to WWW gateway, search WAIS databases through search
terms, public directory maintained by WAIS, Inc.
(http://server.wais.com/directory-of-servers.html).
>SFgate: a CGI script which interfaces to WAIS servers, all freeWAIS
servers can be connected, by Ulrich Pfeifer
(http://ls6-www.informatik.uni-dortmund.de/SFgate/SFgate.html).
>Discussion-WAIS: an unmoderated Usenet newsgroup covering all aspects
of WAIS (news:comp.infosystems.wais).
- WWW = World Wide Web
....
Definition: WWW is a system for disseminating Internet resources
through servers and retrieving hypermedia resources through browsers.
>WWW overview/CERN: overview of the Web, from Conseil Europeen pour la
Recherche Nucleaire (CERN) European Laboratory for Particle Physics,
Geneva, Switzerland (birthplace of WWW)
(http://info.cern.ch/default.html).

>WWW info/EARN: What is World-Wide Web, a narrative introducing and
explaining the Web, from European Academic Research Network Association
(EARN) (http://www.earn.net/gnrt/www.html).

>WWW FAQ/Boutell: Frequently Asked Questions (FAQ) list and answers
about the Web--covers user, provider, and general information,
maintained by Thomas Boutell
(http://sunsite.unc.edu/boutell/faq/www_faq.html).

>WWW FAQ/CERN: Frequently Asked Questions on W3, by Tim Berners-Lee at
CERN (http://info.cern.ch/hypertext/WWW/FAQ/List.html).

>WWW Clients: a list of programs (Web browsers) that allow you to
access the WWW, from CERN
(http://info.cern.ch/hypertext/WWW/Clients.html).

>WWW Servers: a list of programs (Web servers) that allow you to
provide information on the Web, from CERN
(http://info.cern.ch/hypertext/WWW/Daemon/Overview.html).

>EIT WSK: Enterprise Integration Technologies Corporation's
Webmaster's Starter Kit, a resource to help you install a Web server
and optional extensions (http://wsk.eit.com/wsk/doc/).

>WWW ftp info: some information files about the Web, includes papers,
guides, and draft specifications, from CERN
(ftp://ftp.w3.org/pub/www/).

>WWW via telnet: an example of using WWW via telnet (to CERN)
(telnet://telnet.w3.org).

>WWW via email: obtain a web file (e.g., http) via email; URL =
Uniform resource locator; send message body 'www URL', note-use
sparingly, from CERN (mailto:agora@mail.w3.org Body: WWW).

>WWW gateways: interfaces between the WWW and other information or
communication systems
(http://akebono.stanford.edu/yahoo/Computers/World_Wide_Web/Gateways/).

>WWW Guide/Hughes: Entering the World-Wide Web, A Guide to Cyberspace,
by Kevin Hughes (http://www.eit.com/web/www.guide/guide.toc.html).

>WWW Developers: WWW+HTML Developer's JumpStation-a collection of
pointers about WWW and developing HTML, by Barry Raveendran Greene
(http://oneworld.wa.com/htmldev/devpage/dev-page.html).

>WWW Weavers: a collection of links to assist web weavers, includes
pointers to HTML resources, techniques, guides, and information, by
Chris Beaumont (http://www.nas.nasa.gov/RNR/Education/weavers.html).
>Yahoo WWW: Computers-World Wide Web
(http://akebono.stanford.edu/yahoo/Computers/World_Wide_Web/).
>CyberWeb: a resource collection for Web information providers and
users, includes general information and links to various resources
(http://www.charm.net/~web/).
>WWW Spiders: Spiders are a class of software programs that traverse
network hosts gathering information from and about resources
(http://www.rpi.edu/Internet/Guides/decemj/itools/nir-tools-spiders.html).
>webNews: announcements of new Web sites, services, and software
(http://twinbrook.cis.uab.edu:70/webNews.80).
>Discussion-Users: an unmoderated newsgroup for discussing Web client
and user topics, including network resource discovery and new user
questions (news:comp.infosystems.www.users).
>Discussion-Misc: an unmoderated newsgroup for discussing general web
topics not directly related to users or providers, including issues of
the Web's future and development (news:comp.infosystems.www.misc).
>Discussion-Providers: an unmoderated newsgroup for discussing Web
server and information provider topics, including information
presentation and HTML design (news:comp.infosystems.www.providers).
o Interfaces
~~~~~~
- Lists
....
For a longer list of World Wide Web browsers, see: >WWW Browser
source: source code for a variety of Web browsers for different
hardware platformst (ftp://ftp.w3.org/pub/www/bin/).
>WWW Clients: a list of programs to allow you to access the WWW from
your own computer (http://info.cern.ch/hypertext/WWW/Clients.html).
>WWW Browsers/Clients: from UNITE
(http://life.anu.edu.au/links/syslib.html).
>WWW Browsers/Yahoo: list from Yahoo, Computers-World Wide

Web-Browsers
(http://akebono.stanford.edu/yahoo/Computers/World_Wide_Web/Browsers/).
- Biomix
....
Definition: Biomix presents network resources as locations on screen
maps. Note: Not known to be operational >Biomix description: BIOMIX
current status, by Marcus Pattloch
(ftp://mailbase.ac.uk/pub/lists/unite/files/biomix.txt).
- Chimera
....
Definition: Chimera is a HTTP, FTP, Gopher client with an X/Athena
interface. >Chimera source: (ftp://ftp.cs.unlv.edu/pub/chimera/).
>Chimera Home Page: a HTTP, FTP, Gopher client with X/Athena
interface, by John Kilburg (http://www.unlv.edu/chimera/index.html).
- Cello
....
Definition: Cello is a DOS-based Internet browser incorporating WWW,
Gopher, FTP, Telnet, News. >Cello source: source code
(ftp://ftp.law.cornell.edu/pub/LII/Cello/).
- Compass
....
Definition: Compass is a system for Internet access to resources and
tools for CERFnet subscribers; >Compass description: Internet
Compass-your network guide, CERFnet offers new service for easier
Internetting (ftp://mailbase.ac.uk/pub/lists/unite/files/compass.txt).
- Emacs-WWW-browser
....
Definition: Emacs WWW browser is a means to access the World Wide Web.
>Emacs WWW: an Emacs subsystem that allows the user to browse the
World Wide Web (http://cs.indiana.edu/elisp/w3/docs.html).
>Emacs WWW source: (ftp://cs.indiana.edu/pub/elisp/w3/).
- Fred
....

Definition: Fred is an interface to the OSI X.500 white pages directory
service. >Fred: Performance Systems International White Pages Pilot
Project (telnet://fred@wp.psi.net).

- GINA
....
Definition: Gina $ stands for Graphical Interface for Network Access
(client/server) to email, conferencing, bbs, and other information
sources. Contact: The California Technology Project, P.O. Box 3842,
Seal Beach, CA 90740-7842.

- Hyper-G
....
Definition: Hyper-G is a large-scale, multi-user distributed hypermedia
information system. >Hyper-G via WWW: Hyper-G gateway at Graz Univ.
of Technology (http://iicm.tu-graz.ac.at:80/ROOT).

- Hytelnet
....
Definition: Hytelnet provides access to a database of Internet telnet
connects through hypertext (on network or TSR for DOS). >Hytelnet
info/EARN: information and overview of Hytlenet, from European
Academic Research Network Association (EARN)
(http://www.earn.net/gnrt/hytelnet.html).

>Hytelnet source: includes source for PC, Macintosh, Unix, and VMS;
Peter Scott's Hypertext database of publicly accessible Internet sites
(ftp://ftp.usask.ca/pub/hytelnet/).

>Hytelnet via telnet: from the University of Arizona
(telnet://hytelnet@info.ccit.arizona.edu).

>Hytelnet via gopher: from Washington University in St. Louis
(gopher://liberty.uc.wlu.edu/11/internet/hytelnet).

>Hytelnet via WWW: from the University of Kansas
(http://www.cc.ukans.edu/hytelnet_html/START.TXT.html).

>Hytelnet search: given a keyword, returns Hytelnet entries
(gopher://liberty.uc.wlu.edu:3004/7).

>Hytelnet Web search: search all Hytelnet resource entries, via a web
form, from Galaxy (http://galaxy.einet.net/hytelnet/HYTELNET.html).

- Internet-in-a-box
....

Definition: Internet-in-a-box $ gives you graphical user interface access on PCs (standalone or LAN) to news, gopher, mail, telnet, ftp, from O'Reilly/Spry. >Internet-in-a-box: (mailto:info@ibox.com Body: help).

>Internet In a Box web: (http://www.spry.com/intabox.html).

- Minuet

....

Definition: Minuet is graphical interface integrating email, gopher, telnet, Usenet news, and ftp. >Minuet FAQ: Minnesota Internet Users Essential Tool Frequently Asked Questions with Answers (ftp://rtfm.mit.edu/pub/usenet/news.answers/minuet-faq).

- Mosaic

....

Definition: Mosaic is a client for network distributed hypermedia information and discovery. >Mosaic home page: describes Mosaic, Internet information browser and World Wide Web client (http://www.ncsa.uiuc.edu/SDG/Software/Mosaic/NCSAMosaicHome.html).

>Mosaic FAQ:
(http://www.ncsa.uiuc.edu/SDG/Software/Mosaic/Docs/mosaic-faq.html).

>Mosaic: description of how to download and run NCSA Mosaic (ftp://ftp.ncsa.uiuc.edu/Mosaic/README.Mosaic).

>Mosaic paper: NCSA Mosaic Technical Summary, by Marc Andreessen (ftp://ftp.ncsa.uiuc.edu/Mosaic/mosaic-papers/mosaic.ps.Z).

>Mosaic article: an HTML version of a New York Times article about Mosaic by John Markoff (http://www.ugcs.caltech.edu/~kluster/markoff.html).

>Amiga Mosaic: (http://insti.physics.sunysb.edu/AMosaic/home.html).

>Mosaic: bring up Mosaic on system with client installed (unix:mosaic).

- Lynx

....

Definition: Lynx is an ASCII terminal browser for the World Wide Web.

>Lynx info: (ftp://ftp2.cc.ukans.edu/pub/lynx/).

>Lynx Web info: Welcome to Lynx and the world of the web

(http://www.cc.ukans.edu/about_lynx/www_start.html).

- Netscape

....

Definition: Netscape is a WWW browser for MS Windows, Macintosh, and

X. >Netscape Communications: home page of Netscape Communications

Universe, developers of Netscape (http://mosaic.mcom.com).

>Netscape news: information about the free release of Netscape

(http://mosaic.mcom.com/info/index.html).

>Netscape source: FTP site for Netscape source

(ftp://ftp.mcom.com/netscape/).

- Samba

....

Definition: Samba is a Macintosh browser for the World Wide Web.

>Samba source: (ftp://ftp.w3.org/pub/www/bin/mac/).

>Samba Status:

(http://info.cern.ch/hypertext/WWW/Macintosh/Status.html).

- SlipKnot

....

Definition: a Windows-based graphical WWW browser which does NOT

require SLIP or PPP or TCP/IP. Note: restricted shareware >SlipKnot

home page: (http://www.interport.net/slipknot/slipknot.html).

- Viola

....

Definition: Viola is a World Wide Web hypermedia browser for X Window

System. >Viola info: (ftp://ora.com/pub/www/viola/).

- Willow

....

Definition: Willow is a graphical user interface to text-based

bibliographic databases, WWW, and Z39.50. >Willow: Washington

Information Looker-upper Layered Over Windows

(http://www.cac.washington.edu/willow/home.html).

----

* Section -3- CMC = COMPUTER-MEDIATED COMMUNICATION

==

o Interpersonal

~~~~~~

- Email

....

Definition: Email allows a user to send message(s) to another user (or
many users via mailing lists). >Email How: Introduction to Sending
and Receiving Electronic Mail
(ftp://ftp.sura.net/pub/nic/network.service.guides/how.to.email.guide).
>SMTP: Simple Mail Transfer Protocol
(ftp://nic.merit.edu/documents/rfc/rfc0821.txt).
>Email 101: describes how to use email as well as other Internet
features, by John Goodwin
(ftp://mrcnext.cso.uiuc.edu/etext/etext93/email025.txt).
>Finding Email addresses: how do I find someone's email address?
(ftp://sunsite.unc.edu/pub/docs/about-the-net/libsoft/email_address.txt).
>College Email addresses: information on email addresses at colleges
(ftp://rtfm.mit.edu/pub/usenet/soc.college/).
>InterNetwork Mail: methods of sending mail from one network to
another, by John Chew and Scott Yanoff
(ftp://csd4.csd.uwm.edu/pub/internetwork-mail-guide).
>InterNetwork Mail guide via WWW:
(http://alpha.acast.nova.edu/cgi-bin/inmgq.pl).
>Email info: repository of types of email interfaces and tools
(ftp://ftp.uu.net/networking/mail/).
>Email demo: Unix (UCB) mail command (unix:mail user@host.domain).
>Email services: a variety of services offered through an email
account, by Doug Langley; please don't overuse
(mailto:dlangley@netcom.com Subject: "#help").
>POPmail: (ftp://boombox.micro.umn.edu/pub/POPmail/).
>Eudora email: for Mac and Windows (ftp://ftp.qualcomm.com/quest/).
>Eudora info:
(http://wwwhost.cc.utexas.edu/ftp/pub/doc/micro08.html).
>MetaMail: multimedia (ftp://thumper.bellcore.com/pub/nsb/README).
>Hypermail: An EMail to HTML compiler

(http://gummo.stanford.edu/html/hypermail/hypermail.html).

>MIME: Multipurpose Internet Mail Extensions
(http://sodom.mt.cs.cmu.edu/toad-ht/mime.html).

>MIME: Multipurpose Internet Mail Extensions--RFC 1521 and RFC 1522
(http://www.oac.uci.edu/indiv/ehood/MIME/MIME.html).

>Pine info center: links to various Pine help texts, the FAQ, feature
descriptions, discussion archives and the files to download
(http://www.cac.washington.edu/pine/).

>PGP Mail: Pretty Good Privacy, a public key encryption package
(ftp://ftp.uu.net/pub/security/pgp/).

>PGP/PEM: allow you to communicate in a way which does not allow third
parties to read messages, certify that the person who sent the message
is really who they claim they are
(http://hoohoo.ncsa.uiuc.edu/docs/PEMPGP.html).

>PEM: Privacy Enhanced Email (ftp://ftp.tis.com/pub/PEM/FAQ).

>RIPEM: Riordan's Internet Privacy Enhanced Mail
(http://cs.indiana.edu/ripem/dir.html).

- Talk
....
Definition: Talk provides real-time interactive text with another
user. >Talk man page: Unix manual page for talk (unix:man talk).
>Talk demo: where user@host.domain is known (unix:talk
user@host.domain).

- ZTalk
....

Definition: Ztalk provides a low-bandwidth voice communication over
tcp/ip networks. >Ztalk: TCP/IP Voice Communication home page
(http://alfred1.u.washington.edu:8080/~roland/ztalk.html).

>Ztalk source: (ftp://sunsite.unc.edu/pub/Linux/apps/sound/talk/).

o Group
~~~~~~

- Collage
....

Definition: Collage is a client/server group collaboration system which
includes shared dialogue, text, and graphics spaces, from NCSA.
>Collage source: for Mac, PC, and X, from NCSA
(ftp://ftp.ncsa.uiuc.edu/Collage/).
- CU-SeeMe

....
Definition: CU-SeeMe is a real-time, multiparty video-conferencing
system for the Internet. >CU-SeeMe info: includes source code, and
information (FAQ), from Cornell University
(ftp://gated.cornell.edu/pub/video).
>CU-SeeMe use: CU-SeeMe Video conferencing experiments
(http://www.ludvigsen.dhhalden.no/webdoc/video.html).
- Haven

....
Definition: A Haven is a network chat program that allows many people
to talk to each other at once. >Haven info: a repository of
documents, source code, logs and other information
(ftp://kidd.vet.purdue.edu/pub/haven/).
>Haven newsgroup: (news:alt.internet.talk.haven).
- Lily

....
Definition: Lily is a real-time text-based group conferencing system.
>Lily information: ftp site for Lily information, includes
documentation and source code (ftp://lily.acm.rpi.edu/pub/lily).
- Listproc

....
Definition: Listproc is a system that automates mailing lists and
archives. >Listproc info: (mailto:listproc@stormking.com Body: help
listproc).
>Anastasios Kotsikonas: Listproc creator (mailto:tasos@cs.bu.edu).
- LISTSERV

....
Definition: LISTSERV is a mailing-list program for group
communication. >LISTSERV definition: the help file for listserv

(mailto:listserv@uacsc2.albany.edu Body: send listserv memo).

>LISTSERV info/EARN: from European Academic Research Network
Association (EARN) (http://www.earn.net/gnrt/listserv.html).

>LISTSERV tips: (mailto:listserv@bitnic.bitnet Body: get listserv
tips).

>LISTSERV searching: tips on searching a listserv discussion for
information (mailto:listserv@ulkyvm.bitnet Body: get database
search).

>LISTSERV managing: How to Start and Manage a BITNET LISTSERV
Discussion Group, by Kovacs, McCarty, and Kovacs
(mailto:listserv@uhupvm1.uh.edu Body: get kovacs prv2n1).

>LISTSERV tips: List Management Tips for LISTSERV Postmasters and List
Owners, by Lisa M. Covi (mailto:listserv@bitnic.bitnet Body: get
listserv tips).

>LISTSERV guide: The Listserv Guide for General Users
(mailto:listserv@earncc.bitnet Body: get lsvguide memo).

>PAML: Publicly Available Mailing Lists, by Stephanie da Silva
(http://www.neosoft.com/internet/paml).

>Search LISTSERV: search for interesting email lists to join
(http://alpha.acast.nova.edu/cgi-bin/lists).

>Search LISTSERV WAIS: WAIS-based search for a Usenet and LISTSERV
conferences (wais://munin.ub2.lu.se:210/academic_email_conf).

>Search LISTSERV gopher: searching and retrieval of archived LISTSERV
messages
(gopher://dewey.lib.ncsu.edu:70/11/library/disciplines/library/listgopher).

>Dartmouth Merged SIGL: Special Interest Group Lists
(ftp://dartcms1.dartmouth.edu/siglists/).

>Electronic Conferences: Directory of Scholarly Electronic
Conferences, by Diane K. Kovacs (ftp://ksuvxa.kent.edu/library/).

>Search Academic Conferences:
(wais://munin.ub2.lu.se:210/academic_email_conf).

- Majordomo

....

Definition: Majordomo is a mailing list manager. >Majordomo:
(mailto:Majordomo@GreatCircle.COM Body: help).

>Brent Chapman: creator of Majordomo (mailto:brent@greatcircle.com).

>Majordomo Problems: (mailto:Majordomo-Owner@mv.mv.com).

- Maven

....

Definition: Maven is a Mac-based audioconferencing tool. >Maven Info:
a Mac-based audioconferencing tool; powerful when used in conjunction
with, Cornell's CU-SeeMe
(http://pipkin.lut.ac.uk/WWWdocs/LUTCHI/misc/maven.html).

>Maven source: (ftp://k12.cnidr.org/pub/Mac/).

- MU* = Multiple-User Dialogue/Domain/Dungeon

....

Definition: MU*s are real-time interaction systems (usually text)
traditionally used for social role-playing. Note: Variants include
MUD, MUCK, MUSH, MUSE, MOO. Definition: A MOO is an object-oriented
Multiple User Dialogue (MUD). >MU* types: a discussion of differnet
kinds of MU*s, by Eli Burke
(http://csugrad.cs.vt.edu/soc/mud_types.html).

>MUD FAQ: frequently asked questions and answers about MUDs
(ftp://ftp.math.okstate.edu/pub/muds/misc/mud-faq/).

>MUD Archive: documents pertaining to the history of MUDS, by Lauren
P. Burka (http://www.ccs.neu.edu/USER/lpb/muddex.html).

>MUD resources: includes many resources, documentation, general
information, by Lydia Leong
(http://www.cis.upenn.edu/~lwl/mudinfo.html).

>MUD research: includes archives of Notes, Papers (archives from MIT,
MediaMOO, Xerox PARC), and References
(gopher://actlab.rtf.utexas.edu/11/MUD/Research).

>MUD/Lysators: Info about Lysators MUDs, and MUDs in general
(http://www.lysator.liu.se:7500/nobw/mud/main.html).

>MediaMoo: example of a MOO at MIT's Media Lab
(telnet://purple-crayon.media.mit.edu:8888).

>Diversity University: example of MOO used for education
(telnet://erau.db.erau.edu:8888).

>Moo/Web-JHM: Jay's House Moo, a Moo with some Web access and interaction (http://jh.ccs.neu.edu:7043).

>Moo/Web(Mosaic)-WAXWEB: Mosaic users can interact with a Moo (http://bug.village.virginia.edu:7777).

>Moo Gopher blurb: a short description of Moo gopher at Jay's House Moo (ftp://mailbase.ac.uk/pub/lists/unite/files/jays_house.txt).

>Moo info: a collection of MOO information, answers, documentation, paper archives (gopher://actlab.rtf.utexas.edu/11/MUD/MOO).

>Moo papers/Xerox: a collection of information and papers about Moos (ftp://ftp.parc.xerox.com/pub/MOO).

>Moo papers/MIT: information and papers from MIT Lab's MediaMOO (ftp://media.mit.edu/pub/MediaMOO).

>Yahoo List: (http://akebono.stanford.edu/yahoo/Entertainment/Games/MUDs__MUSHes__MUSEs__MOOs__etc_/).

>MUD Announcements: an unmoderated Usenet newsgroup for general announcements related to MU*s (news:rec.games.mud.announce).

>MUD Administration: an unmoderated Usenet newsgroup for MU* administration issues (news:rec.games.mud.admin).

>MUD Miscellaneous: an unmoderated Usenet newsgroup for miscellaneous MU* issues (news:rec.games.mud.misc).

- Procmail
....
Definition: Procmail is a mail manager—create mail-servers, mailing lists, sort your incoming mail. >Procmail source: (ftp://ftp.informatik.rwth-aachen.de/pub/packages/procmail/).

>Procmail mailinglist: (mailto:procmail-request@informatik.rwth-aachen.de).

- WIT = Web Interactive Talk
....
Definition: Web Interactive Talk is a means to create a shared discussion space in hypertext on a number of topics and threads.

>WIT: W3 Interactive Talk, a forms-based discussion system (http://info.cern.ch/hypertext/WWW/WIT/User/Overview.html).

>Example WIT session: an example of a WIT, branching off into many

threads (http://info.cern.ch/hypertext/WWW/Discussion).

- WW = Web World

....

Definition: A Web World is a virtual community enabled by the
interactive HTML Forms (Interactive Webbing, see below). >WebWorld:
an example of a WW--allows users to create structures and link these to
any resource on the Net
(http://sailfish.peregrine.com/ww/welcome.html).

- Yarn

....

Definition: Yarn is a text-based networked meeting system. >Yarn web:
Yarn User Manual (http://dstc.bond.edu.au:91776/YarnMan.html).

o Mass

~~~~~~

- ICB = Internet Citizen's Band

....

Definition: ICB is an internet teleconferencing application which
allows Internet users to communicate. >ICB web: information about ICB
(http://www.echo.com/~kzin/icb.html).
>ICB FAQ: (mailto:majordomo@majordomo.bbn.com Body: get icb-social
ICB-FAQ).

- IW = Interactive Webbing

....

Definition: Interactive Webbing gives people a common space for network
distributed multimedia writing. >Free For All: an example of
IW—allows user to place an entry in a list of WWW entries (not known
to be operational 19 Aug 94)
(http://south.ncsa.uiuc.edu:8241/Free.html).
>Related Projects: some other WWW projects that let readers see
feedback from others
(http://union.ncsa.uiuc.edu/HyperNews/get/hypernews/related.html).
>Ping: a global communication experiment in multimedia created by
users (http://www.artcom.de/ping/mapper).

- IRC = Internet Relay Chat

....

Definition: IRC provides real-time, many-many text discussion divided
into channels. >IRC definition: Internet Relay Chat Protocol, by
Oikarinen and Reed (ftp://nic.merit.edu/documents/rfc/rfc1459.txt).
>IRC Web: includes an overview, client/server pointers, and general
information, by Helen Trillian Rose (http://www.kei.com/irc.html).
>IRC info: includes frequently asked questions and answers list from
newsgroup, IRCprimers, tutorials
(ftp://cs.bu.edu/irc/support/alt-irc-faq).
>IRC sources/Larsson: IRC related documents and other sources of
information, by Jonas Larsson
(http://eru.dd.chalmers.se/home/f88jl/Irc/ircdocs.html).
>IRC Library: pointers to IRC-rleated information, picture database,
archives, etc., by Nicolas, Pioch
(http://mistral.enst.fr/~pioch/IRC/IRC.html).
>IRC guide: Basic Guide to IRC
(ftp://dorm.rutgers.edu/pub/Internet.documents/irc.basic.guide).
>IRC connections: some example IRC sites available via telnet (if you
don't have an IRC client yet)
(http://alpha.acast.nova.edu/irc/connect.html).
>IRC discussion: an unmoderated Usenet discussion about IRC
(news:alt.irc).
>IRC recovery: an umoderated Usenet discussion group about weaning
oneself off of IRC (news:alt.irc.recovery).
- ITR = Internet Talk Radio
....
Definition: ITR is an audio multicast on the Internet. >ITR FAQ:
Frequently Asked Questions on ITR (Usenet FAQ)
(ftp://rftm.mit.edu/pub/usenet/news.answers/internet-talk-radio/).
>ITR FAQ via email: Frequently Asked Questions on ITR
(mailto:info@radio.com).
>ITR ftp site: Internet Talk Radio information, including intro and
FAQ (ftp://sunsite.unc.edu/pub/talk-radio/).
>ITR Web: general information, and connections to broadcast archives
(http://www.ncsa.uiuc.edu/radio/radio.html).
>ITR sites: a partial listing of places to download ITR information

and broadcasts (mailto:sites@radio.com).

>ITR discussion: an unmoderated Usenet discussion group about ITR
(news:alt.internet.talk-radio).

- Mbone
....

Definition: Mbone is a live audio and video multicast virtual network
on top of Internet. >MBONE Home Page:
(http://www.eit.com/techinfo/mbone/mbone.html).

>Mbone FAQ (text): Virtual Internet Backbone for Multicast IP
(ftp://venera.isi.edu/mbone/faq.txt).

>Mbone FAQ Web: Frequently Asked Questions (FAQ) on the Multicast
Backbone (MBONE) (http://www.research.att.com/mbone-faq.html).

>Mbone Tools: lists suite of tools used with Mbone
(http://www.eit.com/techinfo/mbone/mbone.html).

>Mbone Intro: (http://www.cs.ucl.ac.uk/mice/mbone_review.html).

- Usenet
....

Definition: USENET provides asynchronous text discussion on many topics
separated into newsgroups. >USENET description: What is Usenet?
(ftp://rtfm.mit.edu/pub/usenet/news.answers/what-is-usenet/).

>USENET FAQs: collection of frequently answer questions and answers
about Usenet (ftp://rtfm.mit.edu/pub/usenet/news.announce.newusers/).

>Usenet guide: An Introduction to Usenet News and the trn Newsreader,
by Jon Bell (http://ocf.berkeley.edu/pub/trnint-3.3.html).

>USENET info/EARN: from European Academic Research Network Association
(EARN) (http://www.earn.net/gnrt/usenet.html).

>USENET documentation: special issue of Amateur Computerist Newsletter
about Usenet (ftp://wuarchive.wustl.edu/doc/misc/acn/acn4-5.txt.Z).

>NNTP: Network News Transfer Protocol, by Kantor and Lapsley (February
1986) (ftp://nic.merit.edu/documents/rfc/rfc0977.txt).

>Usenet FAQs/rtfm: news.groups FAQ directory
(ftp://rtfm.mit.edu/pub/usenet/news.groups/).

>Usenet FAQs/hyper: a hypertext list of all USENET FAQs found in
news.answers

(http://www.cis.ohio-state.edu/hypertext/faq/usenet/FAQ-List.html).
>Usenet filter: personalized netnews delivery service
(http://woodstock.stanford.edu:2000).
>Usenet filter: personalized netnews delivery service
(mailto:netnews@db.stanford.edu Body: help).
>Usenet post via email: post to newsgroup via email
(mailto:hierarchy-group-name@cs.utexas.edu Subject: Your Subject
Body: Your Contents).
>Usenet via WWW: access newsgroups via WWW
(http://info.cern.ch/hypertext/DataSources/News/Groups/Overview.html).
>Usenet connections: publicly accessible news servers, including
gopher access to Usenet, by Arnold Lesikar (list removed; however,
instructions are given on how to locate these)
(gopher://tigger.stcloud.msus.edu:79/0lesikar).
>Usenet periodics: list of Usenet periodic postings
(gopher://stavanger.sgp.slb.com:79/0nichol).
>Usenet posters: find when and from what host person with name FIRST
LAST posted to Usenet (mailto:mail-server@rtfm.MIT.EDU Body: send
usenet-addresses/FIRST LAST).
>Discussion Beginners: for people new to USENET
(news:news.announce.newusers).
>Discussion humor: an unmoderated Usenet discussion group about
humorous Usenet posts (news:alt.humor.best-of-usenet).
>Discussion culture: an unmoderated Usenet discussion group about
Usenet practices, people, issues (news:alt.culture.usenet).
>Usenet reader: nn, xrn)mand for hosts with newsreader, rn (other
readers (unix:rn newsgroup-name).
o Interfaces
~~~~~~
- exMOO
....
Definition: exMOO is a graphical user interface to a MU* >ExMOO Home
Page: (http://www.dl.ac.uk/CBMT/exMOO/HOME.html).
- htMUD
....

Definition: htMUD is a distributed graphical tinymud combining telnet
and web forms client windows.   >htMUD Home Page:
(http://www.elf.com/~phi/htmud.html).

----

* Section -4- STANDARDS

==

Protocols and standards are the basis for operating tools and forums on
the Internet. In this section, I summarize some sources of information
about Internet and other protocols. Protocols associated with
individual tools are listed with the tools above.

o Collections

~~~~~~

>ASN.1: resources for the ASN.1 language, by Philipp Hoschka
(http://zenon.inria.fr:8003/rodeo/personnel/hoschka/hoschka.html).

>Internet Protocols/NRL: listings of working groups and information
about protocols--applications, internet, next generation, network
management, operational requirements, routing, security, and much more,
from Naval Research Lab
(http://netlab.itd.nrl.navy.mil/Internet.html).

>Internet STDs: Internet Standards, sub-series of notes within the RFC
series which document Internet standards
(ftp://nic.merit.edu/documents/std/).

>MM Survey List: Distributed Multimedia Survey Standards List,
includes CCITT/ISO, Internet, Proprietary
(http://cui_www.unige.ch/OSG/MultimediaInfo/mmsurvey/standards.html).

>Organizations: players in setting technical standards for
telecommunications and networking
(http://www.rpi.edu/Internet/Guides/decemj/icmc/organizations-standards.html).

>Protocols: Computers-Software-Protocols category from Yahoo
(http://akebono.stanford.edu/yahoo/Computers/Software/Protocols/).

>Standards List/LLNL: Documentation from Lawrence Livermore National
Laboratory (http://www-atp.llnl.gov/atp/standards.html).

o Internet

~~~~~~

>HTTP: a protocol for networked information
(http://info.cern.ch/hypertext/WWW/Protocols/HTTP/HTTP2.html).
>IP: Internet Protocol
(ftp://nic.merit.edu/documents/rfc/rfc0791.txt).
>Kerberos: network authentication system for physically insecure
networks (ftp://rtfm.mit.edu/pub/usenet/comp.protocols.kerberos/).
>NFS: Network File System will mount remote file systems across
homogeneous and heterogeneous systems
(ftp://rtfm.mit.edu/pub/usenet/comp.protocols.nfs/).
>PC-MAC TCP/IP + NFS FAQ: by Rawn Shah
(ftp://ftp.rtd.com/pub/tcpip/pcnfsfaq.txt).
>PC-MAC TCP/IP + NFS FAQ WWW: by Rawn Shah
(ftp://www.rtd.com/pcnfsfaq/faq.html).
>PC-NFS: (ftp://ftp.york.ac.uk/pub/pc/pc-nfs/FAQ/).
>PPP: Internet Standard for transmission of IP packets over serial
lines (ftp://rtfm.mit.edu/pub/usenet/comp.protocols.ppp/).
>PPP FAQ: comp.protocols.ppp frequently wanted information
(http://cs.uni-bonn.de/ppp/faq.html).
>SIPP: Simple Internet Protocol Plus (SIPP) is one of the candidates
being considered by the Internet Engineering Task Force (IETF) for the
next version of the Internet Protocol
(http://town.hall.org/sipp/sipp-main.html).
>SLIP: Serial Line Internet Protocol
(ftp://vtucs.cc.vt.edu/filebox/nyman/whatslip.txt).
>SNMP FAQ: Simple Network Management Protocol Usenet FAQ
(ftp://rtfm.mit.edu/pub/usenet/comp.protocols.snmp/).
>SNMP Web: the SNMP project group at the University of Twente (the
Netherlands), develops a freely-available implementation of SNMP
(http://snmp.cs.utwente.nl).
>SOCKS: A proxy server for IP hosts behind firewalls
(ftp://ftp.nec.com/pub/security/socks.cstc/What_Is_SOCKS.CSTC).
>TCP: Transmission Control Protocol
(ftp://nic.merit.edu/documents/rfc/rfc0793.txt).
>TCP-IP FAQ: (ftp://rtfm.mit.edu/pub/usenet/comp.protocols.tcp-ip/).

>Winsock: accessing the Internet using tcp/ip applications under
Microsoft Windows
(ftp://nebula.lib.vt.edu/pub/windows/winsock/wtcpip03.asc).
>Winsock FAQ: (mailto:lcsinfo@id1.indirect.com Subject: faq).
o Other
~~~~~~
>ACC: anonymous credit card (ACC) protocol, used for anonymous funds
xfer and delivery on the Internet
(ftp://research.att.com/dist/anoncc/accinet.ps.Z).
>EPIC: Effects Protocol for Interactive Communications, a proposal
designed to provide enhanced formatting, display control for
interaction interactive internet communications
(http://netcom7.netcom.com/pub/stewarta/html/stewarta.html).
>HTML FAQ: hypertext markup language
(http://www.umcc.umich.edu/~ec/www/html_faq.html).
>HTML+: (http://info.cern.ch/pub/www/dev/htmlplus.dtd).
>ISO Protocols: newsgroup (news:comp.protocols.iso).
>ISO FAQ: (ftp://rtfm.mit.edu/pub/usenet/comp.protocols.iso/).
>OSI: Open Systems Interconnection protocols
(ftp://rftm.mit.edu/pub/usenet/news.answers/osi-protocols).
>OSI/GOSIP Protocols: (http://netlab.itd.nrl.navy.mil/GOSIP.html).
>Other Protocols: XTP, HIPPI, Fibre Channel
(http://netlab.itd.nrl.navy.mil/OP.html).
>Telecom stds: International Standards for telecommunication
(ftp://rftm.mit.edu/pub/usenet/news.answers/standards-faq).
>Unicode: a Character Encoding Standard, a 16-bit set to encode all of
the characters used for written languages throughout the world
(ftp://ftp.u.washington.edu/pub/user-supported/reader/text/standards/unicode/unicode.std.z).
>URI/URL/URN/URC: Addressing for the WWW
(http://info.cern.ch/hypertext/WWW/Addressing/Addressing.html).
>URL guide: A Beginner's Guide to URLs
(http://www.ncsa.uiuc.edu/demoweb/url-primer.html).
>URL syntax: Uniform Resource Locator Syntax
(http://info.cern.ch/hypertext/WWW/Addressing/URL/5_BNF.html).

>X.400: a set of ISO/CCITT standards that defines electronic mail, the
only non-proprietary standard for interchange of electronic mail that
has the sanction of an official standards body
(ftp://ftp.u.washington.edu/pub/user-supported/reader/text/standards/X.400/).
>Z39.50 W3 Page: (http://www.vtls.com/market/z39/z39page.html).
>Z39.50 Resources: a reference point for resources related to the
Information Retrieval Service and Protocol standard, ANSI/NISO Z39.50
(http://ds.internic.net/z3950/z3950.html).
----

* Section -5- REFERENCES

==
>Internet Tools EARN: The Guide to Network Resource Tools, from
European Academic Research Network Association (EARN)
(ftp://ns.ripe.net/earn/earn-resource-tool-guide.txt).
>Internet Tools EARN/WWW: The Guide to Network Resource Tools, from
European Academic Research Network Association (EARN)
(http://www.earn.net/gnrt/notice.html).
>Internet Tools NIR: A status report on networked information
retrieval tools and groups
(ftp://nic.merit.edu/documents/fyi/fyi_25.txt).
>Internet Systems UNITE:
(ftp://mailbase.ac.uk/pub/lists/unite/files/systems-list.txt).
>Net Mgt Tools: Tools for Monitoring and Debugging TCP/IP Internets
and Interconnected Devices
(ftp://nic.merit.edu/documents/fyi/fyi_02.txt).

GLOSSARY

:-)—This odd symbol is one of the ways to portray mood in the very flat medium of computers. This is metacommunication, and there are literally hundreds of such symbols, from the obvious to the obscure. This particular example, the "smileyface," expresses happiness. Don't see it? Tilt your head to the left 90 degrees. Smiles are also used to denote sarcasm.

abstract syntax—A description of a data structure that is independent of machine-oriented structures and encodings.

Abstract Syntax Notation One (ASN.1)—The language used by the OSI protocols for describing abstract syntax. This language is also used to encode SNMP packets. ASN.1 is defined in ISO documents 8824.2 and 8825.2. See also: *Basic Encoding Rules*.

acceptable risk—In *risk analysis*, an assessment that an activity or system meets minimum requirements of security directives.

acceptable use policy (AUP)—Many transit networks have policies that restrict the use to which the network may be put. A well known example is NSFNET's AUP, which does not allow commercial use. Enforcement of AUPs varies with the network.

access—(1) In data processing, interaction between a subject and an object that allows information to flow from one to the other; (2) in physical security, the ability to enter a secured building area.

access authorization—Granting permission to an object (i.e., person, terminal, program) to execute a set of operations in the system. Generally, a profile matrix grants access privileges to users, terminals, programs, data elements; type of access (e.g., read, write); and time period.

access control—In a network or its components; the tasks performed by hardware, software, and administrative controls to monitor a system operation, ensure data integrity, perform user identification, record system access and changes, and grant access to users.

access control list (ACL)—Most network security systems operate by allowing selective use of services. An access control list is the usual means by which access to, and denial of, services is controlled. It is simply a list of the services available, each with a list of the hosts permitted to use the service.

access method—A software routine accessible by the network control program that performs the transmitting/receiving of data and may include error detection and correction mechanisms. See also: *medium access control.*

ACK—See: *acknowledgment.*

acknowledgment (ACK)—A type of message sent to indicate that a block of data arrived at its destination without error.

ACL—See: *access control list.*

active threat—Unauthorized use of a device attached to a communications facility to alter transmitting data or control signals; or to generate spurious data or control signals.

AD—See: *administrative domain.*

address—There are three types of addresses in common use within the Internet: email address; IP, internet or Internet address; and hardware or MAC address. See also: *IP address.*

address mask—A bit mask used to identify which bits in an IP address correspond to the network and subnet portions of the address. This mask is often referred to as the subnet mask because the network portion of the address can be determined by the encoding inherent in an IP address.

address resolution—Conversion of an internet address into the corresponding physical address.

Address Resolution Protocol (ARP)—Used to dynamically discover the low-level physical network hardware address that corresponds to the high-level IP address for a given host. ARP is limited to physical network systems that support broadcast packets that can be heard by all hosts on the network. It is defined in RFC 826.

administrative domain (AD)—A collection of hosts and routers, and the interconnecting network(s), managed by a single administrative authority.

Advanced Research Projects Agency Network (ARPANET)—A pioneering longhaul network funded by ARPA (now DARPA). It served as the basis for early networking research, as well as a central backbone during the development of the Internet. The ARPANET consisted of individual packet switching computers interconnected by leased lines. [Source: FYI4]

agent—In the client-server model, the part of the system that performs information preparation and exchange on behalf of a client or server application.

alias—A name, usually short and easy to remember, that is translated into another name, usually long and difficult to remember.

American National Standards Institute (ANSI)—This organization is responsible for approving U.S. standards in many areas, including computers and communications. Standards approved by this organization are often called ANSI standards (e.g., ANSI C is the version of the C language approved by ANSI). ANSI is a member of ISO. See also: *International Organization for Standardization.*

American Standard Code for Information Interchange (ASCII)—A standard character-to-number encoding widely used in the computer industry.

amplifier—In a broadband system, a device for strengthening the radio frequency signal to a level needed by other devices on the system.

anonymous FTP (File Transfer Protocol)—The procedure of connecting to a remote computer, as an anonymous or guest user, in order to transfer public files back to your local computer. (See also: *FTP* and *protocol*). Anonymous FTP allows a user to retrieve documents, files, programs, and other archived data from anywhere in the Internet without having to establish a user ID and password. By using the special user ID of "anonymous" the network user will bypass local security checks and will have access to publicly accessible files on the remote system. See also: *archive site, File Transfer Protocol.*

ANSI—See: *American National Standards Institute.*

answer modem—See: *modem.*

API—See: *Application Program Interface.*

Appletalk—A networking protocol developed by Apple Computer for communication between Apple Computer products and other computers. This protocol is independent of the network layer on which it is run. Current implementations exist for Localtalk, a 235 Kbps local area network; and Ethertalk, a 10 Mbps local area network.

application—A program that performs a function directly for a user. FTP, mail, and TELNET clients are examples of network applications.

application layer—The top layer of the network protocol stack. The application layer is concerned with the semantics of work (e.g., formatting electronic mail messages). How to represent that data and how to reach the foreign node are issues for lower layers of the network.

Application Program Interface (API)—A set of calling conventions that define how a service is invoked through a software package.

archie—A system to automatically gather, index, and serve information on the Internet. The initial implementation of archie provided an indexed directory of filenames from all anonymous FTP archives on the Internet. Later versions provide other collections of information. See also: *archive site, wide area network*.

archive site—A machine that provides access to a collection of files across the Internet. An "anonymous FTP archive site," for example, provides access to this material via the FTP protocol. See also: *anonymous FTP, archie*.

ARP—See: *Address Resolution Protocol*.

ARPA—See: *Advanced Research Projects Agency Network*.

ARPANET—See: *Advanced Research Projects Agency Network*.

AS—See: *Autonomous System*.

ASCII—See: *American Standard Code for Information Interchange*.

ASN.1—See: *Abstract Syntax Notation One*.

assigned numbers—The RFC [STD2] that documents the currently assigned values from several series of numbers used in network protocol implementations. This RFC is updated periodically and, in any case, current information can be obtained from the Internet Assigned Numbers Authority (IANA). If you are developing a protocol or application that will require the use of a link, socket, port, protocol, etc., please contact the IANA to receive a number assignment.

Asynchronous Transfer Mode (ATM)—A method for the dynamic allocation of bandwidth using a fixed-size packet (called a cell). ATM is also known as "fast packet."

ASCII—American (National) Standard Code for Information Interchange, X3.4-1968. A seven-bit-plus parity code established by the American National Standards Institute to achieve compatibility among data services and consisting of 96 displayed upper- and lowercase characters and 32 nondisplayed control codes.

asymmetric encryption—See *public key cryptosystem*.

asynchronous transmission—A mode of data communications transmission in which time intervals between transmitted characters may be of unequal length. The transmission is controlled by start and stop elements at the beginning and end of each character; hence it is also called start-stop transmission.

ATM—See: *Asynchronous Transfer Mode*.

attachment unit interface (AUI)—The cable, connectors, and transmission circuitry used to interconnect the physical signaling (PLS) sublayer and MAU.

audit of computer security—As defined by NBS (now NIST) Special Publication 500-57, an independent evaluation of the controls employed to ensure:

1. The appropriate protection of the organization's information assets (including hardware, software, firmware, and data) from all significant anticipated threats or hazards.

2. The accuracy and reliability of the data maintained on or generated by an automated data-processing system.

3. The operational reliability and performance assurance for accuracy and timeliness of all components of the automated data-processing system.

An examination of data security procedures and measures for the purpose of evaluating their adequacy and compliance with established policy.

AUP—See: *Acceptable Use Policy*.

authentication—(1) ensuring that a message is genuine, has arrived exactly as it was sent, and came from the stated source; (2) verifying the identity of an individual, such as a person at a remote terminal or the sender of a message. In OSI nomenclature, authentication refers to the certainty that the data received comes from the supposed origin; it is not extended to include the integrity of the data being transmitted. (See also: *peer-entity authentication*.) Protection against fraudulent transactions by establishing the validity of messages, stations, individuals or originators.

Autonomous System (AS)—A collection of routers under a single administrative authority using a common Interior Gateway Protocol for routing packets.

availability—That aspect of security that deals with the timely delivery of information and services to the user. An attack on availability would seek to sever network connections, or tie up accounts or systems.

backbone—The top level in a hierarchical network. Stub and transit networks that connect to the same backbone are guaranteed to be interconnected.

back door—A feature built into a program by its designer, which allows the designer special privileges that are denied to the normal users of the program. A back door in a logon program, for instance, could enable the designer to log onto a system, even though he or she did not have an authorized account on that system.

bacterium (informal)—A program that, when executed, spreads to other users and systems by sending copies of itself; since it infects other programs, it may be thought of as a system virus as opposed to a program virus. It differs from a *rabbit* in that it is not necessarily designed to exhaust system resources.

bandwidth—The range of frequencies assigned to a channel or system. The difference, expressed in Hertz, between the highest and lowest frequencies of a band. As typically used, the amount of data that can be sent through a given communications circuit.

bang—An exclamation point (!) used to separate machine names in an extended UUCP path. See also: *bang path*.

bang path—A series of machine names used to direct electronic mail from one user to another, typically by specifying an explicit UUCP path through which the mail is to be routed. See also: *Unix-to-Unix CoPy*.

baseband (signaling)—Transmission of a signal at its original frequencies, i.e., unmodulated. A transmission medium through which digital signals are sent without complicated frequency shifting. In general, only one communication channel is available at any given time. Ethernet is an example of a baseband network. See also: *broadband, Ethernet*.

Basic Encoding Rules (BER)—Standard rules for encoding data units described in ASN.1. Sometimes incorrectly lumped under the term ASN.1, which properly refers only to the abstract syntax description language, not the encoding technique. See also: *Abstract Syntax Notation One*.

batch—A group of records or programs that is considered a single unit for processing on a computer.

batch processing—A technique in which a number of data transactions are collected over a period of time and aggregated for sequential processing.

baud—A unit of transmission speed equal to the number of discrete conditions or signal events per second. Baud is the same as "bits per second" only if each signal event represents exactly one bit, although the two terms are often incorrectly used interchangeably.

BBS—See: *bulletin board system*.

BCNU—Be Seein' You.

BER—See: *Basic Encoding Rules*.

Berkeley Internet Name Domain (BIND)—Implementation of a DNS server developed and distributed by the University of California at Berkeley. Many Internet hosts run BIND, and it is the ancestor of many commercial BIND implementations.

Berkeley Software Distribution (BSD)—Implementation of the Unix operating system and its utilities developed and distributed by the University of California at Berkeley. "BSD" is usually preceded by the version number of the distribution, e.g., "4.3 BSD" is version 4.3 of the Berkeley Unix distribution. Many Internet hosts run BSD software, and it is the ancestor of many commercial Unix implementations.

BGP—See: *Border Gateway Protocol.*

big-endian—A format for storage or transmission of binary data in which the most significant bit (or byte) comes first. The term comes from *Gulliver's Travels* by Jonathan Swift. The Lilliputians, being very small, had correspondingly small political problems. The Big-Endian and Little-Endian parties debated over whether soft-boiled eggs should be opened at the big end or the little end.

BIND—See: *Berkeley Internet Name Domain.*

Birds of a Feather (BOF)—Birds of a Feather (flocking together) is an informal discussion group. It is formed, often ad hoc, to consider a specific issue and, therefore, has a narrow focus.

bisynchronous transmission—Binary synchronous (bisync) transmission. Data transmission in which synchronization of characters is controlled by timing signals generated at the sending and receiving stations, in contrast to *asynchronous transmission.*

BITNET—A cooperative computer network interconnecting over 2,300 academic and research institutions in 32 countries. Originally based on IBM's RSCS networking protocol, BITNET supports mail, mailing lists, and file transfer. Now merged with CSNET and running the RSCS protocol over TCP/IP protocol (BITNET II), the network will be called Computer Research and Education Network (CREN). An academic computer network that provides interactive electronic mail and file transfer services, using a store-and-forward protocol, based on IBM Network Job Entry protocols. BITNET II encapsulates the BITNET protocol within IP packets and depends on the Internet to route them.

bit-mapped graphics—A method of representing data in a computer for display in which each dot on the screen is mapped to a unit of data in memory.

bit rate—The data throughput on the trunk coaxial medium expressed in Hertz.

block—A group of digits, characters, or words that are held in one section of an input/output medium and handled as a unit, such as the data recorded between two interblock gaps on a magnetic tape or a data unit being transmitted over a data communications system; a block may or may not contain control information. A group of *N*-ary digits, transmitted as unit. An encoding procedure is generally applied to the group of bits or *N*-ary digits for error-control purposes.

BNC-connector—A bayonet-type coaxial cable connector of the kind commonly found on RF equipment.

BOF—See: *Birds of a Feather*.

BOOTP—Bootstrap Protocol, described in RFCs 951 and 1084, used for booting diskless nodes.

Border Gateway Protocol (BGP)—The Border Gateway Protocol is an exterior gateway protocol defined in RFCs 1267 and 1268. Its design is based on experience gained with EGP, as defined in STD 18, RFC 904, and EGP usage in the NSFNET backbone, as described in RFCs 1092 and 1093.

bounce—The return of a piece of mail because of an error in its delivery. [Source: ZEN]

bps (bits per second)—See: *baud*.

branch cable—The AUI cable interconnecting the data terminal equipment (DTE) and MAU system components.

bridge—The hardware and software necessary for two networks using the same or similar technology to communicate; more specifically the hardware and software necessary to link segments of the same or similar networks at the data link layer of the OSI reference model, i.e., a MAC level bridge; a router that connects two or more networks and forwards packets among them. Usually, bridges operate at the physical network level. Bridges differ from repeaters because bridges store and forward complete packets while repeaters forward electrical signals. A device that forwards traffic between network segments based on data link layer information. These segments would have a common network layer address. See also: *gateway, router*.

broadband—A communications channel having a bandwidth characterized by high data transmission speeds (10,000 to 500,000 bits per second). Often used when describing communications systems based on cable television technology. In the 802 standards, a system whereby information is encoded, modulated onto a carrier, and band-pass filtered or otherwise constrained to occupy only a limited frequency spectrum on the coaxial transmission medium. Many information signals can be present on the medium at the same time without disruption provided that they all occupy nonoverlapping frequency regions within the cable system's range of frequency transport. A transmission medium capable of supporting a wide range of frequencies. It can carry multiple signals by dividing the total capacity of the medium into multiple, independent bandwidth channels, where each channel operates only on a specific range of frequencies. See also: *baseband*.

broadcast—A special type of multicast packet that all nodes on the network are always willing to receive.

broadcast storm—An incorrect packet broadcast onto a network that causes multiple hosts to respond all at once, typically with equally incorrect packets, which causes the storm to grow exponentially in severity.

brouter—A device that bridges some packets (i.e., forwards based on data link layer information) and routes other packets (i.e., forwards based on network layer information). The bridge/route decision is based on configuration information. See also: *bridge, router.*

BSD—See: *Berkeley Software Distribution.*

BTW—By the Way.

bug—An error in the design or implementation of a program that causes it to do something that neither the user nor the program author had intended to be done.

Bulletin Board System (BBS)—A computer, and associated software, which typically provides electronic messaging services, archives of files, and any other services or activities of interest to the bulletin board system's operator. Although BBSs have traditionally been the domain of hobbyists, an increasing number of BBSs are connected directly to the Internet, and many are currently operated by government, educational, and research institutions. See also: *electronic mail, Internet, Usenet.*

bus—The organization of electrical paths within a circuit. A specific bus, such as the S-100, provides a standard definition for specific paths.

carrier sense—The signal provided by the physical layer to the access sublayer to indicate that one or more stations are currently transmitting on the trunk cable.

CATV—Community Antenna Television. See: *broadband.*

CCITT—Consultative Committee International Telegraph and Telephone. An organization established by the United Nations to develop worldwide standards for communications technology as, for example, *protocols* to be used by devices exchanging data.

central processing unit—See: *CPU.*

centralized network—A computer network with a central processing node through which all data and communications flow.

Centronics—A manufacturer of computer printers. Centronics pioneered the use of a parallel interface between printers and computers and that interface, using Centronic standards, is sometimes referred to as a Centronics parallel interface.

character user interface (CUI)—Classical character-based system for computer/human communications.

checksum—A fixed-length block produced as a function of every bit in an encrypted message; a summation of a set of data items for error detection; a sum of digits or bits used to verify the integrity of data.

cipher—An algorithm for disguising information according to a logical principle by working within the elements of whatever alphabet is in use, such as by shift-substitution of the letters of the alphabet by other letters a certain number of places toward the beginning or end of the alphabet. Not to be confused with a *code*.

ciphertext—Encrypted text that cannot be read without decryption; data are cryptologically protected; the opposite of *plaintext* or cleartext.

client-server—The model of interaction in a distributed system in which a program at one site sends a request to a program at another site and awaits a response. The requesting program is called a client; the program satisfying the request is called the server. It is usually easier to build client software than server software.

Client-Server Interface—A program that provides an interface to remote programs (called clients), most commonly across a network, in order to provide these clients with access to some service such as databases, printing, etc. In general, the clients act on behalf of a human end-user (perhaps indirectly).

code—A technique by which the basic elements of language, such as syllables, words, phrases, sentences, and paragraphs, are disguised through being replaced by other, usually shorter, arbitrarily selected language elements, requiring a codebook (table) for translation. A term not generally used in relation to encryption. Not to be confused with *cipher*.

cold-site—DP hardware-ready room, or series of rooms, that is ready to receive hardware for disaster recovery. See also: *hot-site* and *warm-site*.

collision—Multiple concurrent transmission on the cable resulting in garbled data.

command languages—Software in which commands are typed in, rather than selected from, a set displayed on the screen.

communications—See: *data communications*. Transmission of intelligence between points of origin and reception without alteration of sequence or structure of the information content.

communications network—The total network of devices and transmission media (radio, cables, etc.) necessary to transmit and receive intelligence.

communications security (COMSEC)—The protection resulting from the application of cryptosecurity, transmission security, and emission security measures to telecommunications and from the application of physical security measure to communications security information. These measures are taken to deny unauthorized persons information of value that might be derived from the possession and study of telecommunications. COMSEC includes: (1) cryptosecurity; (2) transmission security; (3) emission security; and (4) physical security of communications security materials and information. (a) Cryptosecurity: the component of communications security that results from the provision of technically sound cryptosystems and their proper use. (b) Transmission security: the component of communications security that results from all measures designed to protect transmissions from interception and exploitation by means other than cryptanalysis. (c) Emission security: the component of communications security that results from all measures taken to deny unauthorized persons information of value that might be derived from intercept and analysis of compromising emanations from cryptoequipment and telecommunications systems. (d) Physical security: the component of communications security that results from all physical measures necessary to safeguard classified equipment, material, and documents from access thereto or observation thereof by unauthorized persons.

communications security (COMSEC) equipment—Equipment designed to provide security to telecommunications by converting information to a form unintelligible to an unauthorized interceptor and by reconverting such information to its original form for authorized recipients, as well as equipment designed specifically to aid in, or as an essential element of, the conversion process. COMSEC equipment is cryptoequipment, cryptoancillary equipment, cryptoproduction equipment, and authentication equipment.

computer conferencing—A process for holding group discussions through the use of a computer network.

computer network—One or more computers linked with users or each other via a communications network.

computer security—The technological safeguards and managerial procedures that can be applied to computer hardware, programs, data, and facilities to ensure the availability, integrity, and confidentiality of computer-based resources. It also can ensure that intended functions are performed as planned.

confidentiality—The property that information is not made available or disclosed to unauthorized individuals, entities, or processes; an attack on confidentiality would seek to view databases, print files, discover a password, etc., to which the attacker was not entitled.

connectionless applications—Those applications that require routing services but do not require connection-oriented services.

connectionless service—A class of service that does not establish a virtual or logical connection and does not guarantee that data-units will be delivered or be delivered in the proper order. Connectionless services are flexible, robust, and provide connectionless application support.

connection-oriented services—Services that establish a virtual connection that appears to the user as an actual end-to-end circuit. Sometimes called a virtual circuit or virtual connection. See also: *virtual circuit*.

connectivity—In a local area network, the ability of any device attached to the distribution system to establish a session with any other device.

CP/M—Control Program for Microcomputers. Manufactured and marketed by Digital Research, Inc.

CPU—Central Processing Unit. The brain of the general-purpose computer that controls the interpretation and execution of instructions. The CPU does not include interfaces, main memory, or peripherals.

CREN—Computer Research and Education Network is the new name for the merged computer networks, BITNET and Computer Science Network (CSNET). It supports electronic mail and file transfer.

cryptochannel—A complete system of cryptocommunications between two or more holders. The basic unit for naval cryptographic communication. It includes: (a) the cryptographic aids prescribed; (b) the holders thereof; (c) the indicators or other means of identification; (d) the area or areas in which effective; (e) the special purpose, if any, for which provided; and (f) pertinent notes as to distribution, usage, etc. A cryptochannel is analogous to a radio circuit.

cryptogram—The ciphertext.

cryptography—The branch of cryptology devoted to creating appropriate algorithms.

crypto-information—Information that would make a significant contribution to the cryptanalytic solution of encrypted text or a cryptosystem.

cryptology—The science that treats of hidden, disguised, or encrypted communications. It embraces communications security and communications intelligence. The art of creating and breaking ciphers.

cryptomaterial—All material, including documents, devices, or equipment that contains cryptoinformation and is essential to the encryption, decryption, or authentication of telecommunications.

CSMA/CD—Carrier Sense Multiple Access with Collision Detection. A network access method for managing collisions of data packets.

CTS/RTS (clear to send)/(request to send)—RS-232 signals sent from the receiving station to the transmitting station that indicates it is ready to accept (CTS) or send (RTS) data. Typically, a means of hardware flow control. See also: *flow control*. Contrast with *xon/xoff*.

CUI—See: *character user interface*.

cursor—A position indicator frequently employed in video (CRT or VDT) output devices or terminals to indicate a character to be corrected or a position in which data are to be entered.

cyclic redundancy check (CRC)—An algorithm designed to generate a check field used to guard against errors that may occur in data transmission; the check field is often generated by taking the remainder after dividing all the serialized bits in a block of data by a predetermined binary number.

daemon—A Unix program that is invisible to users but provides important system services. Daemons manage everything from paging to networking to notification of incoming mail. BSD Unix has many different daemons—perhaps two dozen. Daemons normally spend most of their time sleeping or waiting for something to do, so that they do not account for a lot of CPU load.

database—A nonredundant collection of interrelated data items processable by one or more applications.

data communications—The transmission and reception of data, often including operations such as coding, decoding, and validation.

data encryption standard (DES)—An algorithm to be implemented in electronic hardware devices and used for the cryptographic protection of digital, binary-coded information. For the relevant publications see "Data encryption standard," *Federal Information Processing Standard (FIPS) Publication 46*, January 15, 1977, also published as *American National Standard Data Encryption Algorithm*, American National Standards Institute, Inc., December 30, 1980, and supplemented with "DES modes of operation," *Federal Information Processing Standard (FIPS) Publication 81*, December 2, 1980; "Telecommunications: Interoperability and security requirements for use of the data encryption standard in the physical layer of data communications," *Federal Standard of the General Services Administration*, August 3, 1983, FED-STD-1026; "Telecommunications: General security requirements for equipment using the data encryption standard," *Federal Standard of the General Services Administration*, April 14, 1982,

FED-STD-1027; and "Telecommunications: Interoperability and security requirements for use of the data encryption standard with CCITT Group 3 facsimile equipment," *Federal Standard of the General Services Administration*, April 4, 1985, FED-STD-1028.

data file—A collection of related data records organized in a specific manner. In large systems data files are gradually being replaced by databases in order to limit redundancy and improve reliability and timeliness.

datagram—A finite-length packet with sufficient information to be independently routed from source to destination without reliance on previous transmissions; typically does not involve end-to-end session establishment and may or may not entail delivery confirmation acknowledgment.

datagram service—One that establishes a datagram-based connection between peer entities. In OSI parlance this type of service is called a *connectionless service*.

data link—An assembly of two or more terminal installations and the interconnecting communications channel operating according to a particular method that permits information to be exchanged.

data link layer—The conceptual layer of control or processing logic existing in the hierarchical structure of a station that is responsible for maintaining control of the data link.

data management system—A system that provides the necessary procedures and programs to collect, organize, and maintain data files or databases.

data origin authentication—The corroboration that the source of data received is as claimed. For an OSI network, this refers to authentication in the context of a connectionless service.

data security—Procedures and actions designed to prevent the unauthorized disclosure, transfer, modification, or destruction, whether accidental or intentional, of data.

data set ready—An RS-232 signal that is sent from the modem to the computer or terminal indicating that it is able to accept data. Contrast with *data terminal ready*.

data terminal ready—An RS-232 signal that is sent form the computer or terminal to the modem indicating that it is able to accept data. Contrast with *data set ready*.

DB-25—A 25-pin connector commonly used in the United States as the connector of choice for the RS-232-C serial interface standard.

dialog box—A rectangle that appears onscreen, prompting the user to enter data or mutually exclusive selection.

digital signature—A number depending on all the bits of a message and also on a secret key. Its correctness can be verified by using a public key (unlike an authenticator, which needs a secret key for its verification).

disaster—A condition in which an organization is deemed unable to function as a result of some natural or human-created occurrence.

disaster recovery operation—The act of recovering from the effects of disruption to a computer facility and restoring, in a preplanned manner, the capabilities of the facility.

disaster recovery plan—The preplanned steps that make possible the recovery of an organization's computer facility and/or the applications processed there. Also called a contingency plan or business resumption plan.

disk storage—Information recording on continuously rotating magnetic platters. Storage may be either sequential or random access.

distributed data processing (DDP)—An organization of information processing such that both processing and data may be distributed over a number of different machines in one or more locations.

distributed network—A network configuration in which all node pairs are connected either directly or through redundant paths through intermediate nodes.

Domain Name System (DNS)—The Internet naming scheme that consists of a hierarchical sequence of names, from the most specific to the most general (left to right), separated by dots, for example, **nic.ddn.mil**. (See also: *IP address*.)

DOS (disk operating system)—A general term for the operating system used on computers using disk drives. See also: *operating system*.

download—The ability of a communications device (usually a microcomputer acting as an intelligent terminal) to load data from another device or computer to itself, saving the data on a local disk or tape.

DSR—See: *data set ready*.

DTR—See: *data terminal ready*.

EDI—See: *electronic data interchange*.

electronic bulletin board—A shared file where users can enter information for other users to read or download. Many bulletin boards are set up according to general topics and are accessible throughout a network.

electronic data interchange (EDI)—The intercompany, computer-to-computer exchange of business documents in standard formats.

electronic mail—A system to send messages between or among users of a computer network and the programs necessary to support such message transfers.

email message—A message consists of header fields and, optionally, a body. The body is simply a sequence of lines containing ASCII characters. It is separated from the headers by a null line (i.e., a line with nothing preceding the CRLF).

emulator, terminal—See: *terminal emulator*.

encryption—The translation of one character string into another by means of a cipher, translation table, or algorithm in order to render the information contained therein meaningless to anyone who does not possess the decoding mechanism. It is the reverse of *de*cryption.

encryption algorithm—A group of mathematically expressed rules that render information unintelligible by producing a series of changes through the use of variable elements controlled by the application of a key to the normal representation of the information.

end-to-end encryption—The encryption of data in a communications network at the point of origin with decryption occurring at the final destination point.

envelope—A group of binary digits formed by a byte augmented by a number of additional bits that are required for the operation of the data network; the boundary of a family of curves obtained by varying a parameter of a wave.

Ethernet—A local area network and its associated protocol developed by (but not limited to) Xerox. Ethernet is a baseband system.

F-connector—A 75-Ohm F-series coaxial cable connector of the kind commonly found on consumer television and video equipment.

fax (facsimile)—Devices that consist of three basic components—an image scanner, a fax modem, and a printer—often integrated in a single unit with each fax file treated as a cohesive image (rather than character data).

FEP (front-end processor)—A communications device used for entry into a computer system. The FEP typically provides either or both asynchronous or synchronous ports for the system.

fiber optics—A technology for transmitting information via light waves through a fine filament. Signals are encoded by varying some characteristic of the light waves generated by a low-powered laser. Output is sent through a light-conducting fiber to a receiving device that decodes the signal.

file transfer protocol—A communications protocol that can transmit files without loss of data. It implies that it can handle binary data as well as ASCII data.

floppy disks—Magnetic, low cost, flexible data disks (or diskettes) usually either 5.25 inches or 8 inches in diameter.

flow control—A speed-matching technique used in data communications to prevent receiving devices from overflowing, thus losing data.

frame—In data transmission, the sequence of contiguous bits bracketed by and including beginning and ending flag sequences. A typical frame might consist of a specified number of bits between flags and contain an address field, a control field, and a frame check sequence. A frame may or may not include an information field. A transmission unit that carries a protocol data unit (PDU).

FTP—File Transfer Protocol allows a user to transfer files electronically from remote computers back to the user's computer. Part of the TCP/IP/TELNET software suite.

gateway—The hardware and software necessary to make two technologically different networks communicate with one another; a gateway provides protocol conversion from one network architecture to another and may, therefore, use all seven layers of the OSI reference model; a special-purpose, dedicated computer that attaches to two or more networks and routes packets from one to the other. The term is loosely applied to any machine that transfers information from one network to another, as in a mail gateway.

graphical user interface (GUI)—A means for computer/human communications characterized by ease of use, interaction, and intuitive feel providing visual, direct, immediate feedback in a *WYSIWYG* environment.

GUI—See *graphical user interface.*

handheld password generators (HPGs)—Sometimes called tokens, are pocketsized devices that generate a unique onetime password for each access attempt to a properly equipped host or network.

HDLC—Hierarchical Data Link Control. A highly structured set of standards governing the means by which unlike devices can communicate with each other on large datacommunications networks.

headend—In a broadband local area network or CATV system, the point at which a signal processor upconverts a signal from a low inbound channel to a high outbound channel.

Hertz—A unit of frequency equal to one cycle per second. Cycles are referred to as Hertz in honor of the experimenter Heinrich Hertz. Abbreviated as Hz.

highsplit—In a broadband system the organization of the spectrum that places the guard band at about 190 MHz. The midsplit system offers the greatest amount of spectrum for return path channels (14 channels).

host computer—In the context of networks, a computer that directly provides service to a user. Contrast with a network server, which provides services to a user through an intermediary host computer.

hot-site—A backup facility that is fully operational and compatible with the site's hardware and software. It provides security, fire protection, and telecommunications capabilities. See also: *cold-site* and *warm-site*.

IBM—International Business Machines. One of the primary manufacturers of computer equipment (usually, though not exclusively, large-scale equipment).

icon—A small graphic image on a computer screen that represents a function or program.

IEEE—Institute of Electrical and Electronics Engineers.

impedance—In a circuit, the opposition that circuit elements present to the flow of alternating current. The impedance includes both resistance and reactance.

information security—The protection of information assets from accidental or intentional but unauthorized disclosure, modification, or destruction or the inability to process that information.

integrity (of data)—The property that data have not been altered or destroyed in an unauthorized manner; an attack on integrity would seek to erase a file that should not be erased, alter an element of a database improperly, corrupt the audit trail for a series of events, propagate a virus, and so on.

interactive processing—Processing in which transactions are processed one at a time, often eliciting a response from a user before proceeding. An interactive system may be conversational, implying continuous dialogue between the user and the system. Contrast with *batch processing*.

interface—A shared boundary between system elements defined by common physical interconnections, signals, and meanings of interchanged signals.

Internet—The series of interconnected networks that includes local area, regional, and national backbone networks. Networks in the Internet use the same telecommunications protocol (TCP/IP) and provide electronic mail, remote login, and file transfer services. The

Internet is the largest internet in the world. Is a three-level hierarchy composed of backbone networks (e.g., NSFNET, MILNET), mid-level networks, and stub networks. The Internet is a multiprotocol internet. See also: *backbone*, *IP* (*Internet Protocol*).

IP (Internet Protocol)—The Internet standard protocol that provides a common layer over dissimilar networks, used to move packets among host computers and through gateways if necessary.

IP address—The numeric address of a computer connected to the Internet; also called Internet address.

ISO/OSI—International Standards Organization Open Systems Interface. A seven-tiered network model.

kernel—The fundamental part of a program, such as an operating system, that resides in memory at all times.

key—A piece of digital information that interacts with cryption algorithms to control cryption of information and, thus, must be protected from disclosure.

key distribution center (KDC)—The element in a system that generates and distributes cryptographic key variables.

key generator—An object for encrypting-key generation.

key hashing—The method in which a long key is converted to a native key for use in the encryption/decryption process. Each number or letter of the long key helps to create each digital bit of the native key.

key management—Control of key selection and key distribution in a cryptographic system.

key notarization—A method for encrypting information at a terminal site before transmission to a host computer, over communications media that might not be secure. It is necessary for the host and the terminal to maintain the same encryption key and algorithm. This is frequently accomplished by *downloading* (sending information) from the host to the terminal on key changes. The downloaded information must also be encrypted.

kilohertz—One thousand Hertz. See: *Hertz*.

leaf—In database management, the last node of a tree; in network design and administration, the last (or lowest) node of a hierarchical network.

link encryption—Application of on-line crypto-operations to a communications system link so that all information passing over the link is completely encrypted. The term also refers to end-to-end encryption within each link in a communications network.

line extender—In a broadband system, an amplifier used to boost signal strength usually within a building.

Listserv lists (or listservers)—Electronic discussion of technical and nontechnical issues conducted by electronic mail over BITNET using LISTSERV protocols. Similar lists, often using the Unix readnews or rn facilty, are available exclusively on the Internet. Internet users may subscribe to BITNET listservers. Participants subscribe via a central service, and lists often have a moderator who manages the information flow and content.

LLC—See: *logical link control.*

local area network—A computer and communications network that covers a limited geographical area; allows every node to communicate with every other node; and that does not require a central node or processor.

logical link control (LLC)—That part of a data station that supports the logical link control functions of one or more logical links.

logical record—A collection of items independent of their physical environment. Portions of the same logical record may be located in different physical records.

logic bomb—A program routine that destroys data; for example, it may reformat the hard disk or randomly insert garbage into data files. A logic bomb may be brought into a personal computer by downloading a public-domain program that has been tampered with. Once executed, it does its damage right away, whereas a virus keeps on destroying. See: *virus* and *worm.*

MAC—See: *medium access control* or *message authentication code.*

Mail Transport Agent—The software responsible for transporting mail from source to destination, possibly transforming protocols, addresses, and routing the mail.

Mail User Agent—The user interface to the mail system; the software that the user uses to read, store, and send mail.

mainframe computer—A large-scale computing system.

malicious software—Any software, such as a virus, worm, logic bomb, bacterium, rabbit, rogue, time bomb, or Trojan Horse, that has the unauthorized capacity to modify or erase data or software and/or to reproduce itself.

manager's workstation—A microcomputer containing an integrated package of software designed to improve the productivity of managers. A workstation will usually, though not exclusively, include a word processor, a spreadsheet program, a communications program, and a data manager.

Manchester encoding—A means by which separate data and clock signals can be combined into a single, self-synchronizable data stream, suitable for transmission on a serial channel.

manipulation detection code—See: *MDC*.

Masquerading—The attempt to gain access to a system by posing as an authorized client or host.

master-slave computer system—A computer system consisting of a master computer connected to one or more slave computers; the master computer provides the scheduling function and jobs to the slave computers(s).

MDC—Manipulation (Modification) Detection Code. A redundancy check field included in the plaintext of a chain before encipherment, so that changes to the ciphertext (an active attack) will be detected.

medium access control (MAC)—The portion of the IEEE 802 data station that controls and mediates the access to the medium.

medium attachment unit (MAU)—The portion of the physical layer between the MDI and AUI that interconnects the trunk cable to the branch cable and contains the electronics that send, receive, and manage the encoded signals impressed on and recovered from the trunk cable.

medium-dependent interface (MDI)—The mechanical and electrical interface between the trunk cable medium and the MAU.

menu—A multiple-choice list of procedures or programs to be executed; a list of command options currently available to the computer user and displayed onscreen.

menu trees—Succession of menu displays that become more detailed.

message—See type of message, such as *email message*.

message authentication code (MAC)—A method by which cryptographic check digits are appended to the message. They pertain to the transaction type, transaction account number, destination, and point of origin in computer security. Specifically, by using MAC, messages without the additional check digits are rejected by the computer system, and valid transactions cannot be modified without detection.

MHS—(1) Message Handling Service; an electronic mail system developed by Action Technologies, Inc., and licensed by Novell for its NetWare operating systems. It allows for the transfer and routing of messages between users and provides store-and-forward capabilities. MHS also provides gateways into IBM's PROFS, Digital's All-in-1 office automation system, and X.400 message systems. (2) Message Handling System; an electronic mail system. MHS often refers to mail systems that conform to the OSI (Open Systems Interconnect) model, which are passed on CCITT's X.400 international message protocol.

microcomputer—A computer system of limited physical size and in former times limited in speed and address capacity. Usually, though not exclusively, a single-user computer.

microprocessor—The central processing unit of a microcomputer that contains the logical elements for manipulating and performing arithmetic or logical operations on data.

midsplit—In a broadband system, the organization of the spectrum that places the guard band at about 140 MHz. The midsplit system offers a substantial amount of spectrum for return path channels (14 channels).

minicomputer—A computer system, usually a timesharing system, sometimes faster than microcomputers but not as fast as large mainframe computers.

modem—Modulator/demodulator. A device that modulates and demodulates signals transmitted over communication facilities. A modem is sometimes called a data set.

modification detection code—See: *MDC*.

MTA—See: *Mail Transport Agent*.

MUA—See: *Mail User Agent*.

multimedia—Software that permits a mix of text, speech, and static and dynamic visual images.

multitasking—The ability of a computer to perform two or more functions (tasks) concurrently.

multiuser system—A system where two or more people, using different access systems (terminals), can access one computer concurrently or simultaneously. Such a system must have multitasking capabilities.

National Institute of Standards and Technology—See: *NIST*.

native key—The internal key (string of bits) that is required by the encryption algorithm.

network—See also: *communications network* and/or *computer network*. (1) A system of interconnected computer systems and terminals; (2) a series of points connected by communications channels; (3) the structure of relationships among a project's activities, tasks, and events.

network operating system (NOS)—A control program that usually resides in a file server within a local area network. It handles the requests for data from all the users (workstations) on the network; on a peer-to-peer LAN the NOS may be distributed across all the attached worksations.

network security—The measures taken to protect a network from unauthorized access; accidental or willful interference with normal operations; or destruction, including protection of physical facilities, software, and personnel security.

NIC (Network Information Center)—A NIC provides administrative support, user support, and information services for a network.

NIST—National Institute of Standards and Technology. Formerly (prior to 1988) the National Bureau of Standards (NBS) of the U.S. government.

node—Any station, terminal, computer or other device in a computer network.

notarization—The verification (authentication) of a message by a trusted third-party similar in logic to classic notarization procedures; normally an automated procedure.

NREN—The National Research and Education Network is a proposed national computer network to be built upon the foundation of the NSF backbone network, NSFnet. NREN would provide high-speed interconnection between other national and regional networks. SB 1067 is the legislative bill proposing NREN.

object—An entity (e.g., record, page, program, printer) that contains or receives information.

object protection—(1) In computer system security, the mechanisms and rules used to restrict access to objects; (2) in physical security, a means to protect objects such as safes, files, or anything of value that could be removed from a protected area.

object reuse—Reassigning some subject of a magnetic medium that contained one or more objects. To be securely reassigned, such media must contain no residual data from the previously contained object.

octet—A bit-oriented element that consists of eight contiguous binary bits.

Off-the-shelf—Production items that are available from current stock and need not be either newly purchased or immediately manufactured. Also relates to computer software or equipment that can be used by customers with little or no adaptation, thereby saving the time and expense of developing their own.

office automation—Refers to efforts to provide automation for common office tasks including word processing, filing, recordkeeping, and other office chores.

on-line processing—A general data processing term concerning access to computers, in which the input data enters the computer directly from the point of origin or in which output data is transmitted directly to where it is used.

OPAC—Online Public Access Catalog, a term used to describe any type of computerized library catalog.

operating system—A program that manages the hardware and software environment of a computing system.

originate-only modem—A modem that can originate data communications but cannot answer a call from another device.

OSI (Open Systems Interconnection)—This is the evolving international standard under development at ISO (International Standards Organization) for the interconnection of cooperative computer systems. An open system is one that conforms to OSI standards in its communications with other systems.

outlet—Access point, with an appropriate connector, to a communications medium.

packet—A block of data for data transmission. Each packet contains control information, such as routing, address, and error control, as well as data; a group of data and control characters in a specified format, transferred as a whole; a group of binary digits, including data and call control signals, which is switched as a composite whole; the data, all control signals, and possibly error control information are arranged in a specific format.

packet switching—A discipline for controlling and moving messages in a large data-communications network. Each message is handled as a complete unit containing the addresses of the recipient and the originator.

passive threat—Monitoring and/or recording data while data are being transferred over a communications facility; with release of message contents an attacker can read user data in messages; with *traffic analysis* the attacker can read user packet headers to identify source and destination information as well as the length and frequency of messages. See also: *threats active threat.*

passphrase—A phrase used instead of a password to control user access.

password—A unique word or string of characters used to authenticate an identity. A program, computer operator, or user may be required to submit a password to meet security requirements before gaining access to data. The password is confidential, as opposed to the user identification.

PBX/PABX—Private branch exchange or private automated branch exchange. A switching network for voice or data.

Peer-entity authentication—The corroboration that a peer entity in an association is the one claimed. This exists in an OSI context only when an association has been established between peer entities.

peer protocol—The sequence of message exchanges between two entities in the same layer that utilize the services of the underlying layers to effect the successful transfer of data and/or control information from one location to another.

peer systems—Computer/communication systems capable of performing equal or comparable tasks within defined limits or parameters.

peer-to-peer LAN—A local area network regulated by a network operating system that does not require a central server; a LAN where each node on the LAN is capable of performing equal or comparable tasks.

peripheral—Computer equipment external to the CPU performing a wide variety of input and output functions.

personal computer—An alternative name for microcomputer suggesting that the computer is to be used for personal and individual work production or entertainment.

personal identification number (PIN)—A sequence of decimal digits (usually four, five, or six) used to verify the identity of the holder of a bank card; a kind of password.

physical access control—The procedures used to authorize and validate requests for physical access to computer, communication, or network physical facilities to help ensure the physical integrity of those systems and facilities.

physical record—A basic unit of data that is read or written by a single input/output command to the computer.

physical security—Measures necessary to protect the computer and related equipment and their contents from damage by intruders, fire, accident, and environmental hazards.

plaintext—Text that has not been encrypted (or has been decrypted) and can be easily read or acted upon.

private key cryptosystem (encryption)—A type of encrypting system that uses a single key to both encrypt and decrypt information. Also called *symmetric*, or single-key, encryption.

program—A set of instructions in a programming language used to define an operation or set of operations to a computer.

protocol—A formal set of conventions governing the format and relative timing of message exchange in a communications network.

protocol data unit (PDU)—The sequence of contiguous octets delivered as a unit from or to the MAC sublayer. A valid LLC PDU is at least three octets in length, and contains two address fields and a control field. A PDU may or may not include an information field in addition.

public key—A cryptographic key used for encipherment but not usable for decipherment. It is therefore possible to make this key public.

public key cryptosystem—An encryption methodology that depends on two keys: A public key—made available to anyone who wants to encrypt information—is used for the encryption process, and a private key—known only to the owner—is used for the decryption process. The two keys are mathematically related. Also termed *asymmetric encryption*.

pull-down menu—A menu that appears onscreen when accessed by a cursor placed on a box or bar at the top of the display.

questionnaire—A method of identity verification that makes use of information known to the authorized user but unlikely to be known to others.

rabbit (informal)—A program designed to exhaust some resource of a system (CPU time, disk space, spool space, etc.) by replacing itself without limit; it differs from a *bacterium* in that a rabbit is specifically designed to exhaust resources; it differs from a *virus* in that it is a complete program in itself; it does not infect other programs.

RAM—Random Access Memory. Semiconductor memory devices used in the construction of computers. The time required to obtain data is independent of the location.

reference monitor concept—An information systems access control concept that refers to an abstract machine that mediates all access to objects by subjects.

reliability—In data communications or computer equipment, the extent to which hardware or software operates in a repeatable manner, often characterized (for hardware) as a low mean-time-between-failures.

remote access—The ability to access a computer from outside a building in which it is housed, or outside the library. Remote access requires communications hardware, software, and actual physical links, although this can be as simple as common carrier (telephone) lines or as complex as TELNET login to another computer across the Internet; pertaining to communication with a computer by a terminal distant from the computer.

remote batch terminal (RBT)—A terminal used for entering jobs and data into a computer from a remote site for later batch processing.

remote job entry (RJE)—Input of a batch job from a remote site and receipt of output via a line printer or other device at a remote site.

repeater—A device used to extend the length, topology, or interconnectivity of the physical medium beyond that imposed by a single segment, up to the maximum allowable end-to-end trunk transmission line length by copying electrical signals from one network segment to another. Because repeaters transfer electrical impulses rather than data packets they may also transfer noise.

repudiation—The denial by a message sender that the message was sent, or by a message recipient that the message was received.

resource—Anything used or consumed while performing a function. Categories of resources include time, information, objects (information containers), or processors (the ability to use information).

risk analysis—A process of studying system assets and vulnerabilities to determine an expected loss from harmful events, based upon probabilities of occurrence of those harmful events. The object of risk analysis is to determine the degree of acceptability of each risk to system operation.

ROM—Read-Only Memory. A memory device used in computers that cannot be altered during normal computer use. Normally a semiconductor device.

router—The hardware and software necessary to link two subnetworks of the same network together; the hardware and software necessary to link two subnetworks at the network layer of the OSI reference model; any machine responsible for making decisions about which of several paths network traffic will follow. At the lowest level, a physical network bridge is a router because it chooses whether to pass packets from one physical wire to another. Within a long haul network, each individual packet switch is a router because it chooses routes for individual packets. In the Internet, each IP gateway is a router because it uses IP destination addresses to choose routes.

security—See also: *communications security, data security.* (1) The state of certainty that computerized data and program files cannot be accessed, obtained, or modified by unauthorized personnel or the computer or its programs. Security is implemented by restricting the physical area around the computer system to authorized personnel, using special software, and the security built into the operating procedure of the computer. (2) When applied to computer systems and networks denotes the authorized, correct, timely performance of computing tasks. It encompasses the areas of confidentiality, integrity, and availability.

security audit—See: *audit of computer security.*

security mechanisms—Operating procedures, hardware and software features, management procedures, and any combinations of these that are designed to detect and prevent either passive or active threats on any component of an information system.

security service—Activity or provision of an activity that enhances the security of information systems and an organization's information transfer. In the OSI model the defined services consist of five groups: confidentiality, authentication, integrity, nonrepudiation, and access control.

security threat—Any action that compromises the security of information owned by an organization. See also *active threat*, and *passive threat*.

server—A computer in a network that is shared by multiple users such as a file server, print server, or communications server; a computer in a network designated to provide a specific service as distinct from a general-purpose, centralized, multiuser computer system.

session—Active connection of one device to another over a communications system, during which interactions can or do occur.

Shareware—Microcomputer software, distributed through public domain channels, for which the author expects to receive compensation.

shell—An outer layer of a program that provides the user interface, or way of commanding the computer. Shells are typically add-on programs created for command-driven operating systems, such as Unix and DOS. The shell may provide a menu-driven or graphical icon-oriented interface to the system in order to make it easier to use.

socket—The abstraction provided by Berkeley 4.3 BSD Unix that allows a process to access the Internet. A process opens a socket, specifies the service desired (e.g., reliable stream delivery), binds the socket to a specific destination, and then sends or receives data. While the functional characteristics remain as defined, the concept has been generalized to include processes that access networks other than Internet.

software—A term used to contrast computer programs with the iron or hardware of a computer system.

spectrum—A range of wavelengths usually applied to radio frequencies.

spreadsheet programs—Computer programs that allow data to be entered as elements of a table or matrix with rows and columns and manipulate the data. Programs widely available on microcomputers are Lotus 1-2-3 and SUPERCALC.

start-stop transmission—See: *asynchronous transmission*.

station—A physical device that may be attached to a shared-medium local area network for the purpose of transmitting and receiving information on that shared medium.

subject—An active entity—such as a process, person, or device—that causes information to flow among objects or changes the system's state.

subject security level—The security level of a subject that is the same as the security level of the objects to which it has both read and write access. The clearance of the user with whom the subject is associated always dominates the security level of the subject.

subsplit—In a broadband system, the organization of the spectrum that places the guard band at about 40 MHz. The subsplit system offers the least amount of spectrum for return path channels (4 channels).

symmetric encryption—See: *private key cryptosystem.*

tap—A device that allows an exit from a main line of a communications system.

TCP/IP—Transmission Control Protocol/Internet Protocol is a combined set of protocols that performs the transfer of data between two computers. TCP monitors and ensures correct transfer of data. IP receives the data from TCP, breaks it up into packets, and ships it off to a network within the Internet. TCP/IP is also used as a name for a protocol suite that incorporates these functions and others.

telecommunications—The transfer of data from one place to another over communications lines or channels; the communication of all forms of information including voice and video.

TELNET—A portion of the TCP/IP suite of software protocols that handles terminals. Among other functions, it allows a user to log in to a remote computer from his or her local computer.

teletex—One-way transmission of data via a television system.

terminal—A device that allows input and output of data to a computer. The term is most frequently used in conjunction that a device that has a keyboard for data entry and either a printer or a video tube for displaying data.

terminal emulation—Most communications software packages will permit your personal computer or workstation to communicate with another computer or network as if it were a specific type of terminal directly connected to that computer or network.

terminal emulator—A software or software/hardware system for microcomputers that allows the micro to behave like some specified terminal, such as a DEC VT100 or an IBM 3278/79.

terminal server—A machine that connects terminals to a network by providing host TELNET service.

text editor—A program that provides flexible editing facilities on a computer for the purpose of allowing data entry from a keyboard terminal without regard for the eventual format or medium for publication. With a text editor data (text, copy, or what have you) can be edited easily and quickly.

text formatter—A program for reading a data file created with a text editor and transforming the raw file into a neatly formatted listing.

threat—Threats to an information system or its networks may be either *active* or *passive*. See also *active threats* and *passive threats.*

time bomb—A *logic bomb* activated at a certain time or date.

TN3270—A version of TELNET providing IBM full-screen support.

token—(1) In LAN protocols, the symbol of authority that is passed between stations using a token access method to indicate which station is currently in control of the medium;(2) a hand-held password generator designed to provide a unique password for each access attempt to a LAN (or other network) or multiuser computer system.

token passing—A collision avoidance technique in which each station is polled and must pass the poll along.

traffic—The information moved over a communications channel.

traffic analysis—When communication traffic is in cipher form and cannot be understood it may still be possible to get useful information by detecting who is sending messages to whom and in what quantity.

traffic flow confidentiality—Concealment of the quantity of users' messages in a communication system and their sources or destinations, to prevent *traffic analysis*.

traffic flow security—The protection resulting from features, inherent in some cryptoequipment, that conceal the presence of valid messages on a communications circuit, normally achieved by causing the circuit to appear busy at all times.

traffic padding—A function that generates a continuous stream of random data or ciphertext, thus making it very difficult for an attacker (1) to distinguish between true data flow and noise; and (2) to deduce the amount of traffic.

transaction processing—A style of data processing in which files are updated and results generated immediately as a result of data entry.

trojan horse—Any program designed to do things that the user of the program did not intend to do. An example of this would be a program that simulates the logon sequence for a computer and, rather than logging the user on, simply records the user's user ID and password in a file for later collection. Rather than logging the user on, it steals the user's password so that the trojan horse's designer can log on as the user.

trunk cable—The trunk (usually coaxial) cable system.

trusted computer system—A system that can simultaneously process a spectrum of sensitive or classified information, because it employs sufficient hardware and software security measures.

trusted computing base (TCB)—Refers to the hardware, firmware, and software protection mechanisms within a computer system that are responsible for enforcing a security policy.

trusted path—The way in which a person at a terminal can communicate directly with the trusted computing base. Only the person or the trusted computing base can activate this mechanism; it cannot be imitated by untrusted software.

trusted software—A trusted computing base's software segment.

turnkey system—A system in which the manufacturer or distributor takes full responsibility for complete system design and installation, and supplies all necessary hardware, software, and documentation.

twisted pair—The two wires of a signaling circuit, twisted around each other to minimize the effects of inductance.

Unix—A multitasking, multiuser interactive operating system developed by Ken Thompson, Dennis Ritchie, and coworkers at Bell Laboratories (AT&T in the 1970s); a powerful operating system implemented on a wide variety of computers from mainframes to microcomputers. Now owned by USL, which was, in turn, sold by AT&T to Novell in 1993.

Unix-to-Unix CoPy (UUCP)—This was initially a program run under the Unix operating system that allowed one Unix system to send files to another Unix system via dialup phone lines. Today, the term is often, if somewhat inaccurately, used to describe the large international network that uses the UUCP protocols to pass news and electronic mail. See also: *electronic mail, Usenet, UUCP.*

upload—Refers to the ability to send data from an originating terminal (usually a microcomputer) to another computer or terminal.

Usenet—A collection of thousands of typically named newsgroups, the computers that run the protocols, and the people who read and submit Usenet news. Not all Internet hosts subscribe to Usenet and not all Usenet hosts are on the Internet. See also: *Unix-to-Unix CoPy.*

user—A human being or computer process that possesses the right to log in to a particular computer system.

UUCP—Unix-to-Unix CoPy. A system of closely integrated programs providing file transfer capabilities; originated in the Unix world, but has expanded to many other operating environments. Can also apply to the uucp command that is part of the UUCP system, thus resulting in some confusion. See also: *Unix-to-Unix CoPy.*

videotex—A two-way method of communications integrating video and a related communications system.

virtual circuit—A communication arrangement in which data from a source user may be passed to a destination user over various real circuit configurations during a single period of communication (during a single session). Also called a logical circuit. See also: *connection-oriented service.*

virus—A program that is used to infect a computer. After virus code is written, it is buried within an existing program. Once that program is executed, the virus code is also activated and attaches copies of itself to other programs in the system. Whenever an infected program is run, the virus copies itself to other programs. A virus cannot be attached to data. It must be attached to an executable program that is installed on a computer. The virus-attached program must be executed in order to activate the virus. See also: *logic bomb* and *worm.*

warm-site—Similar to a *cold site* but with telecommunications facilities.

wide area network—In communications, a network that interconnects other networks and computers across geographical boundaries such as cities, states, or nations.

Winchester disks—Hard magnetic disk storage media in sealed containers. Not all sealed disks are Winchester drives.

window—A rectangular onscreen image within which the user accesses particular features of a system. With operating environment software windowing is often combined with multitasking capabilities.

windows (Microsoft)—The graphical user interface (GUI) developed by Microsoft for use on microcomputers using Intel 80286 and higher CPU chips.

Windows UUCP leaf system—A Microsoft Windows-based UUCP system that is the last node in an hierarchically arranged network using UUCP as the method for communications. See also: *leaf, UUCP.*

word processing—The transformation of ideas and information into a human-readable form of communication through the management of procedures, equipment, and personnel. Generally refers to text editing and formatting on a computer.

worm—(1) A destructive program that replicates itself throughout disk and memory, using up the computer's resources and eventually putting the system down (See: *virus* and *logic bomb*); (2) a program that moves throughout a network and deposits information at each node for diagnostic purposes, or causes idle computers to share some of the processing workload; (3) WORM (Write Once Read Many) a storage device that uses an optical medium that can be recorded only once. Updating requires destroying the existing data (zeroes [0] made ones [1]), and writing the revised data to an unused part of the disk.

WYSIWYG—What You See Is What You Get.

xon/xoff—In communications, a simple asynchronous protocol that keeps the receiving device is synchronization with the sending device. When the buffer in the receiving device if full, it sends an xoff signal (transmit off) to the sending device, telling it to stop transmitting. When the receiving device is ready to accept more, it sends the sending device an xon signal (transmit on) to start again. A means of software flow control. See also: *flow control*. Contrast with *CTS/RTS*.

Z39.50 Protocol—Name of the national standard developed by the National Information Standards Organization (NISO) that defines an applications-level protocol by which one computer can query another and transfer result records, using a canonical format. This protocol provides the framework for *OPAC* users to search remote catalogs on the Internet using the commands of their own local systems. Projects are now in development to provide Z39.50 support for catalogs on the Internet. SR (Search and Retrieval), ISO Draft International Standard 10162/10163 is the international version of Z39.50.